EDUCATIONAL PSYCHOLOGY

by

Alice Crow, Ph.D.

About the Author

1. *Activity:* Formerly, Associate Professor of Education, Brooklyn College; chairman and program adviser of the Graduate Guidance and School Counseling Curriculum.
2. *Teaching Experience:* Elementary school, junior high school, senior high school, teacher training college, college and university.
3. *Publications:* Co-author

   Child Psychology, Barnes and Noble, 1953.

   Readings in General Psychology, Barnes and Noble, 1954.

   Readings in Abnormal Psychology, Littlefield, Adams, 1958.

   Introduction to Guidance, 2nd ed., American Book, 1961.

   Human Development and Learning, rev. ed., Van Nostrand Reinhold, 1963

   How To Study, Collier-Macmillan, 1963.

   The Student Teacher in the Secondary School, McKay, 1964.

   Education Psychology, New rev. ed., Van Nostrand Reinhold, 1965.

   Adolescent Development and Adjustment, 2nd ed., McGraw-Hill, 1965.

   Organization and Conduct of Guidance Services, McKay, 1965.

   Introduction to Education, 2nd ed., Van Nostrand Reinhold, 1966.

About the Editor of the Revised Edition

Dr. Francesco Cordasco is Professor of Education at Montclair State College, and has served as a consultant to the U.S. Office of Education and to federal, state, and community antipoverty programs funded under the Economic Opportunity Act. Dr. Cordasco's recent books include *Jacob Riis Revisited: Poverty and the Slum in Another Era* (Doubleday, 1968); *Puerto Rican Children In Mainland Schools* (Grolier, Scarecrow, 1968); *Education in the Urban Community* (American Book Co., 1969); *The School In The Social Order* (Intext, 1970); and *Minorities In the American City* (McKay, 1970). An educational historian and sociologist, Dr. Cordasco has edited the classic 19th century work of the psychologist-physician, Edouard Seguin, *Idiocy and its Treatment by the Physiological Method* (1971).

EDUCATIONAL PSYCHOLOGY

by

Alice Crow

Brooklyn College

REVISED EDITION

Edited by

FRANCESCO CORDASCO

Montclair State College

1972

LITTLEFIELD, ADAMS & CO.

Totowa, New Jersey

First Edition 1956
Reprinted, 1958, 1961, 1964, 1965, 1968

Library of Congress Catalog Card Number—56-13917

Revised 1972

Printed in the United States of America

PREFACE

This *Educational Psychology* is an overview of such human relationships as growth and development, dynamics of human behavior, significance of individual differences in learning and teaching, problems involved in human learning, principles and techniques of evaluation, reporting pupil progress and pertinent factors of human adjustment. The editor has attempted to present current psychological approaches to the various facets of human learning. Brief, but careful consideration has been given to (1) the significant aspects of child and adolescent growth and development; (2) the functioning of the principles of integrated learning; (3) the techniques utilized in the evaluation of intelligence; (4) the educational implications of personal and social development and adjustment; and (5) the role of the teacher in the motivation of learners.

Of necessity, the many complex phases of the developmental and learning processes are treated briefly but succinctly. At the same time, the presentation is aimed at helping men and women who are planning to enter the teaching profession as well as aiding teachers already on active duty to acquire insights concerning human behavior and the nature of learning, and a better understanding of the functions and responsibilities of teaching.

Short-form examination questions with answers have been provided. Also included is a list of selected books in Educational Psychology; and a selection of titles in the area of social deprivation and minority contexts which are of special value to the educational psychologists. A section on the statistical treatment of data is appended. Over the years this text has been favorably received by teachers and their students; the current revision will hopefully continue to receive this favorable response. The editor welcomes suggestions for its continuing improvement.

F.C.

TABLE OF CONTENTS

Part 1. Scientific Bases of Education

Part 2. Human Growth and Development

Part 3. Aspects of Differences Among Learners

Part 4. The Psychology of Learning

Part 5. Evaluation and Education

Part 6. Psychological Aspects of Adjustment

EDUCATIONAL PSYCHOLOGY

OTHER PSYCHOLOGY AND EDUCATION BOOKS PUBLISHED BY LITTLEFIELD, ADAMS & CO.

A BRIEF HISTORY OF EDUCATION
By Francesco Cordasco
"The reappearance of this volume in this series—a 'quick review' of the history of Western education—should be welcomed by undergraduate students."—*Choice* (March, 1971).
2nd edition 1970 188 pages (No. 67) Paper $1.75

TEACHER IN THE URBAN COMMUNITY
By Leonard Covello
"Leonard Covello is an idealist with his feet firmly planted on the earth. His book (autobiography) is readable, written in a candid, engaging and moving style . . . It has a quality of social commentary and is therefore, at times, stirring writing."—*Modern Language Journal.*
1970 288 pages (No. 242) Paper $2.25

APPLIED RESEARCH IN EDUCATION
Edited by E. Wayne Courtney
The collection of readings by outstanding educators and scientists in this book will be of particular interest to the classroom teacher and graduate student in education.
1965 341 pages (No. 92) Paper $2.25

AN OUTLINE OF GENERAL PSYCHOLOGY
By Lester D. Crow and Alice Crow
The significant areas of psychology are given full coverage in a clear, simple style. Technical terms are explained when used. Because of its comprehensive coverage and its terse clarity of style, it is a valuable book for everyone interested in psychology. Fully illustrated. Self-testing questions and answers—both objective and subjective—are included.
Revised edition 1971 316 + pages (No. 28) Paper $2.25; Cloth *$5.95

SYLLABUS OF LECTURES ON THE HISTORY OF EDUCATION
with Selected Bibliographies and Suggested Readings
By Ellwood P. Cubberley. Introductory Note by Francesco Cordasco.
The Syllabus of Lectures on The History of Education evolved out of courses in the History of Education which Cubberley gave at Stanford University. Cremin has characterized the *Syllabus* as ". . . a rather remarkable work that remains unique in the literature."
1904, reprinted 1971. 360 pages Cloth* $20.00

THE SOCIAL IDEAS OF AMERICAN EDUCATORS
By Merle Curti
A study of the social philosophy developed by leading educators and the factors that influenced this development. This edition includes an important new chapter on the last twenty-five years.
1971 613 pages. (No. 105) Paper $3.45

PHILOSOPHY OF EDUCATION: Problems of Men
By John Dewey
This collection of essays by Dewey offers an invaluable and convenient sourcebook of writings by the most important philosopher of education which America has produced.
1966 311 pages (No. 126) Paper $1.95

HANDBOOK OF PSYCHOLOGICAL TERMS

By Philip L. Harriman

A helpful, inexpensive guide for students and the general reader through the maze of technical vocabulary in scientific psychology.

1969 222 pages (No. 35) Paper $1.95 Cloth *$5.95

MODERN PSYCHOLOGY

By Philip L. Harriman

A comprehensive survey of the principles of modern psychology. Terms are defined in context. The book includes a glossary, self-testing exercises, a series of functional illustrations, a bibliography, and extensive appendix that includes foreign terminology and professional societies.

Revised edition 1963 316 pages (No. 20) Paper $1.95 Cloth *$5.95

SIMPLIFIED STATISTICS FOR STUDENTS IN EDUCATION AND PSYCHOLOGY

By Robert H. Koenker

A simplified approach for students in education and psychology who have no mathematical background beyond high school algebra.

This completely revised edition includes short work problems and answers with simple explanations, references for further study, helpful glossaries, tables to assist students with computations, and a special section relating the subject to the increasing use of computers in school.

Revised edition 1971 192 pages (No. 251) Paper $2.95

REVIEW OUTLINE OF PSYCHOLOGY

Edited by Wilbert J. McKeachie

This outline is organized around basic questions students ask about general psychology. Includes charts, self-help tests with answers, glossary.

3rd edition 1967 326 pages (No. 77) Paper $1.95

THE HISTORY OF MODERN ELEMENTARY EDUCATION

By Samuel Chester Parker

This "classic in education" is, in essence, a social history in which the progress of elementary education is cast in a context which makes it valuable as history and instructive and useful in terms of contemporary problems.

1970 505 pages (No. 245) Paper $2.95

THE CHILD'S CONCEPTION OF PHYSICAL CAUSALITY

By Jean Piaget

An evaluation of the significance of the child's explanation of his conceptions and the use he makes of his notions of cause and law.

Reprinted 1969 309 pages (No. 212) Paper $2.25

THE CHILD'S CONCEPTION OF THE WORLD

By Jean Piaget

A study of the various conceptions of the world formed by the child at different stages of his development—the child's notion of reality and of causality.

Reprinted 1969 397 pages (No. 213) Paper $2.25

JUDGMENT AND REASONING IN THE CHILD

By Jean Piaget

In this enquiry into the nature of logical relations Piaget studies the child's behavior when confronted with those conjunctions denoting causality or logical relations and with those expressing antithetical relations.

Reprinted 1968 260 pages (No. 205) Paper $1.95

THE PSYCHOLOGY OF INTELLIGENCE

By Jean Piaget

The author gives a brief presentation and critique of the main theories of intelligence and develops his own view based on the formation of "operations."

Reprinted 1972 182 pages (No. 222) Paper $1.95

ESSAYS ON EDUCATIONAL REFORMERS

By Robert Hebert Quick. With an introductory Note by Francesco Cordasco

This reprint of a work which W. S. Monroe called "unquestionably the most influential book on the history of education ever published in the English language", deals with the history of education from the Renaissance down to Quick's own nineteenth century.

Reprinted 1970 568 pages (No. 244) Paper $2.95

ESSAYS ON EDUCATION

By Herbert Spencer

The four essays in this book develop theories on education held by one of the leading and most influential philosophers of the nineteenth century.

Reprinted 1963 283 pages (No. 151) Paper $1.95

BIBLIOGRAPHY OF PUBLICATIONS OF THE UNITED STATES OFFICE OF EDUCATION

Introductory Note by Francesco Cordasco

The present volume brings together three indexes (each of which has been long out-of-print and generally unobtainable) which constitute a bibliography of the publications of the Office of Education from 1867 through 1959.

Reprinted 1972 372 pages 3 volumes in one Cloth *$20.00

VIVES: ON EDUCATION. A Translation of the *De Tradendis Disciplinis* of Juan Luis Vives.

Introduction by Foster Watson. Forword by Francesco Cordasco.

The main educational work of the man who ranks with Erasmus as one of the greatest thinkers on educational matters of the Renaissance, The *De Tradendis Disciplinis* was first published in Antwerp in 1531. The introduction by Dr. Watson is 158 pages in length and constitutes a study in depth of Vives and his work.

1913; reprinted 1971 497 pages Cloth *$15.00

**Cloth editions are published by Rowman & Littlefield* (*Library Division of Littlefield, Adams & Co.*)

PART I

SCIENTIFIC BASES OF EDUCATION

CHAPTER 1

EDUCATIONAL PSYCHOLOGY AS AN APPLIED SCIENCE

The traditional concept of education or "schooling" emphasized the mastery of subject matter and competence in specific study or practice and/or stubbornness. As now interpreted, education (1) touches every aspect of an individual's personality, (2) represents a continuous learning process, (3) is affected by conditions and experiences both within and outside the school situation, and (4) is conditioned by the abilities and interests of the learner, the appropriateness of the learning situation, and the efficacy of the teaching approach.

The modern concept of education is an outgrowth of continuing research concerning human development and behavior. Educational psychology represents the application of scientifically derived principles of human reaction that affect teaching and learning.

Functions and Areas of Psychology

Viewed historically, the science of psychology is in its early youth. Scientific study of the behavior of living organisms began in the nineteenth century; the first psychological laboratory probably was established in 1879. From then onward, research and experiment in the field have progressed rapidly. Psychologists are broadening and intensifying their study of human reaction patterns as well as those of other organic species.

Functions of Psychology. Early psychological research was concerned mainly with the reactions of animals to varying types of environmental stimulation. Psychological principles that appeared to evolve from experiments with animals then were tested for their validity in regard to human reactions.

Gradually an increasing number of experimental studies

---

* For general historical background, see F. Cordasco, *A Brief History of Education* (Totowa, N. J.: Littlefield & Adams, 1970).

came to deal with the behavior of human beings in specific stimulus-response situations. As a result of laboratory-conducted research, much has been learned by psychologists concerning specific types of human behavior, such as reaction time, threshold of sensitivity, reflex activity, rote memory, and similar basic behavior patterns.

To the extent that psychology is a "pure" science it is concerned primarily with systematic theories of behavior and their verification. The functions of the theoretic psychologist therefore are: (1) to establish accurate and appropriate research conditions and situations, (2) to keep accurate and detailed records of behavior responses, (3) to evaluate data carefully, (4) to interpret objectively the results of study, (5) to formulate an adequate generalization or psychological principle, and (6), through continued experimentation, to test the validity of evolved principles of behavior.

To have utilitarian value, psychological principles must be established that can be applied to practical life problems. Hence some psychological research must be conducted outside the laboratory. Investigations need to be made in stimulus-response situations that do not lend themselves to definite control techniques but rather represent everyday, relatively informal conditions. The value of continued laboratory study is recognized, but psychologists are tending to give increasing attention to the point of view of applied science. Thereby they are enabled to extend their research into every phase of personal and social behavior.

Areas of Psychological Study. As the term suggests, general psychology deals with the fundamental principles of behavior. Since these principles represent to-be-expected or generally characteristic reactions, they cannot explain adequately every phase of human development, behavior or interrelationship. It is an accepted psychological fact that, from birth onward, an individual's developing personality constitutes an integrated whole. It would be difficult if not impossible, however, for a student of psychology to gain an adequate appreciation of the many existing variations in personal attributes and life relationships, unless he concentrated on one aspect of study at a time.

To clarify their findings concerning the various behavior aspects of living organisms, psychologists have organized the results of their study according to specific classified areas. It must be remembered, however, that the various areas of psychology included in the following list are not mutually exclusive of one another. Each represents a detailed consideration of scientific principles that apply particularly to a relatively specific aspect of psychological study. In addition to general psychology, some of the commonly studied areas of psychology are explained briefly here.

Genetic psychology is the study of the developmental aspects of individuals. The origin and development of individual behavior are considered.

Physiological psychology deals with the study of anatomical structure and organic functioning, especially of the nervous system.

Animal psychology is concerned with the nature and reactions of animals.

Child psychology is the study of the behavior of individuals from the prenatal period through the developing years to maturity.

Adolescent psychology is the study of the behavior of individuals during the adolescent years, usually 12 to 20.

Adult psychology is concerned with the behavior of individuals after their period of adolescence.

Dynamic psychology is a study of the inner urges, drives, and motives as they affect the behavior of an individual or of groups.

Social psychology is the study of the behavior of individuals in group situations and of the interrelationships among individuals or among groups.

Differential psychology is concerned with appraising the differences among individuals and groups.

Abnormal psychology is the study of maladjustments among mental and emotional deviates.

Pathological psychology is concerned with the study of mental diseases.

Experimental psychology is concerned with discovering psychological facts by means of experiments scientifically conducted. The laboratory or another controlled situation is utilized.

Clinical psychology is concerned with diagnosis and treatment of mental, emotional, and behavior disorders. A clinic or other place specifically organized for this purpose is utilized.

Comparative psychology is concerned with comparing the behavior of different species.

Educational psychology is concerned with individual learning, growth, and maturation.

Psychology applied to industry, business, law, medicine, etc. concerns the study of human reactions as related to the problems in each area.

A survey of the foregoing list of areas indicates that the categories include developmental aspects, study approaches and emphases, behavior patterning, and applications of scientifically derived principles to respective areas of life activity. Of particular interest to teachers and teacher trainees is the psychology of learning, commonly referred to as *educational psychology.*

Function and Scope of Educational Psychology

According to its derivation from the Latin, the term *to educate* means *to draw out.* Hence the function of education can be regarded to be the provision of situational stimulations whereby inherent potentialities are enabled to express themselves in the form of appropriate skills, knowledge, and attitudes.

Psychologically, education implies change. Education as a *process* refers to those continuing experiences that help develop innate abilities. The *products* of education are those changes that result from participation in educational or learning experiences. Every environmental situation tends to effect changes within the individual experiencing it. The application of certain psychological principles that deal particularly with the learning process yields some assurance that changes resulting from learning will be beneficial for the learner as well as for the society of which he is a member. The area of psychological science that is concerned with the learning process and learning outcomes constitutes the content of educational psychology.

Scope of Educational Psychology. Educational psychology can be considered to be an applied science in so far as it utilizes those scientifically determined psychological principles and facts that deal with human behavior in learning situations. At first, the content of this relatively new area of psychology was limited to a consideration of so-called laws of learning that had evolved, for the most part, as a result of laboratory-controlled experiments with animals and children.

By the end of the second decade of the twentieth century, when school learning still placed major emphasis upon skill development and subject matter mastery, the content of educational psychology represented a detailed treatment of the mental aspects of learning.[1] Gradually, the scope and content of educational psychology have undergone considerable expansion and shift of emphasis. These changes have resulted partly from practical experimentation and other forms of research conducted by educational psychologists, and partly from a continuing trend toward broadening educational objectives.

The broad implications of theories concerning the learning process promulgated by laboratory psychologists may have value for the school man, but many of the principles thus established needed to be adapted for use in group learning situations. Hence educational psychologists have been and are continuing to contribute considerable research material concerning learning in school situations. Much of the content of educational psychology now deals with the ways in which and the means by which the teacher can utilize the results of practical study and experimentation in the field.

Since the goals of modern education are pointed toward what is commonly termed the "all-round" development of the learner, teachers and other school personnel need to possess as thorough understanding of human nature as is possible for them to achieve. Consequently, the scope of educational psychology has become increasingly extensive as well as intensive. It utilizes relevant scientific data from biology, social anthropology, sociology, medicine, and psychiatry, as well as from other branches of psychology.

The adaptation and/or modification of these contributions and the results of research in the field of learning have yielded a body of significant facts and principles that constitute the content of educational psychology. There probably are no two textbooks in educational psychology that include completely similar material or that agree exactly in their mode of approach, point of view, or specific emphases. Yet most books in this field contain a more or less detailed treatment of each of the following areas of study concerning human nature and learning:

Biological inheritance and social heritage
Physical, mental, emotional, and social growth and development
Learner potentialities and behavior characteristics
Personal and social outcomes of education
Mental hygiene for the teacher and the learner
Evaluation in education.

[1] See E. I. Thorndike, *Educational Psychology, Briefer Course.* Teachers College, Columbia University, New York, 1914.

Functions of Educational Psychology. Teacher trainees (sometimes their instructors) may experience confusion concerning the specific aims and purposes to be achieved through a study of educational psychology. This attitude is not surprising in view of the fact that there often appears to be considerable crossover between this field of study and other sciences that deal with human well-being, individual behavior, and group relationships. Primarily, however, educational psychology is concerned with the improvement of teaching and learning. Its general functions are: (1) to improve effectiveness in teaching, (2) to induce increased purposefulness, economy, and permanence in learning, and (3) to encourage the achievement by learners and by teachers of better physical, mental, and emotional health.

The functions of general psychology, educational philosophy, and educational psychology revolve around common basic characteristics of human personality, but the purposes to be served by each differ. The general psychologist establishes generalizations and principles that can be regarded as the bases of human behavior. The educational philosopher attempts to evolve theories concerning the "good life." He establishes educational aims or objectives, in terms of which curriculums can be constructed whereby desired educational goals can be attained. The educational psychologist then is responsible for determining those learning situations and teaching approaches and techniques that can become effective personality molders.

In other words, the function of general psychology is to further the understanding of an individual's personality as the total integrated pattern of his behavior reactions at any stage of his development. Educational philosophy is interested in the shaping of personality, and educational psychology concerns itself with all of a learner's inner motivations and the multitudinous environmental stimulations that do or can exert a potent influence upon his developing personality. General psychology describes and explains personality; education recommends the *what* for personality shaping; educational psychology suggests the *when* and *how* of the educational process.[2]

Study Approaches in Educational Psychology. Although educational psychology is gaining in repute as a science, its attempted approach to the solution of an educational problem may be

[2] For a more complete discussion of this topic see B. R. Bulgeski, *Psychology of Learning Applied to Teaching*, Bobbs-Merrill, 1971; P. E. Johnson, *Psychology of School Learning*, Wiley, 1971; and R. F. Beihler, *Psychology Applied to Teaching*, Houghton-Mifflin, 1971.

limited by the nature of the problem itself or by the difficulty of establishing adequate controls. The researcher in education usually is dealing with dynamic, often unpredictable, children and adolescents. Moreover, in so far as the research is related to improvement of teaching techniques, objectively determined scientific principles may fail to function adequately.

Teaching is an art. The subtle factors that make for "master teaching" may defy detection according to a scientifically applied yardstick. In addition, the many variables that exist in teaching-learning situations make it unwise or even educationally dangerous to conclude, for example, that a learning procedure evolved and applied successfully in one learning situation will function adequately in another. In spite of these and similar unavoidable difficulties, educational psychologists and educators have been conducting a tremendous amount of research that, through continuous evaluation and re-evaluation, is increasing teacher understanding of learners and revolutionizing educational practice and procedures.

Currently utilized tools and techniques of educational evaluation are discussed in Chapter 20. There are several other commonly used methods of approach to the study of learner reactions, the learning process, and teaching techniques, however.

Although these methods vary in degree of scientific objectivity; many valuable data have been obtained from nonscientific and semiscientific studies. Teacher observation of his pupils' classroom behavior is helpful. Learner and/or teacher utilization of introspection to discover inner feelings and mental activities that cannot be measured objectively can yield worth-while practical data. Information concerning learner behavior, attitudes, and interests obtained by way of controlled observation or through utilization of the questionnaire technique may or may not have scientific validity but can improve insight into a particular teaching-learning situation or set of conditons.

Educational experimentation probably has proved to be one of the most reliable sources of psychological information in the field of education. Conclusions based upon data obtained by application of experimental procedures to group-learning situations or conditions may be less valid, however, than are the results of experiments conducted in a scientific laboratory. When one is dealing with complex human behavior, it is difficult, sometimes impossible, to isolate completely one variable for study. Neither can the experimenter be certain that the members of the experimental group and those of the control group are equated, member with member, except for the one variable that is to be studied. Yet comparative studies of learner reactions, teaching-learning situations and conditions, and teaching techniques have contributed much valuable information concerning educational problems.

Valuable as are the results of psychological research in education, the inadvisability of basing broad generalizations upon one or a few studies cannot be stressed too strongly. Individual potentialities and characteristics, cultural background, economic and social status, and educational advantages differ from community to community. For example, educational research conducted in one school community may yield data that are extremely valuable as the basis of improved curriculum organization of learning procedures in that community. Attempts to introduce similar educational changes in another school community will be successful only in so far as the two are fundamentally similar.

Likewise, conclusions based upon the study of the interests of one age group may be invalid for another older or younger group. Many cases could be cited to emphasize the danger of accepting as a broad generalization the conclusions resulting from a relatively narrow, specific study. This fact holds for all scientific research, but it is especially important in the field of educational research. Solutions to educational problems that grow out of the many complex variables inherent in physical, mental, and emotional differences among learners and teachers can be achieved only through continuous application and reapplication of research methods in every area of study.

Regardless of the study technique used, the resulting conclusions must be applied with discretion. For example, many studies of human behavior have centered around research concerning individuals who have been reared in middle-class urban communities. We constantly need to be alert to any generalizations resulting from research applicable to members of the group studied, and not to the population at large. Also within the group studied there are likely to be some individuals who, for one reason or another, deviate widely from the generally accepted norm of behavior of the majority of the group.

CHAPTER 2

EDUCATIONAL PSYCHOLOGY AND TEACHER PREPARATION

The effective teacher possesses a broad cultural background, gained at least partially from college-level study in the liberal arts and the basic sciences. Moreover, he has achieved thorough mastery of subject content relevant to his particular teaching area. In addition, it is imperative that the teacher on any educational level shall understand and be prepared to apply in his teaching activities the psychological principles that are basic to successful teaching and effective learning.

Psychological Aspects of Teaching

In few, if any, school communities is a teacher's function regarded to be no more than to hear and to rate pupils' answers to questions based entirely upon assigned home study. Yet many lay people and some inexperienced or poorly trained teachers still seem to be unaware of the many areas of service in which a modern teacher is expected to engage and the breadth and depth of psychological knowledge and human understanding he needs to fulfill adequately his teaching responsibilities.

Professional and Personal Needs of Teachers. Regardless of the level or area of study, the mastery of learning content is the learner's responsibility. Teachers cannot do a young or older person's learning for him; their function is to guide or direct learning activities toward the achievement of appropriate educational goals. To achieve success in their work, teachers must (1) be thoroughly grounded in their subject matter, (2) believe that the content of their teaching has value for the learner, and (3) be able to motivate him toward a desire to learn.

The foregoing analysis of teaching responsibilities represents an oversimplified description of his functions. It is unrealistic to assume that every learner can or does react favorably to teachers' attempts to arouse his interested coöperation in learning activities. Furthermore, educational aims, as now interpreted, are not pointed only toward the mastery of particular subject matter or the gaining of specific skill competencies, even though these learnings help prepare a young person to assume adult responsibilities for effective self-dependent living.

It is possible for a teacher, as a result of his own enthusiasm for and interest in his teaching field, to arouse a similar interest among his pupils. They may be stimulated thereby toward a recognition of the *why* of learning. The *how* of mastering the material depends upon the teacher's ability to utilize those teaching techniques and tools that will ensure successful learning progress. He needs to understand the principles of learning readiness and know how they function in respect to each of his pupils. His teaching procedures then should be adapted accordingly.

Although there sometimes is value in having ideas presented to learners in logical sequence, better learning results usually are achieved through a psychological approach that takes into consideration learner readiness to understand and to appreciate the concepts that he is expected to learn. Various psychologically effective teaching and learning procedures can be utilized, but educational psychologists are not in complete agreement concerning their relative value in differing learning situations. Yet effective teachers usually are those who, through their knowledge of psychological principles and their understanding of learner abilities, are able to adapt their teaching procedures to meet learner needs.

An increasingly important function of education is to guide the learner toward the development of attitudes and behavior patterns that are socially acceptable. The social aspect of education cannot be divorced from the personal. The emotional reactions of the child or young person in his home, school, or community become attitude-developing experiences. Although psychologists, sociologists, educators, and community leaders are attempting to improve those home and community conditions that are likely to encourage antisocial attitudes among young people, responsibility for attitude development is becoming a primary function of the school.

The teaching-learning situation has emotional implications. Teacher attitudes toward learners and teaching conditions, as well as toward life in general, exert a tremendous impact upon the emotionalized attitudes of young people. Consequently, the kind of person a teacher is can be a more significant factor of teaching and learning success than what he knows and how he teaches, important as the latter are.

Common Teacher Problems

The implementation of modern educational philosophy is placing increasingly heavy demands upon school personnel. Modern educational objectives and resulting school curriculums, as well as programs of cocurricular activities, are aimed at caring for the learner's physical, mental, emotional, and social needs. In addition, state-enacted compulsory education laws keep some young people in school who, in spite of attempts to meet their educational needs, are uninterested in or antagonistic toward staying in school until the law permits them to become "dropouts."

Areas of Teacher Problems. The broadening of educational goals and the lengthening of the school life of the learner are increasing the responsibilities of teachers. Attempts by school people to meet the individual needs of a heterogeneous school population give rise to certain serious problems of teacher adjustment.

Difficulties encountered by a teacher in classroom and other school situations may be caused by (1) insufficient knowledge concerning the individual children or adolescents with whom he is working, (2) inadequate appreciation of the fundamental goals of education, (3) lack of skill in diagnosis, or (4) inexpertness in the utilization of good teaching methods and classroom procedures. Fundamentally, however, professional problems experienced by teachers are the resultants of nonconstructive personal and social attitudes, lack of self-confidence, and emotional instability. In Chapter 24 is discussed the significance of teacher personality as a psychological factor of teaching. At this point are considered briefly some of the major problem situations experienced especially by beginning teachers.

Psychological Factors of Teacher Adequacy. Various studies have been conducted to discover the factors inherent in good or in inadequate teaching. According to the findings of a study by the American Council on Education, the characteristics that are associated with teaching success include: personal and social adequacy, classroom rapport, professional interest, professional information, subject-matter knowledge, mental abilities and basic skills, general cultural background, experience, training, and physical fitness.[1]

As a result of investigatory findings based upon the responses of teachers and educational supervisors, it would appear that a common inadequacy of teachers is lack of professional skill and psychological understanding rather than of mastery of subject matter. Some of the specific difficulties encountered by teachers are related to the following aspects of their teaching responsibilities: motivating learners, providing for individual differences, diagnosing and correcting learning difficulties, developing learner self-discipline, selecting appropriate subject matter, inculcating good study habits, testing and evaluating learner readiness and progress, and achieving professional and social relationships with administrators, supervisors, fellow teachers, and parents.

Although the points of view expressed by teachers themselves and their supervisors are significant indices of teacher problems, important also are the attitudes of learners toward what they consider to be desirable teacher characteristics. A study conducted by the author and her husband of the opinions of high school and college students concerning successful teacher traits yielded the following traits that were considered most important by both groups of responders: knowledge of subject matter, interest in students, encouragement of students, patience, adaptability, organization of subject matter, definiteness of aim, accuracy, sincerity, enthusiasm, and friendliness.[2]

It is interesting to note that these students emphasized the importance of a teacher's knowing his subject but that they also appreciated the display of those skills and attitudes that have psychological significance. In general, when children and adolescents are asked to list the outstanding characteristics of teachers who have helped them most, they name attributes such as interest in and understanding of learners, helpfulness in explaining learning tasks clearly and thoroughly, friendliness, ability to adjust their vocabulary to that of the pupils without "talking down to them." (See Chapter 24.)

Effective teaching skill and attitudes are not acquired accidently or incidently. Experience on the job probably is an important factor of improved performance, but many years of teaching may do no more than intensify early difficulties unless the

[1] *Brochure No. 11,* American Council on Education, Washington, 1947.
[2] L. D. Crow and A. Crow, *Mental Hygiene,* 2d ed., McGraw-Hill Book Company, Inc., 1951, pp. 232-233.

young teacher brings to his task adequate preteaching preparation for it.

Value of the Study of Educational Psychology

Many beginning teachers assert that their student-teaching experience was the most valuable phase of their preteaching program of teacher education. Some claim that their other courses consisted "only of a lot of theory that has no practical value." The basis of this neophyte-teacher attitude can be explained in either or both of two ways: (1) the theory courses were too academic, and/or (2) the young man or woman had not yet achieved sufficient maturity of judgment to recognize the extent to which his background study helped him meet his teaching responsibilities.

Preteaching Psychological Preparation. Before a teaching candidate is ready to assume responsibility for guiding the learning activities of children or adolescents, he should (1) possess adequate knowledge and understanding of the psychological bases of human development and behavior, and (2) have acquired at least minimal skill in utilizing appropriate techniques for studying young people's capacities, interests, and degree of learning readiness. In addition, he should have achieved some competence in judging the relative psychological values of differing teaching procedures. Moreover, as the teacher trainee studies the psychological aspects of education, he can analyze his own learning approaches and evaluate his learning strength and weaknesses.

Although a study of much of the content of educational psychology can benefit parents and members of professions other than teaching, the psychological study of education is an essential area of preteaching preparation. The teacher must understand the psychological aspects of child and adolescent behavior and the psychology of the many phases of learning and teaching. Since educational psychologists do not yet agree upon a best approach to the solving of all learning problems, teacher trainees as well as the active participants in the teaching profession constantly must be alert to the significant findings of continued psychological reseach.

The classroom teacher usually has little opportunity to engage in extensive and intensive research activity. Yet many simple teacher-conducted classroom studies yield data that have practical value in the particular school situation in which they were obtained. Every teacher, however, should be able to read research materials intelligently and to apply appropriate findings to his own teaching-learning situations.

The Teacher and Research. During his preteaching period, the prospective teacher may not appreciate to the degree that he will later the importance of research dealing with psychological problems, such as:

1. Extent and ways in which learning is affected by biological inheritance and social heritage.
2. Maturational factors of learning.
3. Relation between teaching procedures and learning outcomes.
4. Effectiveness of evaluating techniques.
5. Relative influence upon young persons of incidental learnings and formal education.
6. Emotional factors of learning.
7. Bases of attitude changes.

This list includes only a few of the areas of psychological and educational research with which the teacher trainee should become acquainted.

The Mastering of Educational Psychology

Whether a student gains adequate mastery and understanding of educational psychology is dependent upon the way in which the subject matter content is presented and the student's attitude toward the practical value of the course.

Teaching Approaches. An academic-minded college instructor in educational psychology regards it as a content subject, similar to the "pure" sciences and mathematics. In his teaching, he stresses the mastery of psychological theory and the memorization of principles of learning. He may expect his students to reproduce exactly the minutiae of research investigations. Further, traditional and some recent textbooks are devoted mainly to detailed treatment of physical structure and physiological functions, mental and emotional processes, and similar topics that are treated in an erudite fashion, with little or no teaching or learning application.

At the other extreme are instructors who avoid or treat only indirectly theoretical content or sound psychological principles. The atmosphere of the classroom is extremely permissive. Students are encouraged to express their own opinions concerning human development and adequate teaching procedures. In such study situations, students' opinions emerge from three sources: (1) their analyses of personal experiences with teachers on lower school levels, (2) present informal and more formal observational study of individual young learners, and (3) visits to classrooms of neighboring schools.

Usually the permissive instructor does not utilize a textbook to be studied by all members of his class. Whatever readings are assigned include articles, research reports, and some practical materials that deal with the application of psychological theories and principles, without concern for student understanding of them.

These two types of approach to the study of educational psychology represent opposite extremes. Between these there are varying degrees and kinds of teaching emphasis, depending upon instructor interest and knowledge. Consequently, undue time and attention may be given to areas of development, the learning process, techniques of evaluation, or the social aspect of teaching and learning, to the exclusion of equally important areas of educational psychology.

Student Attitude toward Educational Psychology. Many students regard courses in education as "snap" courses. This is especially true of educational electives in a liberal arts college. To the extent that the goal of the first two years of college study has been almost exclusively the mastery of textbook content with little or no application to everyday living, the applicational aspect of education courses causes them to be considered "thin," repetitious, and unworthy of serious, concentrated study attention. Because of the complex nature of teaching and learning, the many aspects of teacher education cannot be understood and appreciated through the study of isolated unitary courses that deal only with specific areas, such as history of education, child development, principles of learning, measurement, methods of teaching, and the like. Preteaching preparation and in-service teacher education represent a continuum of intergrated learning, beginning with the understanding and application of simple psychological and educational concepts upon which gradually are built increasing knowledge, keener insight, and improved application. Teacher education, viewed as a continuing, integrated process, may seem to include repetitious materials, unless the student is enabled to recognize the interrelated and progressive nature of its objectives and curricula.

For the study of educational psychology to include values

other than the earning of college credits, it is the responsibility of the instructor to induce interested, serious, and constructive student attitudes toward it. He must help prospective teachers to:

1. Recognize the functional nature of educational psychology.

2. Gain an adequate understanding of child and adolescent growth or development, through book study, by personal observation of children and young people, and by intelligent classroom discussion based upon facts rather than mere opinion.

3. Assume a professional point of view toward their study.

4. Acquire skill in reading and comprehending reports of psychological research and other pertinent literature in the field, as well as in applying appropriate principles and theories in practical teaching-learning situations.

5. Maintain an unprejudiced and conservatively critical attitude toward differing theories of learning and teaching techniques.

6. Assume an experimental attitude within the limits of proved psychological principles and their applicational values.

7. Achieve the power to adapt habitual modes of thinking and teaching approaches to new but scientifically sound changes in educational theory and practice.

8. Learn ways to cooperate with and assume a professional attitude toward colleagues.

9. Acquire a willingness to apply tested theories that will be helpful to learners of all ability levels.

10. Become independent in thought and action within the framework of good educational leadership.

11. Become a leader in human relations in situations involving the learners with whom associated.

12. Appreciate the contributions of educational psychology to the continuing improvement of the teacher's understanding of learner abilities, attitudes, and behavior and the effects upon learning outcomes.

In the remaining chapters of this *Outline of Educational Psychology* are presented the results of psychological research and the points of view of present-day psychologists, as these materials can be applied by the teacher in his professional activities.

PART II

HUMAN GROWTH AND DEVELOPMENT

CHAPTER 3

BIOLOGICAL AND CULTURAL BASES OF HUMAN DEVELOPMENT

An individual's degree of success in learning depends upon (1) his innate potentiality to benefit from instruction, (2) his acquired interest in mastering learning materials, and (3) teaching content and procedures that are suited to his capacities, interests, and state of learning readiness. To be effective in his work with young people, a teacher needs to understand the biological and cultural backgrounds of his pupils and to adapt his teaching approaches to meet particular learner needs.

Aspects of Human Development

Every person is a unique individual, possessing personal characteristics that differentiate him from others of his age or kind. Fundamentally, however, human beings are more like one another than they are different. Human growth and maturation follow a relatively similar pattern, with some individual deviations in rate and extent of development. The kind of person an individual eventually becomes is the resultant of continuous interaction between the various aspects of his biologically inherited nature and the physical and cultural elements of the environment in which he grows and matures.

Basic Concepts. In any discussion of human nature, constant reference is made to the terms *growth, maturation,* and *development.* Sometimes these words seem to be used interchangeably. Although psychologists do not agree completely concerning their exact interpretation, each term represents a concept that differs somewhat from either of the others, although no two of the three concepts are mutually exclusive.

The meaning of the word *growth* can be restricted to increase in size as a result of multiplication of cells; a broader connotation of the term includes change and development resulting from interactions between an organism and its environment. *Maturation* connotes the processes involved in the sequential progress toward the upper limit of functional adequacy. The concept of maturation as intrinsic or inner growth probably has greater significance during the earlier years of an individual's life than it does later, when experience also is involved. *Development* represents changes in quality or function that accompany growth and that are effected through exercise or experience.

Practically, there is no sharp distinction between growth and development. When we speak of physical, mental, or social growth we tend to stress intrinsic changes; the substitution of the term *development* would seem to place greater emphasis upon the external causes for the inner changes.

General Principles of Growth and Development. Regardless of the kind and limit of growth or development of any individual, growth is a continuous process that tends to progress at a relatively slow, regular pace. Moreover, the growth pattern represents sequential advancement rather than a series of additions.

The rate and limit of growth and maturation differ among individuals as well as among the developmental aspects of the same individual. This is a fact that needs to be understood by teachers and applied in their teaching of pupils whose chronological ages are similar but whose growth and maturation levels may be very different from one another.

Although the many aspects of personality may vary in rate and limit of growth or development, an individual develops as a unified whole. The patterns of physical, mental, emotional, and social growth or maturation are interrelated in such way that change in one area influences progress in others. Hence any learning that takes place is conditioned to some degree at least by the learner's total growth or maturational level.

Observable behavior is related closely to growth status. The young child displays attitudes and engages in activities that later are modified or abandoned. For example, during childhood, a girl who is not inhibited by cultural pressures may participate in so-called "tomboy" play activities. With the onslaught of puberty, her recreational interests become less strenuous. Her changing physiological state is accompanied by changing attitudes toward boys and her relations with them.

Stages of Development. Although growth is continuous, for practical purposes the growth process can be divided into artificially established age sequences. The divisions most commonly used are: prenatal growth (from conception to birth), infancy and early childhood (from birth through the age of five), later childhood (from about six through eleven), and adolescence (from puberty to adulthood).

These developmental states usually are associated with the individual's learning experiences. During the prenatal period, the organism is concerned mainly with the growth process; during infancy and early childhood, behavior and attitudes are developed in the home, and physical care is provided almost entirely by the members of the family group. Later childhood often is referred to as the elementary school years, and adolescence is the period during which the developing individual usually is learning on the high school level, and then continues his education on the college level or begins vocational activity.

From one's own experiences or from observation of other growing or developing young people, significant differences can be found in the developmental pattern of an individual at the ages of 3, 9, 15, and 25, respectively. Not only are there evidences of progress in physical and physiological growth and maturation, but also of mental and social advancement. Yet so gradual is the entire process that differences between the 5- and 6-, the 11- and 12-, or the 18- and 19-year-olds may be difficult to distinguish.

It cannot be emphasized too strongly that growth and maturation do not take place in a vacuum. Every phase of an individual's nature is influenced by the environmental factors to which he is exposed from conception to death. There has been much controversy among biologists, psychologists, and sociologists concerning the relative importance during the developmental years of inherited characteristics and of environmental influences.

The implications of the phrase "nature versus nurture" have exerted a tremendous impact upon educational theory and practice. Most educators accept the fact that children differ in their innate capacities and learning potentialities. They also recognize the extent to which cultural factors and environmental elements influence the natural growth and maturation patterns of any young person, regardless of his inborn characteristics.

Contributions of Biological Inheritance

Psychologists have drawn heavily upon biological research for their knowledge concerning the beginnings of life. Educational psychologists select and apply those psychologically accepted principles that have educational significance. The following treatment of heredity, therefore, is limited to a consideration of the major principles and a brief description of the mechanism of heredity.

Basic Principles of Biological Inheritance. Continuing biological and psychological research constantly is disclosing heretofore unknown facts concerning human nature. In so far as we know at present, biological inheritance functions generally according to certain definite principles, as traits or characteristics are transmitted from generation to generation.

1. Since each category of animals or plants tends to follow a pattern of growth or maturation peculiar to itself, the members of the human species have many characteristics in common. In other words, like begets like. Such characteristics as tallness or shortness, brightness or dullness, vivacity or stolidity tend to be transmitted by way of family line.

2. Although human beings are alike in many respects they also differ from one another. Variation from what might appear to be a general family pattern is common among family offspring. Children are not replicas of their parents.

3. The bases of heredity are the germ cells. Specific characteristics of a new organism result from different combinations of the genes or determiners in the germ cells of the parents. The functioning of the element of chance in gene combinations makes it impossible to predict with any degree of certainty the likeness to or variation from parental qualities exhibited by the new organisms. Siblings may differ in various inherited characteristics, but they tend to be more similar to one another than they are to unrelated children.

4. Fifty percent of the new organism's total inheritance (23 chromosomes) is contributed by the maternal line, and 50 per cent by the paternal line. The father may contribute 23 *X* chromosomes, in which case the child will be a girl. If he contributes 22 *X* chromosomes and one *Y* chromosome, the sex of the child will be male.

5. The child does not inherit all his characteristics directly from his parents. According to present estimates, one-half of his inheritance is from his parents, one-quarter from the grandparents, one-eighth from great-grandparents, and lesser fractions proportionately from more remote ancestors.

The fact that a child inherits some of his characteristics by way of his ancestral lines rather than all of them directly from his immediate parents is important to teachers as well as to the parents themselves. Too often siblings are expected to display similar attitudes and to possess comparable potentialities. A young person who differs markedly from other members of the immediate family in one or another characteristic may be treated as a changeling or considered to be queer or unnatural unless adults understand the factors involved.

6. As a result of gene selection and combination, the new organism inherits certain potentialities of development. Whatever skills, attitudes, or knowledge he eventually attains are acquired in accordance with the limits set by his potential learning capacity and the environmental stimulations he experiences. A former common belief among lay people that a child's character, personal appearance, or abilities could be influenced by the mother during the period of gestation has been discarded. These qualities cannot be acquired during the prenatal period. There is some possibility, however, that the growth of the embryo and fetus may be affected by environmental factors such as insufficient or faulty nutrition, strictures or pressures, venereal disease, infection, severe illness, physical hurt, or extreme emotional stress suffered by the mother during the period of pregnancy.

7. In general, certain genes seem to be stronger than others, in that traits produced by the stronger or *dominant* genes appear more often than do those produced by the weaker or *recessive* genes. The functioning of gene dominance or recessiveness is especially apparent when one compares the physical characteristics of relatively "pure" strains of national or geographical groups. Scandinavians, for example, are known for their light hair, fair complexion, blue eyes, and relatively tall stature. Latin peoples, on the contrary, tend to have dark hair and complexion and brown eyes, and to be relatively short. Deviations from the expected characteristics are explained as "sports" or as resulting from intermating between the strains. The behavior traits produced by dominant genes are less easily determined than are physical characteristics because of the great influence of environmental factors upon behavior development.

8. A child's potentialities tend to reflect ancestral characteristics, especially those of his immediate relatives. To the extent that a parental characteristic is superior or inferior, the trait potential in the child is likely to approach the average more nearly than it did in the parent. The tendency for an inherited trait to move toward the average is known as *regression.* This principle of heredity does not always function. Some children

are as tall as or taller than their parents. Some children of apparently dull parents are extremely bright, or vice versa. There is enough evidence available, however, to indicate that regression functions in many instances.

The multiplicity of genes and the complexity of trait determination are such that no principle of heredity is completely infallible. One must always allow for a margin of error, even while an explanation is sought to validate a principle. For example, an individual who possesses an inferior or superior trait may mate with a member of the opposite sex in whom this trait more nearly represents the average. Further, even though both parents are inferior or superior in the same trait, their germ cells may be better or worse than those which produced them, or the combination of the gene determiners.

The Mechanism of Heredity. A new life begins with the union of an ovum or female germ cell with a sperm or male germ cell. The fertilization of the ovum is called conception. The fertilized cell receives 23 cellular structures or chromosomes from each of the parents, thus possessing 23 pairs, totalling 46 chromosomes. These strings of pairs of protoplasmic substances are believed to carry hundreds of genes, invisible particles that act as determiners of native characteristics or traits. Billions of permutations and combinations can result from the variations in combination of a human being's 23 pairs of chromosomes.

The process of mitosis or cell division begins at conception and continues until appropriate body structures appear. An equal number of maternal and paternal chromosomes is received by each cell; the genes arrange themselves in ways that may be different for every new organism.

The average length of a human being's prenatal period is about 270 days, or nine calendar months. The entire period can be divided roughly into three periods of development: *germinal, embryonic,* and *fetal.* During the germinal period (from conception through the second week), the fertilized egg or zygote floats freely and needs little or no nourishment. Through a continued process of cell division and subdivision there is formed a cluster of globules which, having passed during cell division down the Fallopian tube to the uterus, attaches itself to the uterus wall. The placenta (from which the umbilical cord extends to the zygote) develops at the point of implantation, thereby enabling the developing organism to receive nourishment from the mother's blood stream.

Many changes take place during the embryonic period, which extends from the second week to approximately the end of the eighth week or second month after fertilization. There is a division of the cell mass into three germ layers—the outer layer or *ectoderm,* the middle layer or *mesoderm,* and the innermost layer or *endoderm.* In these layers are produced various body structures and organs. Several of the organs begin to function during this period. The heart beats faintly by the end of the third week and the liver and other organs become active during the second month. The organism now exhibits some likeness to a human being and possesses the beginnings of behavior potentialities.

Growth and development begun during the embryonic period are continued during the fetal period. The fetus increases in size; the various organs gradually come to function in much the same way as they will after birth. Some spontaneous movements are possible, as well as feeble crying. For a healthy fertilized ovum experiencing favorable environmental conditions during the prenatal period, entrance into the world as a newborn infant usually is made with little or no traumatic experience. With his first cry, the neonate may show some slight awareness of the new environment which will continue to play a significant role in his process of development as a human being.

Significant Inherited Characteristics. The newborn child does not possess specific traits or behavior patterns. These must be learned. Effective learning depends upon biologically inherited potentialities as well as upon the kind and amount of environmental stimulation the child receives. It is difficult to state with assurance that any one or more of an individual's characteristics are biologically inherited or environmentally acquired. Studies of identical (monozygotic) and fraternal (dizygotic) twins have yielded data that would seem to indicate that there is a closer relationship between the physical characteristics and mental capacity of identical twins than is found between fraternal twins, or siblings who are reared in the same home. Identical twins reared in different environments reflect the difference in their mental and educational abilities, with relatively little change in physical development.

Research concerning family lineage would seem to indicate that the offspring may inherit potentialities which later show themselves variously in the form of feeblemindedness, special talent leading to eminence, insanity, criminality, or social deficiency. The data of such studies should not be accepted as general tendencies that apply to all children, however. In the past, too many parents and teachers assumed a fatalistic attitude toward the younger members of families who, rightly or wrongly, had earned a commendable or unfavorable reputation in the community. A child may be a "chip off the old block" but it is with the potentialities of that particular chip that the teacher especially should be concerned.

Environmental conditions are important but only to the extent that they can function in cooperation with inherited characteristics. The acquiring of skill and knowledge, the developing of personal and social attitudes, and the formation of behavior habits through education are made possible by the child's original or inherited equipment. A human being's body structure is an important basis of learning. The nervous system, the sense organs, and the arms and legs respond to environmental or educational stimulations. The cerebrum especially serves as a medium of adaptation.

The active, dynamic nature of a living organism impels it to move or change position. Much physical activitiy is characteristic of early childhood, during which period movement is gross and undifferentiated, gradually becoming more specialized and refined. Other inherited characteristics that make learning possible include organismic sensitivity or irritability and human plasticity or modifiability. Biological "dispositions" or urges, needs, and wants are fundamental to motivation toward participation in learning activities.

Except in cases of specific hereditary deficencies, all human beings possess an original equipment that has educational significance. Heredity sets individual limitations, however, upon the kind and amount of development that occurs. Each new organism has its own total pattern of potentialities, each of which responds in its particular fashion to accidental or controlled external stimulation. As a result of research and experimentation, it is being discovered that the adaptation of learning content and teaching procedures based upon an improved understanding of inherited potentialities and educational needs of individual learners can affect favorable development to a degree that at one time was considered impossible to achieve.

Contributions of Cultural Background and Social Environment

There is much evidence available concerning the great strength of heredity in determining an individual's developmental progress. Psychologists, however, do not minimize the molding power of the environment into which a new organism is born and of the many differing cultural forces by which he is stimulated throughout his growing years.

Reference often is made to a child's need to be reared and educated in a *favorable* environment. Used to describe an environment, the term *favorable* may have various connotations. One could ask to what the environment should be favorable—the child's physical health, his mental development, his emotional reactions, or his social interrelationships. From another viewpoint, one might be concerned with the standards or ideals of the community considered to be favorable.

Customs, mores, traditional attitudes, and practices differ among social groups and subgroups. What might be regarded to be desirable environmental conditions by one cultural group, one family, one educational system, or one community might be ignored or condemned by another. In the following discussion of the cultural and social basis of development and of the interaction between hereditary and environmental factors, major stress is placed upon factual data concerning environmental influences, with a minimum of evaluation of their effects as favorable or unfavorable.

Areas of Environmental Influences. Broadly interpreted, the physical environment of a growing child includes climatic conditions and geographic terrain. In and of itself, the physical environment has relatively little effect upon the child's development. Climatic or temperature differences may influence an individual's amount and kind of work and recreational activities, and his relative speed of movement. A child reared in hilly country is likely to be more sure footed than a child who spends his early years on the plains. To grow up among richly hued and luxurious flora may develop in the child an appreciation of and love for natural beauty that is not experienced by the young person whose home is in a crowded, almost treeless city, or on a grassy plain. Usually, however, most individuals can adapt themselves easily to changes in physical environment.

Much more powerful are the effects upon an individual of the elements of his social environment. His behavior and attitudes are molded through his relationships with the members of his family, his teachers, his peer-age and older associates, as well as by what he hears about other sections of his own country or more remote parts of the world.

Cultural Background. A child is sensitive to the habitual behavior and attitudes that are characteristic of his cultural background. Although it is difficult to determine exactly what cultural factors influence his developmental pattern, he cannot avoid being affected to some degree at least by the way of life of the society into which he is born.

Regardless of where they are born, the original equipment of human beings is relatively the same. Differences in the behavior of children reared in different cultures, therefore, would seem to reflect cultural influences. Comparisons of the way of life among differing peoples indicate that children reared in New Guinea, for example, display gentle and noncompetitive behavior that is very different from the more individualistic and aggressive attitudes characteristic of children in more competitive societies.

The language of a people is an important medium for transmitting their culture, since not only the literal meaning of words but also the feelings associated with them affect behavior.* The young child is inducted into his particular culture as he learns to put meaning into the words that reflect in their connotations the customs, beliefs, and attitudes of the group. An individual's accustomed language sometimes is referred to as his *native* tongue, implying that he was born with the ability to speak that language. This is a false assumption or a loose use of terms. One inherits vocal organs which enable him to learn how to imitate sounds. Whatever proficiency he gains in a particular language is the product of environmental stimulation. To that extent it becomes his *accultured* tongue or language.

The members of a particular society tend to show certain fundamental behavior and attitude patterns peculiar to their culture. For example, expressions such as *the American way of life, Oriental culture,* or *Latin background* are generally used to describe what are considered by the speaker or writer to represent basic characteristics of the societal groups so designated. A large cultural group, however, usually consists of many subcultures which may be similar to one another in some respect but may differ markedly in others. For a teacher to understand children's attitudes and behavior, it is important that he become acquainted with the kinds of interactions the child has experienced and is in the process of experiencing in terms of the various aspects of his cultural and subcultural backgrounds.

* See F. Cordasco, "The Challenge of the Non-English Speaking Child in American Schools," *School & Society*, Vol. 96 (March 1968), pp. 198-201.

Interaction of Inherited Potentialities and Environmental Experiences

During an individual's prenatal as well as postnatal experiences, his growing characteristics and maturing potentialities continue to interact with numerous and increasingly complex environmental forces. The stimulating conditions and situations to which he responds more or less effectively are rooted in his cultural or subcultural background.

Nature and Nurture. The kind and degree of mating selection exercised by his parents, the amount and kind of medical care the mother receives, and her accustomed activities during her period of pregnancy may exert a significant influence upon the prenatal development of the new organism. Physical structure, including height, weight, and body contours, the organization of the nervous system, and other physical characteristics are largely gene determined, yet their rate and limit of growth are helped or hindered by nurture.

Health and life span are influenced by enivornmental factors. In the United States, for example, medical research and improved health care have reduced infant mortality from a rate of 1 out of 6 in 1850 to a present rate of 1 out of 30, with probable decrease. The average life span has increased from about 35 years at the beginning of the nineteenth century to approximately 70, with an increasing number of persons living through the 80's. Improved dietary knowledge and campaigns against disease, such as typhoid fever, scarlet fever, smallpox, and diphtheria, as well as other preventive measures can be regarded as environmental factors favorable to healthy physical development.

Mental health status, and developed personality qualities and character traits are the resultants of interactions between native endowment and environmental experiences. From the moment of his birth, an individual's inherited characteristics are molded according to the many differing environmental stimuli to which he reacts, at first in the home and later in the neighborhood, school, community, and larger societal units.

Home Influences. That an individual's fundamental behavior patterns and attitudes are formed in the home during his early childhood years is a generally accepted fact. Through precept and example he acquires the habits of thought, speech, and action that are characteristic of the members of the family in their relationships with him. The young child is affected directly or indirectly by the kind of home into which he is born and reared. The social, economic, and educational status of the family determines the amount and kind of situational experiences provided for the development of his organic equipment.

Parental attitude toward the child is important. Rejection or overprotection of the child by either or both parents interferes with the satisfaction of his urge for security or for appropriate independence. Other significant factors of home influence include: (1) his age position among siblings or his status as an only child, (2) whether the home has both parents or is a broken home, and (3) the degree of consistency governing parental treatment of him.

Neighborhood Influences. A young child's developing interests are conditioned by his neighborhood experiences. The child reared in an urban community, especially in an apartment house of an overcrowded section of the city, usually is denied the freedom of activity that he needs and wants and that is available for the child living in a suburban town or a rural area.

Racial or national concentration in a child's home neighborhood may result in his being indoctrinated during his early years in the traditions, customs, and beliefs that are characteristic of the group. Later, the child is likely to come into contact with children who have been reared in the traditions of another, different culture or whose early training reflects more cosmopolitan experience. Difficulties of social adjustment then tend to arise that either require the child's modification of habitual behavior or impel him to retreat from the new social environment to his accustomed neighborhood in which he experiences greater personal security.*

School Experiences. A child's entrance into school is a critical point in the developmental process. Even though he starts in the nursery or kindergarten department of a neighborhood school, he encounters situations and conditions that differ from those experienced in the relatively sheltered environment of his home and immediate neighborhood. New and different physical and

* A vast literature on the minority child and the American school has been assembled over the 1960's. See, generally, F. Cordasco, "The Children of the Poor and The Schools," in William W. Brickman and Stanley Lehrer, *The Disadvantaged In International Perspective* (New York: John Wiley, 1972).

social stimuli require him to make changes in habitual responses.

The new school entrant is affected variously by the school building and grounds and the kind and arrangement of seats, desks, and other classroom furniture and equipment. He finds himself in a school or class group, many members of which are strangers. A mother substitute, in the form of a teacher, issues directives which he is expected to follow. He is challenged by learning tasks that are different in form and content from his customary home activities. Further, he must find a place for himself among his schoolmates, and gain status with his teacher. During his early school experiences, the degree of success achieved by a child in developing his potentialities depends partly upon the kinds of interaction between his organic equipment and the stimulating environmental forces of the home, and partly upon the teacher's understanding of his natural capacities and habitual behavior patterns.

To some extent, the experiences of the young school entrant are duplicated on each new educational level, such as junior high school, senior high school, and possibly college. With increasing maturity, the young person becomes better equipped to adapt himself to increasingly complex educational demands.

Community Influences. At one time, the home and the school were regarded as the sole agencies responsible for a young person's growth and development. The results of studies dealing with the influence of environmental and cultural forces indicate that other factors also have a strong impact upon the behavior and attitudes of growing and maturing individuals.

Important as home rearing and school training may be, the experiences of young people outside the home and school wield a tremendous influence upon the building of their ideals and upon the nature of their personal and social values. Consequently, there is a growing trend toward placing increased responsibility upon the community as a whole for the welfare of its young citizens.*

There are wide differences among communities (rural, urban, and suburban) in the extent to which provision is made, through community institutions and agencies, for child and youth-centered projects. Large cities find it difficult to meet all the needs of all children. Rural areas are faced with the problem

* For the postures of community influences and participation in the schools, see Henry M. Levin, *Community Control of Schools* (Washington: Brookings Institution, 1970), which is more comprehensive than its title suggests and provides a delineation of the new, evolving community-school relationship.

of bridging wide area distances. Some communities lack the financial means to establish adequate opportunities for constructive youth activities. Prosperous suburban communities and middle-sized towns probably are showing most progress in caring for the physical and social needs of their young citizens.

There are various media by the utilization of which a community can help stimulate good physical, educational, and social development. Among projects organized in an increasing number of communities are community-sponsored health centers and medical clinics, indoor and outdoor recreational centers, social and welfare organizations, mental-health and child-guidance clinics, libraries, and community schools serving adults as well as young people. In addition, contrary to traditional practice, not all school learning needs to take place within the school building. Business organizations, industrial plants, government offices, and other community institutions encourage young people to visit them and to study their operations at first hand.

Effect of Physical Status. Human beings have a tendency to respond adversely to those conditions which thwart or interfere with their vital urges. When fulfillment is endangered, there is a possibility that a basic frustration may germinate. For example, both size and strength are influential in assessing a young person's place among his peers.

Physical features exert a powerful influence on the attitudes and behavior of the developing individual. Girls desire to possess those physical features that will help them to be accepted by girls and, especially during adolescence, be attractive to boys. Boys desire to possess those physical qualities that will help them to be regarded as masculine. However, they want people of all ages to admire their physical appearance.

Specifically, a boy is disturbed by such physical features as smaller-than-average stature, extreme stoutness or thinness, facial blemishes and poor physique in general. A girl is bothered by such physical features as shortness, excessive stoutness or thinness, acne, underveloped breasts or any features in which she believes that she is much different from other girls of her age group. However, a strong, healthy adolescent boy or girl usually is at ease with others and relatively free from emotional tensions.

Comment. This chapter has dealt with the basic contributions of heredity and of environment to the developmental progress of human beings. The treatment was limited to a brief survey of the total growth and developmental process. In the remainder of the book, many of the materials included here will be discussed more fully in their appropriate relationships.

The prospective teacher needs to recognize the fact that heredity and environment are equally important in determining the kind of adult a young person probably will become. So interwoven are the influences of the two, however, that it is difficult, if not impossible, to distinguish exactly between what is completely inherited and what is inherited potential modified by environment.

Education, considered broadly as informal, relatively accidental learning or interpreted more strictly as organized purposeful school experiences, is concerned with every aspect of an individual's total behavior. The growth of anatomical structure and the maturation of physiological functions follow a harmoniour pattern, although each aspect of the unified whole of an individual's personality develops at its own particular rate and to its germ-determined limit.

Physical, mental, emotional, or social development does not represent an isolated process. An individual eventually achieves a particular life style through interaction between all the various phases of his inherited tendencies and all the differing environmental forces by which he is stimulated. For convenience of discussion, the growth patterns of human nature are treated separately but the interrelationships that exist among them cannot and should not be ignored.

CHAPTER 4

ANATOMICAL AND PHYSIOLOGICAL GROWTH

Biologically, mammals have some similar physical characteristics. They differ in structure but are warm-blooded and possess much the same life-sustaining organs and physiological functions. Man's superiority lies in the great complexity and sensitivity of his physical nature. He thereby is enabled to respond to environmental stimuli effecting developmental changes within him beyond the natural capabilities even of other primates. Hence human growth potentialities constitute the bases of every phase of human development.

Educational Implications of Physical Development

The kind and effectiveness of an individual's experiences are rooted in his body health. Deviation from what is considered to be physical normality may interfere seriously with personal activities and social acceptance. It is important therefore that parents and school people understand what is meant by normal physical development at every age level. They should be able to recognize the seriousness of possible deviations and be prepared to cope with problems caused by individual variation from accepted norms.

Societal Attitudes toward Physical Fitness. The educational significance of physical development is closely related to cultural ideals and life patterns. Primitive man struggled with the forces of nature to achieve physical survival, and engaged in face-to-face combat with neighboring groups to maintain tribal unity and independence. The women were expected to be physically fit to bear strong, healthy children and to perform their arduous duties in the home.

World conquerors, such as the early Romans, the Spartans, and the Germanic peoples placed great emphasis upon physical growth status. During the relatively peaceful periods of world history, however, and among nonwarlike peoples, the development of physical prowess has been minimized and increasing emphasis placed upon the training of the mental abilities. Consequently, in most cultures, schooling came to be concerned mainly with imparting knowledge. The physical development of children was considered to be a parental responsibility. Except in cases of severe physical impairment, concern about physical health was divorced almost completely from provision for mental development. Through scientifically conducted studies of human growth and development, it was discovered that physical growth is basic to the development of human potentialities. School people began to recognize the educational, personal, and social importance of the factors of structural growth and of physiological maturation during childhood and adolescence.

The Study of Physical Growth. A considerable mass of research data is available concerning the various phases of human growth. Numerous growth studies have been and are being conducted in research areas, such as physiology and biochemistry, morphology, pathology and clinical medicine, psychology, psychiatry and mental hygiene, and public health and hygiene. The Harvard and Yale research centers are in the process of investigating every measurable phase of physical growth and maturation.

Various study approaches are utilized. Regardless of the specific techniques employed in a particular investigation, two commonly used approaches are (1) the cross-sectional, or horizontal, and (2) the longitudinal, or vertical.

Early researchers in the field utilized the cross-sectional, or horizontal approach. Large numbers of children at specific stages of development were subjected to single testings. Conclusions based upon these studies were concerned primarily with sex and nationality or race growth tendencies in height, weight, and body contour. From the averages obtained for different age groups, growth curves were constructed, especially height-weight charts. In addition, the application of statistical techniques to the results of these horizontal studies led to the conclusion that the growth curves of the various aspects of physical development are closely related.

Although the horizontal study approach yields considerable data concerning general growth trends, it fails to provide information about the growth tendencies of a specific individual. Increased interest in child study as a means of discovering and providing for individual differences among children motivated the utilization of the longitudinal or vertical approach. A long-time study can be made of the progressive growth pattern of a particular child or group of children. A combination of the horizontal and longitudinal approaches yields valuable data, in that an individual can be compared with himself and with others at various stages of growth, thereby affording opportunities to discover the underlying causes of uneven individual growth and of individual differences.

The results of growth studies have provided an average for each developmental stage that can be expressed in the form of "age" status for that aspect of growth. A structural or anatomical "age" identifies a stage in the growth of the bony structure; the physiological "age" refers to the developmental stage of the internal organs, especially the sex organs.

It should be noted that it is more difficult to measure organic or physiological changes than it is to obtain accurate records of growth in body structure. Blood pressure, pulse rate, glandular action, and metabolism (physical and chemical process in using and releasing energy) are not constant in their functioning. They may be affected by variables, such as exercise or rest, time of day, and emotional state. In general, however, growth studies have yielded sufficient data to indicate that the rate of physical growth is rapid during early childhood, slows down during later childhood years, and again increases as the young person nears puberty. Although growth continues during adolescence, the rate gradually diminishes. Moreover, during childhood, the rate of growth is relatively the same for boys and girls. With the onset of puberty, girls surpass boys in growth progress, but by middle adolescence, they lose their advantage to boys, who continue thereafter to hold the lead.

Anatomical Growth

The areas of physical growth usually referred to as anatomical growth include the skeleton, height and weight, body proportions, and dentition. Each individual tends to vary from every other in his rate and limit of physical growth for each of the listed areas. Yet certain general growth trends appear to represent normality for particular groups, and therefore to be predictive of related developmental tendencies. Although norms rarely can be regarded as absolute measures, a teacher can compare the growth levels of his pupils if he knows what is considered the appropriate anatomical age for his grade. He is enabled thereby to recognize cases of serious deviation.

Skeletal Growth. The skeleton of the fetus and of the neonate is mostly cartilaginous. During the neonatal period, the organism's 270 bones are spongy, small, pliable, and loosely connected. Fontanels (soft spots in the baby's skull) usually close by the end of the second year. The bony structure begins to harden or ossify as a result of the depositing of calcium and other minerals into the cartilage.

By the age of 13 or 14, the young person's bones have increased to 350. As the process of ossification continues beyond puberty, some of the small bones fuse, thereby reducing the number in the adult to 206 bones that have broadened and thickened during the adolescent period of ossification. Growth of bony structure appears to be fairly regular, although individual differences can be found here, as in other areas of development. It is believed that ossification is related to nutrition, and that skeletal growth is improved and accelerated by healthful diet.

Growth in Height and Weight. During the developing years, growth in height and weight is continuous. The rate of growth differs for different life cycles, however. The most rapid rate of growth probably occurs during prenatal development. After birth, the periods of most rapid growth are infancy and adolescence, with a diminished growth rate during childhood.

Individual children may vary from supposedly average or normal height and weight trends. One child may maintain a relatively short stature until adolescence and then "shoot up" rapidly; another may be an extremely tall child in comparison with his peer-age associates but then slow down in rate of growth so that, as an adult, he is average or below average in height. Similarly, although the average height and weight ratio is relatively consistent at different growth stages, health conditions or glandular imbalance may cause a child to deviate to a marked degree from the accepted weight norm for his age.

Any extreme height or weight deviation may have an adverse effect upon a child's or adolescent's developing behavior and attitude patterns. The young, physically overdeveloped child may be expected to have reached an accompanying degree of mental and emotional maturity, with the result that he is called upon to assume responsibilities for which he is not ready. A smaller but older sibling or classmate may be coddled or be denied privileges granted the younger, larger child. Peer associates often embarrass a physical deviate by applying to him what they consider appropriate names, such as "Fatso," "Butterball," "Skinny," "Matchstick," and other descriptive terms. Social acceptance is as much desired by children as it is by adults. A child can be made unhappy by the denial of peer acceptance that is caused by a physical abnormality. This poses a challenge to adults to provide whatever health or physical care is needed to improve the situation.

Average Height and Weight Trends. The average length of a newborn boy is approximately 20.5 inches; his weight is about 7 pounds 8 ounces. The average length of a girl at birth is 20.3 inches, and her weight approximates 7 pounds. The child's gain in height during the first year is expected to be about 10 inches, and 4 or 5 inches during the second year. There is a slight slowing down of the rapid rate of growth to the sixth year; from 6 to 12 years the amount of height increase may be no more than 2 or 3 inches. Then there is a sudden spurt.

The weight curve follows a relatively similar pattern, except that the rate is rapid during the first year, when the child probably triples his weight at birth. The slowing down process is such that the monthly gain approximates about ½ pound for the second year. The weight of the average child ranges between 38 and 45 pounds by the fifth year, and from 80 to 95 pounds during the twelfth year.

The boy tends to be taller and heavier than the girl until about the age of 10, at which time there is little if any difference between them. The onset of puberty is usually earlier for a girl than for a boy. The girl becomes taller and heavier than the boy and continues to surpass him in height and weight until middle adolescence, when the situation is reversed; the boy regains and maintains his height and weight advantage.

There is danger in too great definiteness concerning height and weight averages. Although an extreme deviation may cause the child to experience serious problems, parents and teachers should take into account the fact that family tendencies, climatic conditions, or other factors may cause a child's height and weight progress to be normal for him even though it differs from the general average.

Body Proportions and Contours. Growth is from the head downward. For example, the head of a newborn infant comprises about one-fourth of the height of his total body; the adult's head represents approximately one-tenth of the total body length. The relative growth of the features is uneven; hence an adolescent's face may seem to be asymmetrical. Other body proportions, such as relative length of arms, legs, and torso, also change with growth.

During childhood, the body contours of boys and girls are similar. Beginning with pubescence, significant differences between the sexes begin to show themselves. Nature prepares each of the sexes for its expected life functions. The boy's form is identified by relatively broad shoulders, narrow hips, and straight leg lines; the girl's shoulders remain narrow, her legs tend to curve and her hips become wider.

Dentition. Normally, a child experiences the eruption of two sets of teeth—first or "baby" teeth, and permanent teeth. At birth, all the first teeth are formed in the gums; they usually begin to erupt when the child is about 6 months old. By the end of the first year the child should have approximately 8 first, or deciduous teeth, and a complete set by the time he reaches his fourth year.

Rate of physical growth can be measured by the rate of eruption of the permanent teeth. The first permanent tooth should be the six-year molar. The rate at which the teeth erupt differs among individual children. On the average, the eruption of a complete set of permanent teeth occurs before the fourteenth year, although the age at which the full quota is possessed may vary from the age of 9 to about 20.

Cranial Growth. The growth of the skull is relatively complete by the end of the sixth year. Cranial (brain) growth follows a pattern similar to that of height and weight. The head size of boys tends to be larger than that of girls. Yet the rate of growth decreases for both sexes until puberty, after which there is a 2-year spurt, followed by a gradual diminishing of rate.

At birth the child possesses his complete number of nerve cells; the weight of the brain is one-fourth of what it will be in adulthood. By the age of 5, the child's brain weight has increased, especially in the frontal lobes, to about 90 per cent of its adult size.

Skull growth is measured according to length, width, cubic capacity, and cephalic index (ratio of head breadth to head length—the wider the head the greater the index). The cephalic index differs with racial stock, although variations are found within any racial group. At one time, shape and size of head were believed to be closely related to degree of mental ability. Expressions such as, "highbrow" and "lowbrow" were supposed to be indications of a high degree and a low degree of intelligence, respectively. A well-formed, rounded back of head was considered to represent superior mental ability; a "flat" head connoted mental dullness. These beliefs no longer are accepted completely. Among the lower animals, the size of the brain in comparison to that of the skull may be related to mental ability. For example, the elephant has a small brain in a large skull. Among humans, however, except in extreme cases of arrested growth, neural quality rather than skull size or shape probably is the determining factor of degree of mental acuity.

Organic Growth and Physiological Maturation.

Included among the body organs are the respiratory, circulatory, digestive, nervous, muscular, glandular, and reproductive systems. Each of these systems follows its own developmental pattern; but there is no sharp differentiation between anatomical or structural growth and organic or physiological development and their functional maturation. The progressive changes that take place from conception to maturity represent interdependent and overlapping phases of the total growth process.

The Respiratory System. There is no definite evidence of breathing during the prenatal period. At birth the lungs are small; they grow rapidly during the early years and then continue at an uneven rate. Early adolescence is marked by relatively great increase in the weight and volume of the lungs, with a continuous but lower rate of development until adulthood. The shape of the chest remains constant after the age of 13. The growth of the lungs, accompanied by increased breathing capacity, continues until maximum development is reached by girls at about the age of 17 and boys at 19 or 20.

The Circulatory System. The embryo gives evidence of frequent but feeble heartbeats. After the child is born, the functioning of the respiratory system is accompanied by stronger and slower heart action. At about the age of 6, the heart has increased from four to five times over its weight at birth and to approximately seven times at the age of 12, reaching twelve times its birth weight by adulthood. A period of relatively slow growth occurs at the age of 7, with another possible lag during the prepubertal and early adolescent periods.

The heart beat increases in steadiness as the heart grows in size. The pulse rate at birth is high, approximately 130 for boys and 144 for girls. The 3-year-old boy tends to have a pulse rate of 95, and the same-age girl's is 90; at the age of 9 the rate is about 80 for both sexes. The pulse rate of each sex continues to decrease, but at about the age of 13, the girl's is 76 and the boy's is 73. From then on, normally, the girl's heartbeat tends to be higher than the boy's. Variations in the growth rate of the circulatory system need to be recognized by parents and school people lest, during the formative years, too great strain be placed upon the heart as a result of too strenuous and too prolonged physical exercise.

The Digestive System. The kind and amount of food consumed by a child from birth through the developmental period should be controlled in terms of stomach and intestinal organ growth. At birth, the capacity of the stomach is 1 ounce, increasing to about 3 ounces in about 4 weeks. The young child's stomach and intestines are small; the digestive tract is delicate, and the amount of digestive juices is low.

With increased growth of the digestive systems, more food can be eaten and elimination of waste materials is less frequent. Elimination of body wastes and the destruction of bacteria in the body are controlled by the lymphatic system, which develops rapidly during the first 12 or 13 years of life and then diminishes in rate.

Dietary care should continue to be exercised, particularly during the developing years. Physically active children and adolescents need nourishing food to build energy. Unless they are properly guided, however, they may acquire the habit of indulging in foods that are detrimental to the digestive system and to physical growth in general.

The Nervous System. It is estimated that by the end of the sixth month, the nervous system of the fetus probably consists of more than 12 billion nerve cells, and that some nerves are beginning to function. By birth, the nerve cells have been organized into reaction patterns and the structural development of the nervous system has been completed.

The child's nervous system is composed of three types of neural networks. (1) The sympathetic or autonomic neurons control the life-sustaining body organs. (2) The sensory and motor neurons serve as media of communication and control body activity. (3) The association neurons function in voluntary and imaginal activity: perception, ideation, language, and the higher mental processes.

Prenatally differentiated form and functions of the brain produce a well-systematized, highly complex organ of mental activity. The lower brain centers and the spinal cord control the behavior of the very young child. The increasingly complex mental activities of an individual are centered in the cortical layers of the cerebrum or "large" brain. The cortex consists of: (1) the infragranular layer, having attained about 80 per cent of its growth at birth and controlling the various reflex reactions; (2) the granular layer, having reached 75 per cent of its growth by birth and conducting sensory impressions, and (3) the supragranular layer, having only 50 per cent of its growth at birth and serving as organizer and coordinator of the interacting functions of the nervous system.

The Muscular System. The growth of muscle tissue is relatively slow during childhood. The weight of a child's muscles at birth is about 23 per cent of his total weight, progressing to no more than 27 per cent at the age of 8. During adolescence, muscle growth is more rapid, increasing from approximately 33 per cent at 15 to about 44 per cent of total body weight at 16.

With adolescent change in muscle weight, the larger or "fundamental" muscles of the trunk, legs and arms and the small or "accessory" muscles of the feet, hands, and face increase in length and thickness. They become firmer and stronger, with a consequent gain in power.

The Endocrine Glands. The endocrine, or ductless glands discharge their secretion or hormones directly into the bloodstream. Although human development probably is affected greatly by their functioning, relatively little is known about them except their respective locations in the body. (See Figure 1.)

Further research is needed to improve present understanding of their composition and their complex interrelationship. Research in the field has established the fact, however, that these glands follow dissimilar patterns of maturation, indicating that they serve specific functions at different stages of development. A brief description of the tentatively accepted function of each of the endocrine glands follows.

The thyroid gland, secreting a hormone (thyroxin) which affects the rate of basal metabolism, seems to exercise control over developmental and behavior tendencies. Abnormal tensions and extreme physical activity are associated with hyperthyroidism or overactivity of the gland. Hypothyroidism or underactivity

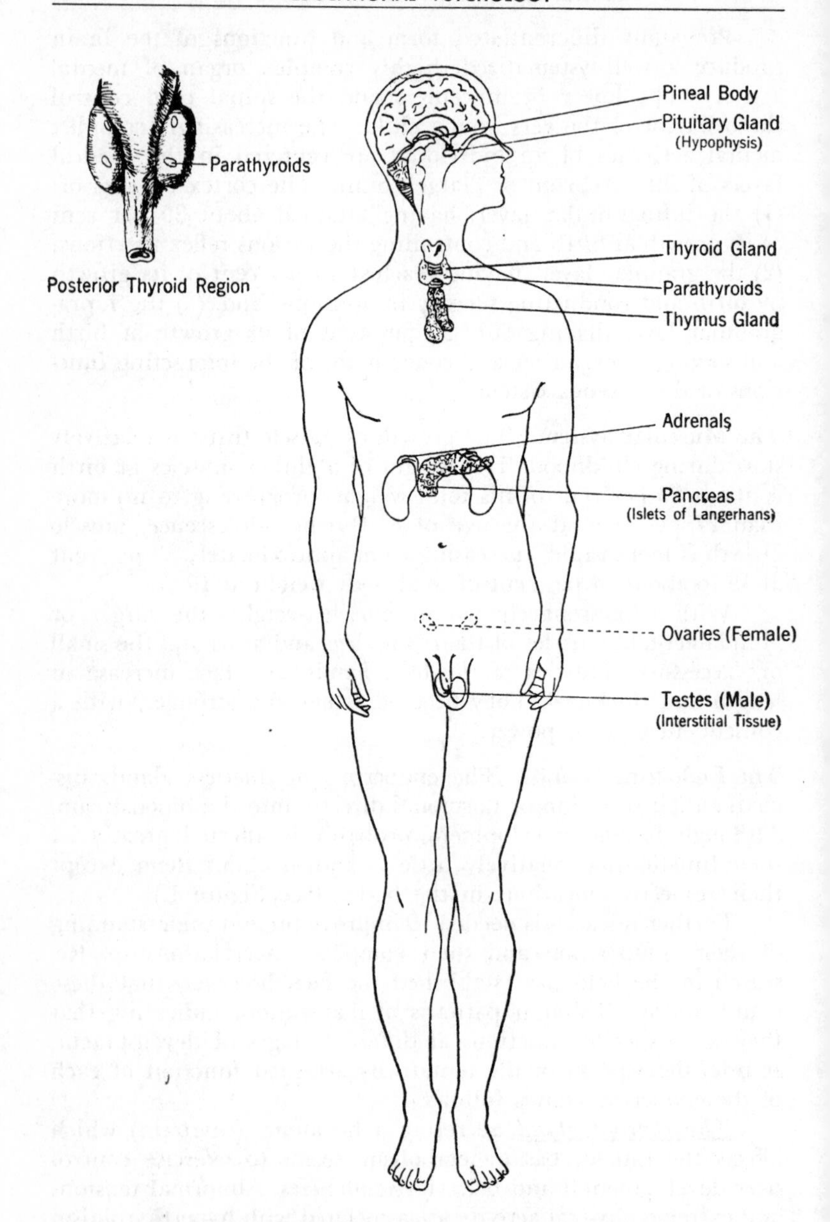

Fig. 1. Diagram showing location of the endocrine glands.
From *Psychology in Nursing Practice* by Crow-Crow and Skinner. Used by permission of the publisher, The Macmillan Company, New York.

of the gland induces generally sluggish behavior. The amount of iodine consumed by an individual affects the functioning of the gland.

The parathyroids, comprising four small glands attached to the thyroid gland, may affect bone ossification through their control of calcium metabolism.

The pituitary gland consists of two lobes—the anterior and the posterior. One hormone of the anterior lobe seems to control skeletal growth. Overfunctioning of this hormone may result in giantism; underfunctioning may induce dwarfism. Another hormone of this lobe activates the sex glands or the gonads. All that is known about the functioning of the hormones of the posterior lobes is that they may affect the tonus of the smooth muscle lining of the digestive tract and may influence the burning of fat and the storing of water in the tissues.

The adrenal and suprarenal glands function in relation to emotionalized states. During anger, for example, an increased amount of adrenin, released into the bloodstream, results in increased blood pressure and more rapid heartbeat. Adrenal action, combined with a greater supply of glycogen or sugar from the liver, increases the physical strength of the angered individual.

The sex glands or gonads are active in sexual development and reproduction. With the onset of puberty, reproductive cells begin to secrete themselves in the reproductive organs—sperm cells in the testes of the male, and ova in the ovaries of the female. The sex glands or the gonads also produce hormones that induce the development of secondary sex characteristics, such as (1) sex changes in body and facial contours, (2) the growth of pubic hair, (3) menstruation and breast development in girls, and (4) deepening of voice and growth of beard in boys.

The thymus and pineal glands, active during childhood, appear to inhibit sexual maturation. They disappear or become less active with the beginning of adolescence.

Factors Affecting Physical Development

The complex pattern of physical growth and development represents a continuity of anatomical and organic changes that have many health implications. If there are no inherited defects and if developmental needs receive proper care, the processes of growth and maturation can be expected to progress smoothly at their natural rates and toward gene-determined limits. The principle of *homeostasis* (self-balance) can be applied to the developmental experience of human beings. An organism can assimilate or repair its resources, thus maintaining balance in its physiological equilibrium. During an individual's growing years, he needs adult assistance in regulating his various activities, such as eating and eliminating, working and relaxing, seeking and avoiding, so that growth equilibrium is not too greatly disturbed.

Reference was made earlier to the improved health conditions of children as well as of adults. Pediatricians are combating the unhealthful effects upon growing children of malnutrition and improper diet. Advances in medical science are operative in preventing or ameliorating physical defects that have an extremely adverse effect upon physical, mental, and emotional development.

Included among the more serious physical defects are (1) sensory defects such as blindness or near blindness, and deafness or impaired hearing; (2) crippling, such as hereditary malformations, birth injuries, and the resultants of disease or accident, and (3) health difficulties—heart disease, cancer, and poliomyelitis. Although all growing children and adolescents should receive intelligent adult care, special attention is needed by the physically handicapped. Otherwise their developing personalities may be so damaged that adequate adjustment in their social relationships becomes increasingly difficult.

The accelerating or retarding effects of environmental factors upon growth and development have been discussed. Certain specific inhibitors of healthy physical development can be noted. Although medical scientists are not in complete agreement concerning the effects upon an individual of some drugs, alcohol, caffeine, and tobacco, it probably is wise to discourage their use by growing young people. Other possible practices of children and adolescents that may need adult control are; overeating or undereating, insufficient sleep, and the wearing of inadequate clothing during inclement weather.

The home and the schoolroom need to be properly ventilated. Artificial lighting should be adequate in power, well diffused, free of glare, and appropriate for the particular type of task for which it is needed. Classroom furniture should be suited to the height, weight, and contours of individual pupils. In fact, school people are becoming increasingly aware of the sitting-posture needs of their pupils. In general, whatever is done to induce healthy physical growth in a healthful environment can eliminate or reduce some of the difficulties experienced by young people in other areas of development.

CHAPTER 5

BASIC ASPECTS OF MENTAL DEVELOPMENT

An individual is equipped by nature with the potentiality to be sensitive to and to react to the many differing physical and social stimuli that surround him. His changing attitudes and behavior patterns reflect his degree of sensitivity and the quickness and appropriateness of his responses. The nature and extent of a person's learning potentiality are described variously as mental ability, mental alertness, mental behavior, intellectual power, or general and specific learning capacity.

This chapter deals with the basic aspects of so-called mental abilities. The meaning, characteristics, and significance of intelligent behavior will be treated in greater detail in Chapter 10.

Aspects of Mental Growth and Maturation

The commonly heard phrase "mind and body" would seem to imply that the mental self and the physical self were two coexisting, tangible entities. Actually, *mind, mental self,* and *mental ability* are terms used to identify one of the functions of the organism. In fact, physical growth can be measured with fair accuracy from the prenatal period to maturity, but mental functioning cannot be studied directly and objectively. Consequently, available data concerning mental maturation are incomplete, and for the most part are obtained indirectly through the study of behavior responses.

Physical Bases of Mental Development. Mental maturation implies change, especially increase in organic capacity to interact with the environment toward the attainment of conscious goals or purposes. Since mental activity pertains to the functioning of the brain and nervous system, mental maturation and neurological growth are interrelated. Structural growth and functional maturation tend to follow relatively similar growth patterns from infancy to adulthood. Moreover, increasing chronological age is accompanied by increasing physical and mental growth. The functioning of the principles of growth is evidenced, for example, in the changes that take place in the physical status and behavior characteristics of the average individual from the first year of life through the ages of 4, 10, 15 and onward to 21 years.

Although physical and mental growth changes give indication of a high degree of correlation, many variations occur among children and within any one child. Structural growth and mental maturation do not parallel each other completely. Physically well-developed children may be mentally slow; some bright children are physically underdeveloped for their age or are delicate. Yet studies show that mentally superior children tend to be above average in physical growth.

The fact that rate of growth differs for the three cortical layers of the brain is basic to the maturational pattern of mental potentiality. Each layer has its function. The early growth of the infragranular layer insures physical survival for the individual through his power as an infant to engage in reflex and related responses. Then, through the slightly delayed functioning of the granular layer, the young child is enabled by way of his developing sensory mechanisms to become acquainted with his environment. Finally, as the supragranular layer continues its growth to maturity, the individual first achieves the ability to engage in simple mental activity and then gradually acquires increasing capacity, within the limits of inherited potentialities, for abstract thinking and the solving of complex problems.

The Influence of Heredity. The relation between an individual's demonstrated mental abilities and his hereditary background continues to be a matter of controversy among researchers in the field of child study. The findings of some well-known studies of mental inheritance, such as the family histories of Max Jukes, Jonathan Edwards, and Martin Kallikak were considered originally to yield conclusive evidence that superior mental ability or feeblemindedness can be explained as a gene-determined characteristic of the family stock. After the potent effect of environmental conditions upon inherited traits was discovered, some doubt has arisen concerning the complete responsibility of the genes for the degree of mental acuity displayed by an individual.

The effect of biological heredity upon mental ability cannot be discounted. Other factors, such as congenital influences, birth injuries, and disease (especially the veneral diseases) are linked with low mental ability; favorable health conditions and enriching experiences can induce mental acceleration.

Characteristics of Mental Maturation. Mental maturation is characterized not merely by increase in ability to do more things and perform them more successfully but also by improvement in the power to comprehend environmental stimulations, to think logically and objectively, to acquire more intensive and extensive interests, and to make sound judgments. Moreover, mental development constitutes a continuous process, each stage of which represents a kind of building upon what has gone before in the way of a preparatory background of mental maturation and previous behavior.

Mental development or learning does not represent an unfolding of the abilities possessed by the child from the beginning of his life; neither should it be regarded as a process of strengthening or of eliminating mental "units," the nature of which is definitely set. The child brings to a learning situation certain inclinations or tendencies, born of earlier experiences, that determine his mental readiness to acquire more adequate behavioral responses. Each succeeding step in mental development is based upon the preceding one. Overstimulation of a child's learning potentialities, the presence of too many different stimuli, or too great gaps in successive stimuli may interfere seriously with an individual's learning progress.

Stages of Mental Development

Mental development implies functioning of continuously formed and re-formed patterns of response that advance from relatively adequate reactions in simple stimulus situations toward complex mental operations. The various aspects of mental reaction and association do not develop in isolation or function independently. Rather do the individual's behavior reponses continue to represent the overt expression of constant interaction among the different phases of mental activity.

Since mental development is continuous, no marked changes differentiate one stage of development from another. Rate of maturation may be more rapid during one age period than another, however, and greater development of one area of mental activity may be more characteristic of one stage than of others. Some of the progressive age-period characteristics of mental development are described briefly.

Infancy. During the neonatal period, the child gives little evidence of mental activity. He is a vegetative organism concerned with the satisfaction of his feeding and sleeping needs, and his physical contacts. Yet an infant can be conditioned to respond to light and touch stimulations. He may turn his head in the direction of light, and respond by startle or body jerk and the closing of the eyelids if a bright light is flashed in front of his eyes. By the third week, his eyes can follow moving objects. Diffused and unorganized responses also may be stimulated by someone's touching him. Relatively few neonates react to loud noises.

Certain reflex actions appear to function well at birth or earlier. These include the pupillary reflex, the extension and fanning of the toes (Babinski reflex), jerking of the body and throwing out of arms in response to a loud noise or the striking of a nearby object (Moro-embrace reflex), and the supporting of body weight by grasping an extended rod with the palm and fingers (Darwinian or Palmer reflex). As the term connotes, a reflex is an involuntary response, giving no evidence of mental activity.

The Child from Infancy to Three Years. During this period, the young child displays some evidence of mental activity. He appears to be conscious of temperature changes and of body needs, such as, food, drink, and sleep. He also is becoming somewhat selective and demanding concerning the ways in which his physical wants are satisfied. Further, his behavior gives evidence of his need to be recognized as a person and to receive attention and approval. During this period, the child experiences rapid growth in the ability to walk, talk, and explore. He becomes curious about things and people in his immediate environment, and starts asking questions about them. His manifested curiosity appears to be concerned not so much with the gaining of information as with his own developing mental processes.

The young child is beginning to display imaginative behavior in so far as he identifies himself with objects or persons around him. For a short time, he is a choo-choo train; then he may become a lion or an airplane. He attempts to imitate the behavior of his father, mother, or any other individual who temporarily attracts his attention. Toward the end of early childhood he comes to recognize the difference between *you* and *me*, but at the same time he is intensely individualistic, evaluating everything about him in reference to himself and his desires.

Possibly as a means of directing attention to himself, the young child is likely to pass through a negativistic state, during which he responds with "No" to any adult request or suggestion. His attitude may seem to an adult to be one of stubbornness or uncooperativeness, even in unimportant matters. Yet, he may do what is asked, as he says "No."

The 3-year-old's rote memory is good. He enjoys listening to the same nursery rhyme or story told to him repeatedly, but is quick to recognize any deviations in the telling from what had been said previously. Simple problem solving in connection with toy arrangement may give evidence of some insight, although much of the activity is trial manipulation.

The Preschool Years. A child's mental abilities develop rapidly from the age of 3 to about 6. His sensory and perceptual powers are increasing. He is becoming much interested in things and situations that are different from those to which he is accustomed. His speaking vocabulary is enlarging. He uses words in meaningful combinations and usually pronounces them accurately.

The preschool child engages in a great deal of make-believe, often reproducing in accurate detail the behavior and experiences of his elders. He is eager to help with home chores but he wants to do things in his own inexperienced fashion, sometimes with what to him may seem to be tragic results.

By the time the average child is ready to enter elementary school he is mentally equipped to engage in more complex activities than those he had experienced earlier. His sensory mechanisms are well developed and powers of perception are relatively accurate. His span of attention has lengthened so that he can concentrate on simple materials and activities. It still may be difficult for him to distinguish between the fanciful and the real, but his interests are becoming less self-centered as he becomes more concerned about other people, especially his peer associates.

The Older Child and Adolescent. During later childhood and adolescence sensory acuity is at its height of development, with accompanying improved organization of perceptual patterns. The power to concentrate increases; logical memory, rather than rote memory, becomes the basis of learning new materials. Remembering and forgetting continue to be associated with feelings of pleasantness and unpleasantness. Yet, during the adolescent period especially, increase in materials to be remembered causes a more objective process of selectivity to operate.

Reasoning and problem solving gradually advance from trial manipulation of concrete objects toward the manipulation of ideas based upon a background of factual knowledge. Creative imagination now is linked to realism so that it can function in the carrying out of goal-directed activity. Actually there are no significant differences between the mental processes of children and those of adults except in degree of relative complexity.

Because of their lack of experience in problem solving, young people sometimes arrive at generalizations that appear to the seasoned adult to be not only erroneous but naive. The cause of this adult attitude probably is the fact that parents and teachers too often expect young people to understand subtle but essential elements in a problem that go beyond this stage of mental maturation and previous experience even to recognize as being present.

The adolescent becomes increasingly able to utilize the higher mental processes, but he may not yet be ready to evaluate conditions, situations, and interpersonal and intersocial relationships according to adult standards or in proper perspective. He may be motivated by an attitude of high idealism to formulate his own opinions and to construct codes of behavior. His ideals are not always founded upon realistic understanding, however, and his thinking often is influenced by strong emotional biases or prejudices.

Adulthood is supposed to connote the attainment of mental maturity. An adult is expected to be able to assume responsibility for his own welfare, and perhaps for the welfare of others. Whether a man or woman, when at the age of 21 he has attained legal adult status, actually has achieved adult mental status is dependent partly upon his inherited potentialities and partly upon environmental or cultural stimulation.

The materials of this book that deal with the teaching-learning process are aimed at helping teachers and teacher trainees gain an understanding of their responsibility for the mental, and consequently the emotional and social development of their pupils.

CHAPTER 6

THE EMOTIONS AND THEIR DEVELOPMENT

The emotions exercise a potent influence upon individuals' responses to environmental situations and conditions. Emotional experiences are integral concomitants of human interrelationships. Since the emotions probably function as significant behavior motivators, teachers should have some understanding of the nature and developing patterns of the emotions and emotional behavior.

Basic Aspects of the Emotions

Emotions are complex responses that are meaningful and modifiable. Emotional maturation represents one aspect of the total integrated pattern of human growth and development. The interactions of the physical and mental aspects of human nature with environmental influences play a significant role in the development of emotional behavior and attitudes.

The Nature of Emotions. The term *emotion,* derived from the Latin verb *emovere*—to move out—signifies a more or less definite "stirred up" or aroused state of the human organism. An emotion is *not* an urge, a desire, a drive, a motive or a feeling, but there may be a cause and effect relationship between an emotion and any one of the other inner experiences. A human being is a dynamic living organism. Hence he continuously attempts to fulfill a need, an urge, a want or a desire. (See Chapter 9.)

An individual's success or failure induces an appropriate emotional reaction that varies in duration and intensity with the strength of the stimulating force. If the motivated behavior is successful, the emotional state may be characterized by pleasant or satisfying feeling tones. A thwarting or frustrating experience, or a conflict between two felt urges, or between a need, urge, or interest and the environment may lead to the arousal of emotions that are unpleasant or annoying. A feeling is not an emotion, however. Affectivity as (1) a feeling of satisfaction (pleasantness), (2) annoyance (unpleasantness), or (3) possible indifference is an accompaniment of all of one's experiences, including emotions. Joy is pleasant, but sorrow is unpleasant. A feeling may be regarded as a relatively passive, sometimes unconscious, response. However, a strong feeling tone attached to an experience usually influences one's future reactions toward it. One seeks to repeat a pleasant experience and to shun or avoid an unpleasant or annoying situation or condition.

Simple emotional states sometimes are referred to as feeling. Yet an emotion (as compared to a feeling) is a conscious experience that involves body activity resulting in organic and kinesthetic (muscular) sensations and overt expression, as well as accompanying impulses and strong feeling tones. An emotion can be regarded as a dynamic, intense adjustment operating for the protection, welfare, and satisfaction of the individual experiencing it. Because of the complex nature of emotional experiences, it is difficult to formulate a simply phrased, adequate definition of an emotion. Essentially, however, an emotion is a conscious, complex, and affective experience that accompanies physiological and mental stirred-up states and generalized inner adjustments and that expresses itself in overt behavior.

Kinds and Components of Emotions. According to the kind and intensity of stimuli to physiological and mental activity and to the accompanying feeling tone and overt behavior, emotions can be considered to differentiate themselves into emotional states, such as, fear, worry, envy, jealousy, awe, anger, rage, resentment, hate, contentment, love or affection, tenderness, sympathy, elation, and ecstasy. Some psychologists classify emotions broadly into three major "constellations"—fear, rage, and love or the "tender" emotions. Other emotional states are considered to be modifications of or combinations of any of these three. The terminology utilized to identify one or another relatively specific emotional state associated with any one of the major categories differs according to the degree of the apparent strength or mildness of the emotional state.

Most human behavior is emotional. Man's struggle for survival is accompanied by many differing emotional experiences. Emotional stresses or strong feeling tones result from the cumulative effect of emotion-arousing stimuli. The organism becomes extremely "stirred up," and lack of reasonable control may be evidenced in overt behavior.

A strongly stirred-up state of fear may be accompanied by an impulse to flee from the cause of the fear state: extreme anger or rage may impel the subject to fight; a tender emotion is characterized by a strong desire to touch, be with, or do things for the object of the emotion. Moreover, because of the possible disturbing or upsetting effects of experiencing strong or continued fear or anger, these emotions sometimes are referred to as *disruptive* emotions; the tender emotions, characterized as they are by friendliness, affection, and pleasant feeling tones, are considered to be constructive emotions.

Attempts to analyze emotion into its component parts or aspects have not yet been completely successful. According to some psychologists, four aspects or components can be identified: (1) intensity, which is felt by the individual experiencing the emotion and which may be detected by an observer; (2) overt response, such as clenching the hands, smiling, shouting, or trembling; (3) feeling tone, of which the subject is aware; (4) impulse of the emotionalized person to approach or to withdraw from the stimulus situation.

Since an emotional experience is subjective, it can be analyzed fully only by the individual experiencing it. As he attempts to study the physiological changes that are taking place, the behavior in which he is engaging and the feeling tones that are present, however, the emotional state may disappear. The mental activity involved in his attempted analysis acts as a distractor of his attention from the emotional state and its arousing stimuli.

Factors of Emotion Arousal and Expression. The arousal of an emotion is dependent upon many subtle elements of stimulation. Whether an individual responds actively to possible emotion-arousing stimuli either within or outside himself depends upon his readiness so to be aroused and the kind and strength of the simuli situation in reference to himself. The situation must be recognized to be an emotion arouser in that it is associated with personal interest or desire.

By nature, an individual tends to be more or less receptive to situations having emotion-arousing possibilities. Other factors that can affect his emotional sensitivity are degree of mental alertness, level of maturation, state of health, extent of fatigue, previous experiences, ideals, aspirations, ambitions, and attitudes toward life values. A person may react differently to two apparently similar situations because of difference in his state of readiness to react or his failure to recognize the likeness of the two sets of stimuli. Two persons may experience the same situational conditions at the same time; because of differences between them, one individual may become extremely emotional, while the other scarcely is affected by the experience.

Two differing emotions cannot be experienced simultaneously. Yet the recognition of even a slight change in the stimulating situation may cause an individual to change quickly from one form of emotional response to a different one. Although change in emotional reaction to change of stimuli operates among individuals of all ages, it is especially characteristic of the emotional behavior of young children.

Sentiment, Mood, and Temperament. An emotion is an active experience that usually can be traced to specific factors of arousal and that may be temporary or more prolonged according to the strength and continuance of the causative stimuli. Most individuals give evidence, however, of the presence of complex emotional states that are related to the emotions but appear to be long-lasting, and effective in determining an individual's susceptibility to a specific emotion. These relatively consistent emotional states include sentiment, mood, and temperament.

Sentiments are complex emotional attitudes. Although they cannot be defined exactly, they appear to develop out of experience and to affect behavior in relationship to people and things. Personal likes and dislikes, admiration, loyalty, and religious, patriotic, or social attitudes are some of the many sentiments that exert a powerful influence upon maturing behavior patterns.

A mood can be regarded as a continued aftermath of an emotional experience. A person may be described as "moody," implying that he is depressed, antagonistic, or apathetic. Although serious frustration or repeated thwartings may lead to development of a social or disruptive mood, pleasant emotional experiences induce constructive moods, such as tendencies to be affectionate, merry, gay, and the like.

Attempted explanations of the causes of temperamental differences among human beings have a long history. Temperament probably can be described as including the moods, emotional attitudes, and feelings that are consistently characteristic of an individual's behavior reactions. People differ in their display of emotion, ranging from extreme emotional expressiveness and volubility to apparent unemotionality, stolidity, and phlegmaticism. Temperament may have its origin in the native constitution. Studies have attempted to explain temperamental differences as resulting from difference in endocrine gland functioning, body build, and other physical or physiological aspects of growth. As yet, however, no explanations have been accepted completely.

Physiological Aspects of Emotion. The stirred-up state of the organism during an emotional experience is associated with physiological changes produced by the stimuli arousing the emotional state. Observable effects upon the skeletal muscles include physical reactions, such as bulging eyes, flushed face, facial contortions, choking voice or peculiar sounds, flowing tears, trembling, fist-clenching or shaking, or movements of physical attack or of fleeing.

The organic or physiological changes taking place are concerned especially with the action of the autonomic nervous system and the endocrine glands. Diffuse neural discharge, involving the visceral organs, glands, and muscles, cannot always be observed easily but can be measured by the physiologist. Complex pattern reactions include (1) changes in the functioning of the breathing apparatus, (2) action of the digestive juices, (3) flow of blood from the trunk into the limbs, and (4) decrease in the flow of saliva.

The physiological changes that occur during an emotional experience such as intensive anger or extreme fear, for example, are believed to serve as aids in meeting the disturbing situation. When or if the emotional state subsides, the changed physiological reactions return to their normal functioning; otherwise they continue their stirred-up activity.

Studies of physiological change during an emotion have shown that an individual may interpret the visceral disturbances suffered by him during an emotional experience to be symptomatic of a disease condition. If the emotional state is prolonged, actual tissue damage may occur. The term psychosomatic disease is applied to the awareness of the supposed disease symptoms and possible tissue damage. If a patient is in a highly disturbed state, it may be difficult for the physician to distinguish between actual symptoms and imagined ones.

Theories Concerning the Emotions

Through observation and measurement, a body of relatively accurate factual material has been accumulated concerning some basic aspects of the emotions. The origin of the many differences among individual emotional tendencies are not yet known, neither have there been discovered any specific patterns of distinctive types of emotional states. The relative significance, in the development of the emotions, of inherited potentialities and of environmentally stimulated experiences still is a moot question. Available literature in the field contains many philosophically arrived at and scientifically produced theories concerning the genesis, functions, and directives of the emotions.

Genetic Theories. As recently as the colonial period in American history, the emotions were explained, from an animistic viewpoint, as resulting from the possession of the human organism by evil spirits that had to be exorcised to save the soul of their victim. According to traditional psychological theory, an emotion is rooted in the organic structure as an aspect of a fundamental instinct, such as self-preservation. Age changes in emotional behavior result from changes in organic structure rather than from environmental experiences.

John Watson believed that the emotions consist of three primary innate patterns: fear, rage, or love. As a result of his experiments with infants, he concluded that the three emotions represent specific responses to specific stimuli. These primary emotional patterns were considered to be basic, instinctive behavior patterns but that they could be modified.

Emotions also are viewed as learned patterns, emerging from diffuse states of general excitement characteristic of so-called emotional reactions during infancy. Emotional behavior develops as a result of the constant interaction between organic growth changes and social conditioning or learning. Emotional reactions are goal determined. The reason for a consistent pattern of emotional behavior to persist is its goal-attaining, satisfying, or tension-reducing quality rather than its innate unchangeable response nature.

Theories Concerning the Functions and Directives of Emotions. Darwin, and later, Cannon and other scientists stressed the functional aspects of the emotions. Darwin emphasized the role of the emotions in the human struggle for survival. Cannon formulated the emergency theory of the emotions. He held that the physiological changes in anger and fear function in preparing the subject to meet a physical emergency. Some of these emergency changes are the release of blood sugar for energy, the carrying away of fatigue products by means of the bloodstream, the increased activity of the heart, and the more rapid coagulation of blood in a wound through the presence of adrenin. In addition, according to Cannon and others, the production of overt emotional response is induced by the passing of the impulse from sensory nerve fibers of the receptors (eye, ear, etc.) through the thalamus, thereby relaying the nerve current to the viscera and skeletal muscles.

The well-known James-Lange theory of the emotions deals with the conscious experiences and the physiological changes in an emotion. As a result of their studies, conducted separately, William James and Carl Lange concluded that bodily changes are direct responses to emotion-arousing stimuli and that the emotion itself is the feeling associated with the bodily symptoms. For example, one is stimulated by an unexpected crash behind him. He jumps; his heart starts to beat rapidly; he screams. His bodily and physiological reactions cause him to "feel" afraid.

Freud's theory of unconscious causes of emotions would seem to give some support to James' theory. Freud, working with deeply disturbed patients, discovered that these men and women suffered many physical and mental symptoms without knowing the basic reason for their difficulties. In fact, they often would insist that they were experiencing no emotional disturbance, except in so far as their physical or mental reactions were causing them worry. Through psychoanalysis, the technique of which he was the founder, Freud would uncover the repressed memories of earlier emotional experiences that were the unconscious bases of the existing neurotic state.

The organismic view of emotions is concerned with the purpose of the emotions in the life of an individual. Emotion, viewed according to the organismic theory, is purposive. Emotions do not act upon behavior but they help an individual achieve desired goals and overcome barriers or obstacles that otherwise might interfere with their attainment.

No definite generalization concerning the emotions has resulted from the various study approaches that have been attempted. No simple list of emotions has been constructed that includes all the various aspects of human reactions. Moreover, stimulating causes, physiological reactions, and behavior patterns characteristic of any emotional state vary with individuals, since the total setting of an emotional experience is important.

Continued study and experimentation are needed to clarify existing understanding of the emotions. At present, however, a considerable amount of information is available concerning general principles that govern the functioning of various emotions and their development.

Developing Patterns of Emotional Experiences

Probably, no emotional state is a discrete experience, nor can a specific label be attached to any emotion. For convenience of discussion, however, it is possible to view various forms of emotional behavior as related to one or more of the complex, major constellations—fear, rage, and love (tenderness). Emotions in mild or more serious form are experienced by individuals of any age. The kind and intensity of stimuli needed to arouse an emotion and the overt expression of emotional reactions tend to follow a relatively similar development pattern for the so-called average individual.

Some General Characteristics of Emotional Development. Emotional potentiality is present at birth. Emotional development depends upon the interactions between the maturational and the learning processes. The general, diffused, all-over state of body excitement characterisitc of the neonate changes gradually to more definite overt forms of emotional behavior, such as facial expressions, gestures, etc.

The overt behavior expressions of emotional activity reflect general cultural influences as well as the individual's experiences in his culture group. Habits of emotional expression and control of the emotions are learned through imitation of the behavior of others and their suggestions or teaching, according to personal or societal standards of behavior. A maturing young person must understand what kind of behavior is acceptable to his group before he can attempt to establish approved habits of emotional expression. Hence degree of mental acuity is an important factor of learning as applied to the emotions.

From infancy to adulthood, the developing individual's emotional patterns continue to change under the influence of newly acquired knowledge, interests, appreciations, and ideals. Beginning his life as an egocentric organism, the child gradually develops interest in other people and their activities. He learns to respect the ideals and points of view of others and to accept personal and social responsibility without undue emotionalism, provided that things run smoothly.

Throughout life, the most important motivator of the emotions probably is the need for security. The form of expression of this need varies with age. The infant or young child seeks emotional satisfaction from his parents, especially his mother or mother substitute; the older child satisfies this emotional need by belonging to a peer group or gang; an older adolescent or adult wants both economic security and social approval.

During the developing years, sometimes even during early adulthood, most individuals want to be secure in parental affection and protection, even though they may not admit this need, especially during adolescence. At any age level, the experiencing of emotional security has positive value, induces successful achievement in learning or work activities and in good interpersonal and intersocial relationships. Actual or imagined threats to one's desire for security excite feelings of thwarting, frustration, or disruptive emotional states that may lead to devastating emotional disturbance.

An individual's general emotional characteristics are patterned gradually during the developing years, from infancy through adolescence. Changes in the causative and behaviorial phases of emotion do not occur suddenly. Yet certain emotional trends and tendencies appear to be more characteristic of one developmental stage than of others. In addition, as in other aspects of human growth and development, there are wide individual differences in rate of emotional development.

Infancy and Early Childhood. The young baby's emotional reactions (if this term can be applied to his general diffused state of excitement) are responses to felt physical needs. Emotional satisfaction is expressed by cooing, gurgling, cuddling, relaxing, stretching, and the beginnings of smiling. Annoying experiences such as hunger or discomfort show themselves in crying, squirming, kicking, and other restless movements.

Increasing physical growth and physiological maturation are accompanied by the display of more definite expressions of emotionalism. The child begins to display affectionate behavior by holding out his arms to be picked up and played with; he snuggles, coos, and laughs. He may show great joy or elation by clapping his hands, jumping up and down and through other body activities. He is likely to respond to strange situations, discomforts, pain, or other things that distress or disgust him or that arouse fear, by withdrawing, crying or whimpering, or clutching.

A young child often displays anger. A toy that won't work, a denial of desired food, and similar thwartings produce kicking, screaming, hitting, and holding of breath that may reach tantrum proportions. Jealousy, caused by attention given to a younger sibling, for example, may be expressed in various ways—

attempts to harm the object of the jealousy (anger), withdrawal from the situation (fear), and demands that he be fed, dressed, and held in his mother's arms (bids for affection and attention.)

In all his emotional reactions the young child is expressing his felt need for security in his family relations and in his possessions. If the child attends nursery school, some of his self-centered emotionalism gradually lessens as he becomes more aware of and more concerned with other children and their activities. Usually small-group relationships are established. Young childrens' groups have no permanency, however. The composition of groups changes constantly in terms of short-span, immediate interests. Yet the child is beginning to develop group consciousness and to adapt his emotional reactions in accordance with temporary group standards. He learns quickly that unduly aggressive behavior, noncooperation, or indifference will deny him desired group acceptance.

During these early years, a child's emotional patterns are beginning to be formed. He tends to imitate or emulate the emotional behavior of his elders and peers. He fears what they fear; he returns angry behavior in kind; he responds eagerly to any affectionate behavior displayed toward him. At the same time, he gives little evidence of sympathy for the troubles of others, except his mother and a favorite playmate. Moreover, although people of any age want for themselves and their problems the sympathetic understanding of family members and friends, this need is extremely strong during the early years.

The Elementary School Years. The child of elementary school age begins to demand freedom of activity and of decision making. At times, he resents his parents' "fussiness" about his appearance or manners, and their seemingly unreasonable demands. Adult denial of an immediate, strong interest, or whim may lead to tantrum behavior, sulkiness, or mutterings, and feelings of self-pity.

Group loyalty is strong. Gangs are formed in terms of common interests and, usually, they are relatively permanent. Boys and girls form separate groups, especially during later childhood. Sex antagonism may develop, but behavior toward the opposite sex differs with sex. Boys tend to tease or torment girls; girls usually try to emulate boys' activities and to employ various devices to attract the attention of neighborhood boys or male schoolmates.

The need for emotional security continues to be a strong

behavior director. A child wants the approval of the teacher and a position of prestige in his peer group or gang. Intense jealousy may be experienced if others in the group or the classroom receive more attention or commendation than himself.

Intense jealousy may stimulate the child to become unduly aggressive, or to utilize socially disapproved methods to attract attention to himself. He may boast about his accomplishments or possessions (usually imaginary); he may steal in order to win approval through the giving of gifts to his teacher and classmates.

The elementary school child continues to experience many of the fears developed earlier, such as fear of the dark, of physical danger, of being alone, or of the supernatural. Fear is strong. Ridicule, teasing, or "shaming" in the presence of his peers can make the child miserable. A child whose parents or teachers expect him to maintain high standards of conduct and school achievement is likely to become a victim of much worry or anxiety. He wants to receive adult approval, so he is afraid that he may say or do something to displease his parents, or that he may fail in a school test, for example. A feeling of guilt arises if or when the child believes that he has done something wrong, cannot solve a problem, or in any other way seems to be inadequate.

A sensitive "only" child who is denied free association with other children, or a child who must "mind his manners," keep his clothing neat, or eat like a "lady" or a "gentleman" may be in an almost constant state of anxiety or worry. If or when this child discovers that other children are not held to rigid rules of conduct, he may become bitter, and be resentful of his parents' strictness. He continues to fear the consequences of apparent shortcomings; at the same time he envies his more fortunate young friends, and regards his own family as cruel and nonunderstanding. Usually, however, the elementary school child is happy and cheerful and his "grudges" are short-lived.

The Adolescent. The adolescent worries about many things; his appearance, his chances of social success and of gaining prestige among his peers (especially members of the opposite sex), parental attitudes, money, school achievement, and health. Moreover, he wants independence, but he recognizes his own inadequacies in matters of decision making.

An adolescent, believing that he is old enough to "live his own life," may refuse to follow his parents' wishes or demands, but he usually realizes that he needs their protection and guidance. The boy, more often than the girl, may complain to his peer associates that his parents are old-fashioned or treat him as a child, yet he is extremely loyal to them and will allow little or no criticism of them by others.

Adolescent Fears and Phobias. During the adolescent years, a young person may continue to experience some of the fears developed earlier. Generally, however, a teen-ager's fears, jealousies, worries, and anxieties are related to his peer associates, his school activities, and his struggles to achieve adult status.

A strong, irrational fear (phobia) may be experienced by an adolescent, exerting so strong an influence over his behavior or attitudes that its effects carry into later years. A phobia is an extreme or morbid dread of a situation. It is a continued emoionalized attitude toward situations or conditions similar to one which previously had aroused great fear. A phobia is a pathological fear that may be symptomatic of mental illness. The phobia may take the form of an abnormal fear of high places (acrophobia), closed rooms (claustrophobia), the dark (nyrophobia), dirt (mysophobia), strong light (photophobia), the sight of blood (hematophobia), animals (zoophobia), water (hydrophobia), being poisoned (toxophobia), or pain (algophobia).

A phobia may be rooted in a childhood emotional experience, especially fear of the dark. The sufferer may be aware of the abnormality of his fear. He cannot resist the impulse to flee from or avoid it. Later, however, with increasing nonharmful experiences in the situations like the one originally arousing the fear, he gradually is helped to overcome it. An adolescent with a phobia may become much disturbed by its effect upon him, especially if it interferes with his achieving desired approval or acceptance from his peers. His struggles to conceal the abnormal fear may induce nightmares about them or cause him to become reckless or foolhardy in situations associated with his great fear.

Adolescent Anger. Anger or one of its concomitant emotional states is aroused in an adolescent mainly through the thwarting of goal-seeking interests or activities. At one time, adolescence was thought to be a period of continued stress and strain caused by a young person's conflicts between his increasing urge to be treated as an independent near-adult and his still immature and inexperienced behavior. Although the teen years no longer are viewed as a period of constant turmoil, most adolescents are sensative to and angered by any real or imagined threat to their need for emotional security.

Unless an adolescent was helped during childhood to control his unbridled expressions of anger, he may continue to engage in temper tantrums. The form of the tantrum behavior differs from that of the enraged child. The adolescent has learned that throwing, kicking, and screaming are socially disapproved. Hence he is likely to employ more subtle techniques, such as caustic language, pouting, or dignified withdrawal from the anger-arousing situation. An adolescent can hold a grudge for a long period of time, but his anger disappears quickly if he believes that he has regained prestige, position, or that he no longer is being thwarted in his goal-seeking activities.

An adolescent's mercurial temperament causes him to pass quickly, sometimes for no observable reason, from one emotional state to another. He hates, he fears, he loves. A slight provocation may bring about a sudden change from affectionate, cheerful, or cooperative behavior to a display of timidity and withdrawal, or of resentment and anger. Usually, however, a young person gives evidence of possessing a relatively selfless interest in and concern about other people, especially his same-age associates.

Same-Sex Groups. Most adolescents tend to organize themselves into same-sex groups, usually functioning more permanently than child gangs. Teen-age groups are characterized by greater similarity among its members in intellectual and educational level and by selectivity of membership. Adolescents and young adults are extremely loyal to the other members of their group and are careful in their choice of a leader. The purpose of the group is known to all its members, and initiated group projects are followed through to a satisfactory conclusion.

High school and college fraternities have value in so far as they help young people (1) gain security in peer relationships and (2) achieve positive, affective emotional development. Membership in a secret society can affect a young person negatively as well as positively, however. Too great emphasis upon selectivity in terms of economic, social, national, racial, or religious status encourages snobbishness and intolerance. Activities of groups formed by idle, authority-resisting, educationally and socially frustrated adolescents have a disruptive influence upon emotional development. The members may engage in antisocial or delinquent behavior, especially if the leader is resentfully aggressive in his community relationships but has the power to gain the strong loyalty of the more submissive, perhaps less mature members of the gang.

Emotional Attitudes toward Opposite Sex. Although adolescents continue to engage in same-sex activities, they become increasingly interested in members of the opposite sex. They seek their approval and strive to achieve prestige among them. Physical attraction is a strong motivator of heterosexual behavior, yet the social factor is equally potent. Young adolescents sometimes become the prey of mixed emotional reactions. They are attracted to and at the same time repelled by the opposite sex.

Since girls mature sexually earlier than boys, they want to be approved by and they seek the company of older boys. At the same time, they assume attitudes of contempt or indifference toward boys of their own age. Consequently, hostility or antagonism may arise between the boys and girls in a freshman high school class.

As boys mature to the point at which physically they catch up to or surpass girls, these antagonisms are replaced by mutually expressed desires for one another's company in romance-imbued situations. Yet many sex-stimulated attachments are of short duration. Both boys and girls appear to fall in and out of love easily and frequently. Usually, one of the two, emotionally hurt by the attitudes and behavior of the other, transfers his affections to another more appealing young person. The new attachment lasts until emotional disruption again occurs.

Adolescent experiences in "puppy love" represent exploratory preparation for final mate selection and marriage, but the maturing process may be accompanied by much emotionalism. Tenderness toward the object of affection, fear of losing the love or respect of the current "idol," and jealousy of and anger directed at a possible rival are characteristic of adolescent heterosexual relationships.

An average adolescent usually is not so involved in his developing interest in members of the opposite sex that he fails to exhibit affectionate attitudes toward other affective stimuli. Adolescent boys, possibly more than girls, like animals. A child may enjoy playing with his dog or other pet, but he is likely to leave the care of it to his parents or another family member. The adolescent, contrariwise, wants to be the sole possessor of his pet, caring for its needs, teaching it tricks, and expecting it to be completely loyal to him.

Adolescent "Crushes." Many adolescents pass through a period of "crushes," the object of which usually is an older member of the same sex—a teacher, religious or community leader, or, more remotely, a well-known athlete or dramatic star. In some instances, same-sex idol worship is a form of compensation for failure to establish desired heterosexual relationships, but not necessarily. The admired adult represents an embodiment of the qualities or characteristics which the young person himself wants or hopes to possess.

Boys tend to express their admiration of an adult male in behavior that is patterned according to the adult's apparent standards and ideals. Girls may exhibit a more sentimental attachment, seeking the attention of the adult; copying her style of dress, mannerisms, and speech patterns, and following her around. If a girl's "crush" is strong enough, she may display it by writing poems to and about her idol, telephoning to her home, visiting her although uninvited, and for the duration of the emotional attachment, engaging in many other attention-seeking devices.

Contrary to popular belief, adolescent idolization of a same-sex adult rarely has homosexual implications. There are individuals, of course, who possess homosexual tendencies which may be exhibited during adolescence as well as in adulthood. In general, teachers of young people can distinguish between an annoying but harmless crush and a sexually stimulated attraction, and deal with each appropriately.

Freudian Stages of Emotional Development. The Freudian school of psychological thought attempts to explain emotional development in terms of emotional fixations, conflicts, and regression. According to this theory the individual's affective emotional experiences begin with birth trauma (shock), resulting from the loss of fetal security; the second stage represents the functioning of the *oedipus complex,* causing the male child to love his mother and hate his father, and the *electra complex,* characterized by a female child's great attachment to her father; during the following stage (narcissism), the child experiences self-love or exploratory interest in his body and body parts, especially the sex organs; the older child's affective interests are homosexual, as evidenced by his desire to become a member of a same-sex "gang"; finally, a normally developing individual reaches the stage of heterosexual love.

Conflict and emotional disturbance are experienced if or when a gradual transition from one period to another is not effected. Fixation at one of the earlier periods or regression to it can have a seriously detrimental effect upon an individual's adult life pattern.

The so-called Freudian theory of affective emotional development is not accepted by all psychologists. Moreover, if in essence his theory is correct, it is difficult to determine the extent to which native tendencies or environmental experiences are responsible. There are adults who appear to be unduly concerned about their own bodies; some adults are so attached to their parents that they refuse to leave them and marry; homosexuality does exist on the adult level. These adult abnormalities may be symptomatic of retarded emotional development associated with unfavorable environmental influences. Resulting conflict situations may induce severe mental disturbance, but it has been found that, in some cases at least, the abnormal emotional condition can be eliminated or ameliorated through appropriate therapy.

Emotional Maturity. The age or stage of development at which complete emotional maturity is reached varies with individuals' innate potentialities and their experiences. Some adults seem never to attain a mature emotional attitude in some of their interpersonal relationships. There are adolescents who exhibit behavior that is better controlled emotionally than that of some of their adult associates. Emotional maturity is conditioned by an individual's readiness (1) to assume responsibility for his own and other's welfare, and (2) to meet thwarting and frustrating situations and conditions with a rational, objective approach. Emotional maturity does not imply that the emotional aspects of behavior are eliminated; rather does it connote a reasonable and constructive control of emotional expression and an intelligent recognition of the factors that are inherent in emotion arousal.

An emotionally mature person is capable of accurate, precise, and realistic thinking and problem solving. If necessary, he can sacrifice immediate satisfactions in order to achieve constructive, long-range goals or purposes. The mature person refrains from hasty, emotion-rooted decision making; his judgments result from careful consideration of the factors involved, and are definite. Once made, his decisions are adhered to, without regret, and with no self-recrimination if the outcomes are not completely satisfactory.

Finally, if the individual is emotionally mature, his attitudes toward and relations with other persons are free from jealousy, envy, or prejudice, and his behavior is characterized by self-confidence and faith in others. The development of mature emotional attitudes is closely related to (1) the individual's childhood and adolescent learning experiences, (2) his relationships with his parents, teachers, and peer associates, and (3) his willingness and ability during the formative years to control disruptive emotional outbursts.

CHAPTER 7

DEVELOPING SOCIAL BEHAVIOR

At birth, the child is neither social, asocial, nor unsocial. He is nonsocial. He does, however, enter into a social world which even before birth has exerted some influence upon him. As a living organism he possesses certain potentialities which at first have a limited readiness for effective functioning. Yet he possesses a high degree of modifiability in his social behavior.

Nature of Social Behavior

The neonate or the very young child is dependent upon others for the fulfillment of his life needs. As his various physical needs are met he begins to respond to those who are responsible for his survival. At the start, his mother and his nurse constitute the important adults in his social environment. Soon personal-social interrelationships are experienced between him and others in or around the home. That is, the child not only is influenced by others but exerts his own influence upon them.

Factors in Social Responses. Since responding depends upon the functioning of the sense organs, the very young child's repsonses are relatively unpatterned. As the sense organs become more receptive to social stimuli through their maturation and use, social adjustments become more evident. Influences, such as the presence of a person who gives approval, the beginnings of self-interest and interest in others, and the use of language (when he is old enough) become powerful forces in the child's social development.

The mother's feeding of the infant marks the beginning of what can be considered social behavior. The baby is nursed, petted, kept warm, dried, and talked to; he responds with relaxed behavior, indicating his satisfied state. Crying or restlessness challenges adults to discover the stimuli needed to bring about a change in response. At first, the baby's feeble vocalization may be misinterpreted, but the mother soon comes to recognize differences in crying and body movements and the meaning of each. Some of the differences seem to be almost imperceptible; but through gurgling, cooing, smiling, and bodily movements the child gradually makes his wants known. He becomes increasingly able to manifest his desires to the person who cares for his needs.

Closely associated with social development are the physical, mental, and emotional aspects of development previously discussed. In fact, the interrelation is so great that it is important for the reader to apply to the pattern of social development what he has learned relative to growth and development in other areas. The attitudes of the people around him constantly stimulate the child. His degree of mental acuity influences the interpretation that he places on adult attitudes or overt behavior. If his wants are satisfied, he responds with affectionate behavior; if they are not satisfied, he may display anger. In turn, the responses of the child arouse in adults one or another kind of emotional attitude as they try to meet his wants.

Factors that influence social behavior include physiological changes, mental and emotional maturation, and the nature and extent of the social stimuli made available. Social behavior develops in conjunction with growth and maturational processes and environmental conditioning. The child who develops the kind of social habits that can function satisfactorily for him in his early social environment is equipping himself to meet those social situations which he will confront in later life.

Value of Social Responses. The child learns early to discriminate. He can distinguish his mother from other persons. At an early age, he recognizes her touch, her voice, her facial expression. A stranger, appearing suddenly, presents a new set of stimuli which may frighten the child. If he is introduced gradually to the newcomer, emotional interferences lessen and the child responds with accepting responses.

During his prolonged infancy, the child is surrounded by numerous social forces by which his behavior is conditioned. These social stimuli affect him favorably or unfavorably long before he is able to do anything about choosing his social environment. It is true that, within limits, he is able to indicate by his behavior whether he accepts or rejects these influences.

Group associations have been recognized to have value for everyone. The child is a social being and is unhappy if he is isolated from others. Gradually he learns to adapt his behavior to that of the various groups in the society into which he is born.

Even as a child, his interactions with the social groups into which he is inducted affect both himself and other group members.

Stages of Social Adaptation

Since a child is born into a particular cultural heritage he eventually develops a pattern of social behavior which in many respects reflects the mores of his cultural group. As is true of other areas of his development, the child's social adaptations gradually are patterned through continuously changing stages in his progress toward social maturity. Although some earlier behavior patterns tend to remain fixed throughout life, many differences can be found among children's changing patterns of social response.

Social Development during Infancy and Early Childhood (from birth through 5 years). Much that has been said to this point concerns the child's social development during his early infancy. Gesell, Thompson, and Buhler have made intensive and detailed studies of children's social behavior during the first year of life. Based upon similarities in the behavior of at least 60 per cent of the cases studied, Buhler reached certain conclusions (substantiated in essence by later investigations) concerning the progress of social consciousness during infancy.

Forms of early social behavior are smiling, crying, and eye movements in response to other persons. By the end of the second month, the infant is quieted by touching, and smiles in response to adult glances at him, although these responses probably have no particular social significance. From the ages of 2 to 3 months, the apparently social responses of the infant include crying when the adult who is attending him leaves, and showing disturbance when he is approached. By the end of the fourth month, he returns approaching glances with "lalling" and shows displeasure at loss of adult glance.

Social consciousness and definiteness of response continue to increase, so that by the eighth month the infant (1) is quieted by caressing, (2) strives for attention by "lalling," (3) stretches out hands toward adults, and (4) cries when an adult stops talking to him. During the last 3 months of the first year, social responses continue to progress. In order of their appearance, the infant strives for attention by movements, pulls at the clothing of adults, offers an object to an adult, imitates movements of an adult with playthings, and finally engages in simple organized play activities, such as, playing pat-a-cake or peek-a-boo with an adult.[1] It must be remembered, however, that the behavior responses listed represent general trends. Some infants display certain social responses much earlier than do others. For example, a small percentage of infants begin to play peek-a-boo as early as the age of about 5 months.

During the first year, the infant's simple social responses are directed, for the most part, by and toward adults. His reactions to other infants give little awareness of them in relation to himself. Although he may seem to observe them or smile at them, imitate their movements, or show distress at their leaving, their presence is not sought. Since the young infant is a vegetative, self-centered organism, much of his behavior toward others is relatively negative, except as he responds positively in terms of his physical and of his vague and diffused emotional needs.

By the age of 2 years, the child's responses are predominantly friendly and cooperative. He laughs a great deal. Laughter is aroused by any action of an adult or of another young child that attracts his attention, as well as by simple games. Moreover, young children of his own age may become more interesting to him than his toys.

To the age of 3, most children still prefer to play with their toys by themselves. Yet they are conscious of other children near them to the extent that they make fleeting contacts with them. A child may attempt to grab another child's toy, but protests strenuously, sometimes displaying tantrum behavior, if another child tries to take one of his toys. A few differences in peer relations show themselves at this early age. Some 2- and 3-year-olds are able to play together amicably for short periods of time; they may offer their toys to other children, at times to the extent of forcing a toy upon a favored playmate. In opposition to these beginnings of peer sociability, self-centered behavior still persists, even in the presence of peers. Several children may be playing in the same sandbox, for example, but each plays independently, with no apparent consciousness of the others.

Four- and 5-year-old children play together more frequently and for longer periods of time. During the play activity a child may display alternating aggressive and cooperative behavior. At this age, children begin to display sympathetic behavior toward their peers. Some give evidence of leadership ability. The role of the leader and the follower varies, however, with the nature of the play activity and other factors in the situation, such as

[1] See C. Buhler, *The First Year of Life*, John Day Company, New York, 1930, pp. 56-57.

ownership of the toy used, initiation of the particular activity, suggestions of elders, and relative degree of displayed aggression or submission.

Growth of competitive behavior during these years tends to parallel that of cooperative behavior. Rivalry usually develops in accordance with the home and community forces that are encountered by the child. If in the culture cooperation rather than competition is stressed, the children tend to be noncompetitive; if the social mores include competition (as in the United States), rivalry is a strong motivator of most children's behavior. Moreover, a child may tend to be cooperative in one group and extremely competitive in another, in terms of group attitudes and his reactions in the group.

The introduction of the nursery school and the kindergarten into the school structure has great value as a means of helping young children develop cooperative social attitudes through peer group activity. Early social experiences under guidance can help reduce the number of children who otherwise might develop "isolate" tendencies. Nursery school and kindergarten experience is especially valuable for the "only" child or the rigidly reared child who otherwise may not have the opportunity to play with other children.

Play situations provide the best outlets for young children's social growth. During the ages of 4 and 5, children of both ages learn to play together and to find their respective niches in the various activities in which they engage. Much attention is being given to provide them with appropriate play equipment. Two important principles of toy construction are: (1) the toy must be small enough for the child to handle, and (2) strong enough so that it does not break easily. A mechanical toy should be simple and workable.

Dr. Edgar A. Doll, who earlier developed a social maturity scale, has organized a number of situations to illustrate behavior milestones along the way to growing up. These portray the interrelationships of the mental, physical, emotional, and social factors of development. Sketches illustrating behavior during the first five years are presented here.[2]

[2] From *Your Child Grows Up*, John Hancock Mutual Life Insurance Company, Boston, Mass. Used with permission.

. . . Before the 1st Birthday . . .

SITS UP unsupported and steadily. Pulls self up to standing position, holding on for support; balance may be a bit "wobbly," but stands alone on firm surface.

MOVES about floor by crawling or creeping; plays with rattle and simple objects for quarter hour or so. Does not need constant watching, but likes attention: "asks" to have parents pick him up.

IMITATES sounds and attempts to say words which only his parents understand. Follows such simple instructions as coming when called, pointing out pictures or objects when asked.

. . . Before the 2nd Birthday . . .

CLIMBS up stairs without help, gets about house and yard with only occasional oversight. Gives up baby carriage to walk, or ride in go-cart.

EATS with spoon from bowl or cup, without help or too much spilling.

Chooses between suitable food and substances unfit for eating. Removes wrappers from candy.

PERFORMS useful little errands such as bringing named objects from nearby places. Opens closed doors, climbs up on chairs to reach, removes simple obstacles from his path. Uses basket to carry things.

"HELPS" with undressing by removing socks and shoes (if untied).

Uses short sentences, and has vocabulary of twenty-five words or more – not mere "parrot talk."

Names familiar objects for practical purposes.

. . . *Before the 3rd Birthday* . . .

Occupies self without "looking after" at own play such as drawing with crayon, building with blocks, dressing dolls, looking at pictures.

Uses blunt-end scissors in cutting paper and cloth—is not destructive.

Uses fork without much spilling, and eats solid food that does not require cutting. Can get drink of water unassisted, turning water tap on and off. Dries own hands if washed.

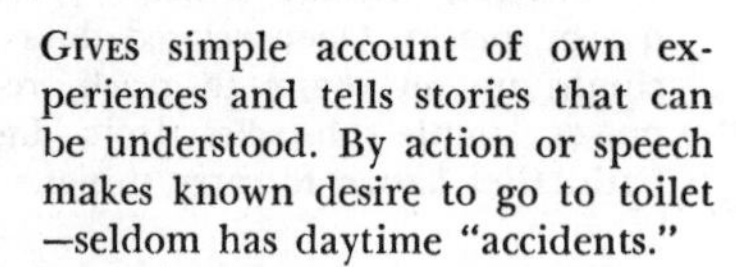

Gives simple account of own experiences and tells stories that can be understood. By action or speech makes known desire to go to toilet —seldom has daytime "accidents."

Avoids simple hazards. "Comes in out of rain." Is careful about falling when on stairs and high places, avoids sharp edges, broken glass, etc., and should keep out of streets.

. . . Before the 4th Birthday . . .

WASHES hands acceptably without help and dries them without soiling towel. Puts on and buttons coat or dress, but may need help otherwise in dressing.

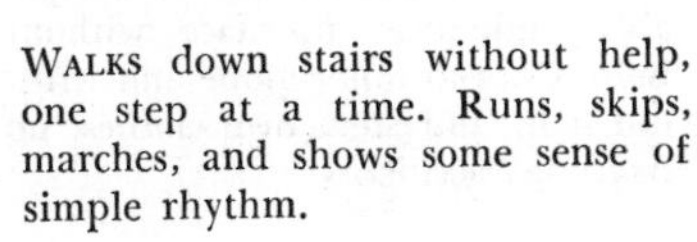

WALKS down stairs without help, one step at a time. Runs, skips, marches, and shows some sense of simple rhythm.

TAKES part in such group activities as simple kindergarten games; joins in simple play tea parties, and activities requiring no skill. "Performs" for others, upon request.

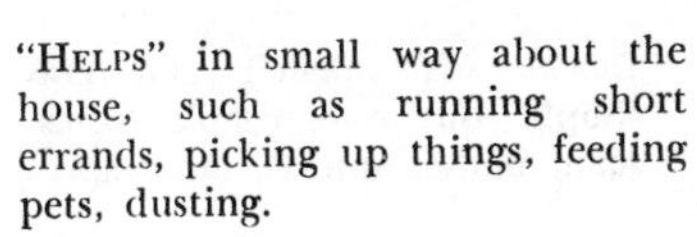

"HELPS" in small way about the house, such as running short errands, picking up things, feeding pets, dusting.

. . . Before the 5th Birthday . . .

DRESSES self except for tying laces, ribbons, or ties. Does all own buttoning, but clothing is laid out. May need help with muffler, rubbers, or overshoes, and with specially difficult or close-fitting clothes.

WASHES face, except ears (!) acceptably and dries his face without help. Goes to toilet alone and without help; unfastens own clothes: no daytime "accidents."

GOES about neighborhood unattended; may be restricted as to areas or "deadlines" so that his whereabouts are known, but is "on his own" within this limitation. Plays in small groups of children of same age such games as tag, hide-and-seek, jump-rope, hopscotch, marbles, etc.

DRAWS with pencil and crayon simple, but recognizable forms as man, house, animal, landscape.

. . . Before the 6th Birthday . . .

TAKES care of self unsupervised, outside own yard; manages roller skates, sled, wagon, velocipede, scooter, or other play vehicle.

PLAYS simple table games with others that require taking turns, observing rules, attaining goals, and does so without undue squabbling. (Games include tiddledywinks, parchesi, dominoes, etc.)

GOES to school unattended. He may go with friends, but no one is in direct charge of him. "On his own" outside his neighborhood. Learns to print simple words of three or four letters without copy—and his own first name. Does so without direction.

IS TRUSTED with small sums of money to make clearly-stated purchases. He carries out directions in returning purchases, but he may not be able to make change.

Social Development during Later Childhood (ages 6 through 12). These are the elementary school years. During these ages, the child exhibits a growing recognition of himself in relation to other people. His attitudes toward others are likely to be influenced by his immediate urges or desires. His emotional pattern is undergoing change and he often does things that appear to have no reasonable basis. He may like his teacher one moment and dislike her the next. He is restless, wants freedom to do as he pleases, whispers, and sometimes draws pictures of the teacher that are unflattering. All these activities are evidences of struggles toward self-realization. By this time he also has become somewhat independent of parental control.

Former self-centeredness is likely to change to participation in group activity. Attendance at a nursery school and kindergarten usually fosters this interest, since the modern school, especially on the lower levels, provides situational opportunities that encourage children to cooperate with others in work and play activities. Moreover, teachers on all levels are trained to plan, organize, and supervise social activities so that social progress can be experienced by each child.

If the 6-year-old enters elementary school without previous experience in the nursery school and/or kindergarten he is likely to be more individualistic than other children who have attended the lower schools. The fact that he probably had received a great deal of attention from his mother during his early formative years causes him (1) to lean heavily upon the teacher, as a mother substitute, for guidance and (2) to lack the ability to submit to the wishes of his peer group. Of course, even a child with earlier training in group relationships may be aggressive and self-centered when he enters the first grade of the elementary school. In fact, he may continue to display such characteristics through much or all of his school life, as a result of too permissive or otherwise unfavorable parental rearing.

With increase in age and maturity, the child wants to participate in social activities that are unrelated to the home. He seeks friends among his peers even though he still needs the satisfaction of knowing that adult help and guidance are within easy reach. Gradually the average 8-year-old is as much or more interested in group-activity participation than in self-centered satisfactions. He wants peer approval and knows that this usually is gained through the show of cooperative behavior.

The need for social approval probably is rooted in the human urge to be with others of one's kind rather than to be completely alone. This growing social awareness is displayed in the tendency of 9- to 12-year-old children to form clubs founded on similar transient interests. These school or neighborhood clubs usually are separated by sex and are short-lived. Occasionally, the purpose of a boys' club is so definite that the interest of the members in its activities gives the club a relative degree of permanency. An organized group of this kind often is referred to as a "gang." Its activities may be characterized by great secrecy. Passwords, badges, rules for membership, and special places for meeting contribute to the emotional overtones associated with a group of this kind. Group loyalty is strong. The gaining of membership into the group is difficult. No matter what restrictions are imposed for eligibility, however, when a child becomes a member he experiences a sense of freedom among the members of the group.

Although children are being given so much freedom of behavior without close supervision that some of them engage in destructive activities, an organized group or gang need not be unfavorable to good social development. Good leadership in a club or a gang can help restrain the members from engaging in asocial activities. In fact, many adults believe that an effective way of curbing uncontrolled behavior among children is to encourage the formation of organized groups, and to help train young leaders to guide the activities of the group members.

Children rally around one of their members who shows leadership qualities. Among the qualities of a leader that are admired and imitated by members of a group are superior physical stature, better than average mental acuity, genuine interest in others, and willingness to cooperate. To the extent that desirable leadership qualities are developed, gangs or clubs are beneficial.

Children, like their elders, are gregarious. Conditions sometimes are such that a child finds it difficult to make friends in a group. He becomes an isolate. Since this experience is distasteful, it may induce socially disapproved behavior unless the situation is corrected by an understanding leader. Antisocial attitudes developed in later childhood are likely to persist, interfering with positive social development during adolescence and early adulthood. In general, however, the prepubescent years represent a happy and socially satisfying period of social growth, maturation, and learning.

The child is interested in discovering all he can about people and things in his own community as well as in more remote places. He enjoys sharing his feelings and experiences with his peer companions. In the following sketches are traced the mental, motor, and social developmental patterns of the 6- to 12-year-old, as evidenced by the progressive changes that are taking place in their attitudes and behavior, according to Doll.

. . . Before the 7th Birthday . . .

At table: uses knife to spread butter or jam on bread. At play: cuts, folds, pastes paper toys. Sews crudely if needle is threaded. Cannot tie knot. Enjoys making simple figures in clay.

Writes (not prints) legibly with pencil a dozen or more simple words, correctly spelled. Does so at own desire, or from dictation, but does not need copy.

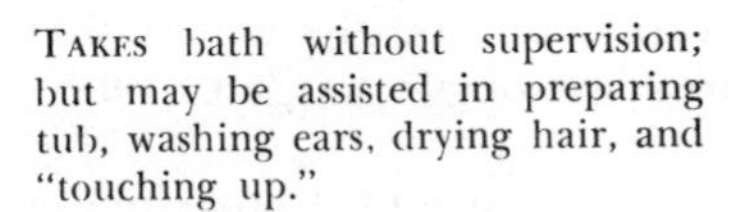

Takes bath without supervision; but may be assisted in preparing tub, washing ears, drying hair, and "touching up."

Performs bedtime operations without help: goes to bedroom alone, undresses, attends to toilet, turns out light according to routine. May be "tucked in" as a matter of sentiment, but requires no assistance.

. . . Before the 8th Birthday . . .

Uses table knife for cutting meat. He may need help with tough or difficult pieces such as on bones, or joints of poultry.

Reads ordinary clock or watch correctly to nearest quarter hour and actually uses clock for practical purposes.

Brushes and combs hair acceptably without help or "going over" when dressing, going out, or receiving company.

Takes part in group play; boys prefer games that do not require much skill, such as unorganized baseball, or basketball, follow-the-leader, fox and hounds, hiking and bicycle riding. Girls prefer playing house, school, nurse-doctor, and other imitations of home and social affairs.

. . . *Before the 9th Birthday* . . .

MAKES practical use of common tools such as hammer, saw, or screw driver; uses household and sewing utensils; handles simple garden implements successfully.

HELPS with such routine household tasks as dusting, sweeping, setting table, washing dishes, making beds, attending furnace, raking lawn. Assumes responsibility for share of household chores.

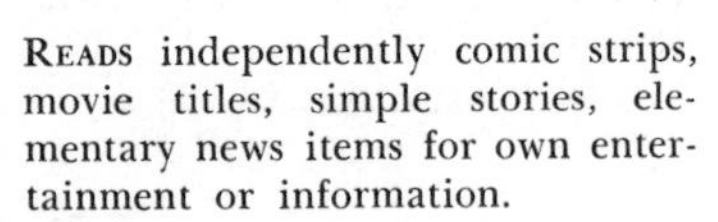

READS independently comic strips, movie titles, simple stories, elementary news items for own entertainment or information.

TAKES bath acceptably without any help; undresses, prepares tub or shower, washes and dries self (except the hair) without need of touching up.

. . . Before the 10th Birthday . . .

LOOKS after all his own needs at table; helps himself, ordinarily prepares such items as baked potatoes, boiled eggs, difficult cuts of meat.

BUYS useful articles and exercises some choice in making purchases. Is responsible for safety of articles, money, and correct change. Does this independently or can be relied upon to follow directions.

GOES about home community freely, alone or with friends. There may be forbidden areas, but the restrictions do not confine the child's activities to his nearby neighborhood.

RUNS useful errands; is trusted as a messenger, or to carry out orders to or from not too distant points, and under clear instructions.

. . . Before the 11th Birthday . . .

WRITES occasional short letters to friends or relatives on own initiative, or following mild suggestions.

Does so without help except perhaps in spelling unfamiliar words.

Addresses envelope and makes ready for mailing.

USES telephone for practical purposes; looks up number, makes call, and carries on sensible, purposeful conversation. Does not attempt long distance calls and automatic dialing may be difficult unless in long usage.

DOES occasional or brief work on own initative about the home or neighborhood, for which small sums are paid or merit payment, such as "odd jobs," housework, helping in care of children, selling magazines.

RESPONDS to magazine, radio, or other advertising by mailing coupons, requesting samples, sending for literature, and ordering from catalogues.

. . . Before the 12th Birthday . . .

MAKES useful articles or does easy repair work. Cooks or sews in small way; does a little gardening; raises pets; writes brief stories; produces simple paintings or drawings.

IS SOMETIMES left alone at home or at work for an hour or so, and is successful in looking after his own needs or those of other children left in his care.

READS for practical information or own enjoyment stories or news items in papers, magazine articles, library book stories of adventure and romance.

WASHES and dries own hair; is responsible for a thorough job at cleaning hair, but may need reminding to do so.

Social Behavior during Adolescence. Social adaptation during adolescence is affected by numerous factors of influence: (1) interest in members of the other sex increases rapidly; (2) maturing primary and secondary sex characteristics bring about marked changes in attitudes and emotional responses; (3) extreme differences in physical growth rate also strongly influence peer relationships, especially the willingness of the very tall girl or the very short boy to participate in social activities with more normal-height peers. Changing attitudes toward themselves, their parents, and others in authority, as well as toward members of the opposite sex, account for some of the conflicts experienced by young people during early adolescence.

During the middle-adolescent period, boys and girls lose interest in same-sex gangs or clubs. Instead, they begin to form social groups, comprising members of both sexes. Usually about five or six members of the group share similar social interests such as dancing, hiking, cycling, and the like; they often refer to their group as a *crowd,* rather than a *gang.* Some of these groups are relatively permanent and exclusive; membership usually is based upon personal merit, in terms of group standards; a young person is excluded from the group if some of his personality characteristics are considered by the group members to be socially undesirable. Because of the freedom permitted adolescents in their social activities, their group activities may or may not be personally beneficial or socially acceptable. The behavior value of an adolescent social group depends upon (1) the habits of self-control possessed by individual members, (2) degree of positive, constructive leadership, and (3) kind and amount of indirect adult supervision.

In addition to group membership an adolescent tends to display an increasing need for close friendship with another teenager. He wants someone of his own age to whom he can talk freely concerning his activities, his hopes and ambitions, and his developing philosophy of life, and who will understand and be sympathetic toward his troubles, thwartings, and conflicts. Many such personal friendships grow out of group relationships. During early adolescence the confidant is likely to be a member of the same sex. A warm close relationship can develop between the two friends that is maintained through all or much of their adult life. The older adolescent usually seeks a satisfying friendship with a member of the other sex, although the earlier-formed, same-sex companionship may continue. Opposite-sex friendships among adolescents can be regarded as a kind of preparation for eventual mate selection and marriage.

In their selection of friends of the opposite sex, adolescents are sensitive to behavior manifestations of certain definite personality characteristics. According to the findings of a study based upon the responses of more than 4000 adolescents, both sexes placed considerable emphasis upon the importance to them of their opposite-sex friends' display of positive, socially acceptable behavior traits. Although they reported that they like their friends to be physically attractive and well-groomed, they seemed to be more interested in personal qualities, such as sincerity, consideration for others, good manners, friendliness, reasonable modesty about self and actual or imagined achievements, and self-control.[3]

Other studies of adolescent attitudes have yielded similar results Regardless of the apparent social undesirability of some adolescents' selection of opposite-sex friends, most young people seem to know the basic personality traits upon which a friendship should be built. Propinquity, sexual attraction, similarity of background experiences, and rejection by more worth-while associates are some of the causes given for unwholesome opposite-sex friendships among adolescents.

In general, adolescent boys and girls engage in similar social activities, but there are differences between the sexes in the relative strengths of certain specific desires. The results of investigators of 15- to 17-year-old adolescents' interests and activities having social implications indicate that both sexes seem to be much concerned about dress and grooming in order to impress members of the opposite sex. Not so important but relatively similar are the interests of boys and girls in (1) attending parties or dances, (2) choosing a mate, (3) being accepted as a member of a social club, (4) developing social skills, (5) attending motion picture programs, and (6) becoming independent of parental control.

Girls appear to be slightly more interested in picnics than boys. The greatest differences between the interests of boys and girls are in sports and dating. Participation in sports activities ranks high for boys, but low for girls. Conversely, girls in their middle teens are extremely interested in twosome dating, while

[3] L. D. Crow and A. Crow, *Human Development and Learning*, rev. ed. Van Nostrand Reinhold, 1965, pp. 110-111.

relatively few boys show a similar interest in dating the same girl. In their words, they want to play the field.

Physical development and tradition are factors of the male's greater interest in physical activity from childhood onward, although there is an increasing trend toward female participation in relatively less strenuous sports activities. Twosome dating becomes a female's interest earlier than a male's because of the former's advantage in rate of physical growth and maturation, and cultural acceptance of a girl's marrying at a young age. The boy is expected to become financially independent before he becomes seriously concerned with twosome dating as a means of mate selection.

Adolescents attempt to model their social activities according to adult standards. Because of their relative immaturity, however, their approach often is experimental. They believe that either by conforming too closely to adult patterns of behavior or deviating too widely from adult or peer standards they may induce one or another kind of social ridicule. Hence, from the viewpoint of social development, adolescence is a period of trial-error-trial-success in personal and social relationships. To the extent that an adolescent experiences more success than errors, the progressive steps of social development during the teen years represent behavior changes as depicted by Doll.

During childhood a boy or girl should be provided with many opportunities of meeting people so that they will have less difficulty in developing social grace and ease. A child, for example, should be permitted to take the initiative in starting or carrying on a conversation in the presence of his elders. Too often he is told that "children should be seen and not heard."

A growing person desires to be an active rather than a passive member of a social group. Participation is essential to good social development. Social grace is furthered through the help of parental and educational guidance in the simple rudiments of acceptable social practices. Growing children, for example, need to be taught proper forms of introductions, ways of starting a conversation, control of voice, desirable eating manners, and the like. Many of these are acquired through imitation. Fortunately, when these habits become functional, the individual is enabled to meet most social situations with ease and enjoyment.

. . . Between 12th and 15th Birthday . . .

TAKES part in games requiring skill, such as card games, basketball, baseball, tennis, pool. Understands scoring and sticks to the rules. Is an active member of athletic team or literary organization. Attends parties, dances, and other activities with children of own age without adult direction.

TAKES complete care of dress; seldom requires help in care of hair, nails, etc. Makes proper selection of clothing according to occasion and weather.

SELECTS and buys minor articles of clothing with regard to appropriateness, cost, and fit, such as ties, underwear, shoes, but not suits, dresses, coats. Authority may come from parents.

PERFORMS responsible routine chores without prodding, doing his share of such recurring household work as waiting on table, house cleaning, caring for garden or furnace, washing windows, cleaning the family car.

. . . Between 15th and 18th Birthdays . . .

WRITES business and social letters that are more than a matter of routine; gives serious information, significant news, and acknowledges instructions. Among friends discusses general news, sports, events, and follows these matters.

GOES outside limits of his home town, and makes his own arrangements. Is "on his own," and able to find his way about unfamiliar places. Is given responsibility for all daytime movements without accounting in advance for his plans.

USES money with common sense. Plans for future needs rather than spending all for mere immediate enjoyment, so is ready for own spending money (either allowance or earned). Usually purchases clothes, including dresses, suits, overcoats, hats. May receive advice, but makes own sensible decisions.

SHOWS personal interest in the opposite sex; is interested in *a* boy or *a* girl, as well as in all boys or girls. Calls or receives callers; but "dates" may be restricted as to time, place, or circumstances.

PART III

ASPECTS OF DIFFERENCES AMONG LEARNERS

CHAPTER 8

INDIVIDUAL DIFFERENCES AND LEARNING READINESS

Two generally accepted statements are: (1) people differ in their appearance and behavior from one another; (2) some children learn better than others. The truth of each of these statements can be checked by observing the day-by-day behavior of any-age individuals and by checking young people's educational progress either through use of artificially constructed tests or by observation of actual behavior. School people and parents need to know the way in which and the extent to which young people differ from one another, as well as the possible reasons for differences that are related to degree of readiness to learn.

Nature of Individual Differences

Some of the basic factors of actual or potential differences among human beings have been considered in previous chapters. The present discussion is concerned with the basic factors of individual success or failure in learning and adjustment.

Possession Aspect of Human Characteristics. Viewed qualitatively, human beings are alike. Except in rare cases of extreme abnormality, human organisms have similar gross body structures and body organs. The general behavior patterns of an individual are predictable, in that they represent human reaction tendencies and reflect culturally acceptable habits and customs.

Quantitatively, people differ. Neither the rates nor the limits of growth and maturation of germ-determined potentialities are exactly alike for any two individuals, even though they are identical twins. Not only inner growth but also the many interactions that take place between the developing organism and environmental forces have quantitative implications.

Broadly interpreted, *individual difference* refers to every aspect of an individual that differentiates him in any way from other human beings. Viewed educationally, those individual differences are significant that affect individual learners' readiness to benefit from instruction in comparison with the readiness stage of their age peers.

Areas of Difference. Observable physical differences include height and weight, body contour, eye, skin, and hair coloring, and facial expression. Body organs differ in their functioning. Unless these differences deviate much from the so-called norms of a geographic group, they do not interfere unduly with organismic adaptation to life demands.

A cross-sectional or horizontal investigation of the mental abilities of unselected same-age children yields data that give evidence of wide variation. Behavior expressions of difference in strength of needs, urges, wants, and desires, and of derived interests can be observed readily. Emotional patterning also differs from person to person.

Relationship among Human Characteristics. It was believed at one time that the law of compensation governs the distribution of an individual's natural characteristics, especially as related to deficiencies. For example, if a person is born blind, nature compensates for the deficiency by endowing the new organism with extremely acute hearing or unusual tactile sensitivity. Other compensating relationships between abilities that are accepted by some laymen are: a physically attractive girl or a man with a strong physique is likely to be mentally slow; a person having a high degree of mental acuity probably will become insane.

Many similar lay views toward the interrelationship of human characteristics or abilities could be cited. There probably is no scientifically determined basis for the apparent functioning of the law of compensation. It is possible that some relatively slight correlation exists among human tendencies, although it is difficult to predict the extent to which the positive or negative possession of one trait affects another.

Theories concerning Individual Differences. Attempts have been made to clarify personality differences among people according to "types," and to attribute specific behavior characteristics to particular type aspects. Personality typing is not a recent approach to the problem of individual differences, but it has a long and interesting history.

Body Fluids. Hippocrates (400 B.C.) and Galen (150 A.D.) attempted to explain personality differences according to excessive amounts of one of four body humors, which was supposed to be accompanied by specific forms of behavior. The four types are: (1) *sanguine* (blood)—quick, gay, emotionally unstable; (2) *choleric* (yellow bile)—easily angered; (3) *melancholic* (black bile)—pessimistic; (4) *phlegmatic* (phlegm)—slow, not easily excited. Following these earlier beginnings in typing, many theories have been propounded, some of which bear some slight relationship to the theory of the four temperaments.

Endocrinologists associate observable differences in human behavior and attitudes with degree of balance or imbalance of the ductless or endocrine glands. Hyperactivity of the thyroid gland and gonads, for example, is accompanied by overambitious, domineering, or aggressive attitudes, while hypoactivity induces less active behavior and more submissive attitudes.

Body Structure. Several attempts have been made to link differences in anatomic structure and physical form with specific behavior concomitants. Kretschmer (1928) classified individuals as: (1) *athletic* (muscular and adaptable); (2) *asthenic* (tall, thin, sensitive to criticism); (3) *pyknic* (short and stout, easy going); (4) *dysplastic* (abnormally built with accompanying abnormal behavior characteristics).

Sheldon and his associates also are attempting to discover relationships between physical characteristics and behavior trends. Accordingly, individuals are classified broadly into three somatypes: (1) endomorphic (soft, round body); (2) mesomorphic (muscular and bony body, heavy physique, and thick skin), and (3) ectomorphic (fragile, sensitive to exposure). According to this theory, techniques of teaching and methods of discipline should be fitted to the child's particular somatype.

Social Development. Individual differences have been typed as aspects of social development. Although deviation in growth and maturation may affect any individual's type of behavior, these classifications represent attempts to differeniate among apparently habitual response patterns in personal and social interrelationships.

One of the most popular theories is that of Carl Jung. According to Jung (1923) people can be classified as (1) *introvert* (socially shy, and retiring, and finding satisfactions in the inner world of their own feelings and imagery), and (2) *extroverts* (socially adaptable, interested in people and social activities). Jung also classified people into four subtypes: (1) sensation type (interested in concrete reality), (2) thinking type (influenced by their thinking and comprehension), (3) feeling type (sensitive to feelings of satisfaction), and (4) intuitive type (given to following hunches and inspirations).

Other forms of typing place emphasis, respectively, upon degree of dominance or submission, self-confidence or inferiority, masculinity or femininity, and similar opposing categories. Springer (1928) classified people, according to their seemingly habitual attitudes toward social institutions and relationships, into sociological types; theoretical, economic, esthetic, social, political, and religious.

Theory Fallacies. There is a fundamental fallacy in any attempt at classification of human beings into distinct types. Extremes of difference among individuals may seem to fall into one or another theoretical category. In general, however, individual characteristics rarely can be explained as completely representative of any particular type. For example, in regard to Jung's theory of introversion and extroversion, so many persons display both extroverted and introverted behavior that it was necessary to add another category, *ambiversion* to the original classification.

Emotional Significance of Differences. Physical, mental, and emotional differences among people, with accompanying differences in abilities, attitudes, and interests have fundamental significance in the furthering of progress. Theoretical explanations of such differences probably are relatively unimportant. Yet, since individual differences in learning and adjustment pose practical educational problems, it is imperative that teachers (1) recognize the presence and significance of differences among their pupils, (2) attempt to discover the reasons for the differences, and (3) adapt instructional materials and methods to the specific needs and abilities of each pupil. To provide experiences for each unique learner is a difficult task that requires the teacher to possess a considerable body of information concerning learning readiness, as well as an intelligent understanding of the behavior and attitudinal tendencies of individual children and adolescents.

Learning Readiness

Differences in anatomical structure may affect children's and adolescents' relationships with their schoolmates, or affect adjustment to classroom conditions, such as size of seats and desks. Except in cases of extreme abnormality, a learner's physical characteristics have little or no connection with his degree of readiness for school learning. That certain differences in inherited potentiality and experiential background are potent affectors of differences in learning ability is becoming increasingly important in curriculum construction and teaching approaches.

Determining Factors. At one time, chronological age was the one general factor of readiness for school grading. At the age of 6 years, children were considered ready to start their elementary schooling. They then were supposed to progress on an age basis. In addition, parents and teachers expected all learners to profit equally well from instructional materials and methods that varied only according to grade level. The cause of failure to meet required standards of learning competence was laziness, naughtiness, or stubbornness. Psychologists and school people now recognize the need of adapting learning content and teaching procedures to meet differences among same-age children.

Since chronological age is a general indicator of level of maturity it must remain a general factor of difference in possible educability. At the same time, the educational experiences of the individual child within a same-age group, rather than the group as a whole, is becoming the focal point of instructional methods and materials.

Readiness to learn in any learning area on any school level is determined by the learner's (1) degree of general mental alertness and of his possession of one or more special abilities, (2) temperament, (3) emotional state, (4) habitual interests, and (5) attitude toward learning. Differences in ability to learn are functional. From the point of view of learning readiness, individual differences refer to behavior in a learning situation. The learning process involves various aspects of mental functioning, such as memorizing, understanding number relationships, solving problems, handling abstract concepts, recognizing similarities and differences, and reasoning.

A young child's degree of readiness to utilize his mental functions is closely related to his maturational progress. With increasing maturity, differences in experiential background tend to determine whether older children or adolescents are ready to engage in learning materials of advanced difficulty.

Maturational limitation sets the point beyond which an individual learner cannot progress, regardless of favorable learning conditions. Although the concept implied in the phrase "limit of maturation" is accepted generally by psychologists and educators, there is a growing belief that in some instances the limits of physiological maturation may be reached later in the life of the developing individual than formerly was thought. It also is known that a rich experiential environment increases a young person's readiness to master progressively difficult learning materials and that meager environmental experiences retard his progress. Yet there are cases which would seem to show that learners having similar learning potentiality, but differing greatly in the richness of background environment, earn acceptable success in learning achievement.

Factors other than mental ability *per se* and environmental conditions function as determiners of learning readiness. Some of these determining factors, mentioned earlier, have their roots in the learner's emotional pattern. The influence of the emotions should not be minimized in any consideration of learning readiness.

Educational Significance of Differences in Learning Readiness. Most classes give evidence of differing degrees of learning readiness. For example, it is a common experience of a fifth- or sixth-grade teacher to find that his pupils differ greatly from one another and within themselves in their levels of achievement in various subjects. Reading grade status may range from second grade to tenth grade reading level. Similar ranges in achievement level occur in arithmetic, language usage, vocabulary, spelling, and the social studies.

The class represents heterogeneous grouping of mental abilities. Yet the various subject area ranges may not parallel one another. That is, the slowest child mentally is not achieving on the lowest level, or near it, in all subjects, nor is the mentally superior child necessarily the top pupil in every subject. There may be a clustering of levels of achievement at one or more points of the distribution; mental ability and relative success in achievement may show some correlation. A study of the performance of each of many of the pupils probably would show wide variations, indicating perhaps differences of interests, attitudes, or other determining factors.

Experimental Approach. Much experimentation with homogeneity of grouping for learning purposes has yielded results that have doubtful significance. Theoretically, learners having similar mental ability and comparable background experience should perform similarly in their learning. This is not always the case. Personal qualities other than mental ability affect learner behavior even in homogeneous group situations.

Various projects or programs have been devised to individualize instruction. Included among them are widely known large-plan projects: (1) the *Dalton Laboratory Plan,* according to which each learner proceeds at his own rate in the study of his various subjects, assigned as "contracts" on a monthly basis; (2) the *Winnetka Plan* which allows the learner to follow his own rate of learning in each of his subject fields; (3) the *Project Method* whereby, through group cooperation in the working out of a project, learning can be individualized according to the interests and ability of each member of the group; (4) the *Activity Program,* which stresses the principle of *learning* through *doing* by encouraging the participation of every pupil in learning situations.

Although it is probable that at present no one of these plans is operating in the form in which it orginally was organized, the fact that educators have been interested enough to develop them is evidence of a growing awareness by school people of the necessity to meet the needs of pupils. In addition, modifications of the purposes and procedures characterizing these projects have been applied in many schools and school systems.

Importance of Reading Readiness. Considerable attention now is being focused upon the importance to a child of learning to comprehend reading materials. Degree of success in any school subject, as well as in many other life activities, depends upon the individual's ability to get ideas from the printed page. Studies of learning failure on upper school levels have shown one of the major causes of failure to be inability to read with adequate understanding.

In many school systems, attempts are made to determine a child's maturational readiness to profit from instruction in reading before he is "taught" to read. Moreover, it has been found that progress in learning to read may be inhibited or retarded by psychological "blocks" having emotional concomitants.

In the following chapters are discussed various aspects of individual differences among learners. The dynamic nature of human behavior, the nature of intelligence and special abilities, and the total pattern of an individual's personality are basic determining factors of differences among children and adolescents. These factors are closely related to their learning experiences from early childhood onward.

CHAPTER 9

DYNAMICS OF HUMAN BEHAVIOR

The behavior of a human being is influenced by the attitudes he acquires, the immediate and more permanent interests he develops, and the other factors of influence both within and outside himself that stimulate him in his daily living. The activity of a human being is purposeful and continuous. He constantly strives to satisfy his body needs and to acquire those behavior habits and ideals which will enable him to function successfully in his various life situations.

Human Drives and Motivation

An organism is not static; it is dynamic, in that it can be activated by an impelling force. The dynamic aspect of human behavior is based upon motivation. Motive connotes causation; it refers to sequence or continuity. Every human experience involves a causation factor that produces one or another response. It is not easy to trace the motive-response sequence in an individual's thinking and behavior, although psychologists are trying by means of various devices to discover ways to explain the functional aspects of behavior motivation. For example, some insight into the deep-seated emotionalized motives of individual behavior is made possible through utilization of psychoanalysis.

Meaning of Motive. The function of motive as an activating force ranges from directing a simple act to the complex processes involved in the selection of a career or the completion of work toward a professional degree. There is evidence, however, that the functioning of human motivation is complex even in what appears to be a simple activity.

Motives can be regarded as those internal conditions or forces that tend to impel an individual toward certain goals. These forces or motives serve to direct behavior toward goals by causing one stimulus pattern to be more forceful than another or by enabling the individual to desire strongly that which is not present to the sense organs at the time. For example, if it starts to rain as a man is leaving his home, he returns for his raincoat or umbrella. His motive may be to avoid damage to his hat, suit, or shoes, or to prevent catching a cold.

The Functioning of Motives. Some motives are persistent; others are fleeting. If a person has a strong desire to attain a distant goal, the likelihood that it will be attained depends upon the persistence of the motive. For example, recognition by a beginning ball player of improved achievement on the field is accompanied by a strengthening of his desire to become a member of the first-string team. This ambition necessitates an increase in his willingness to spend many hours in careful practice and to cooperate wholeheartedly with the team and its manager.

An individual may fail to attain a desired goal. Motive then takes the form of *exploratory variation* that continues until a substitute goal is reached. The behavior of an individual in the process of becoming oriented to a new group or situation also gives evidence of this form of motive functioning. Neophyte teachers, children new to a social group or to a classroom situation, newly drafted servicemen, and newcomers in a community are examples of exploratory variation. The leaders of a group can do much to help the newcomer reduce the amount and number of his different acceptance-seeking activities by introducing him to the group, with appropriate comments concerning possible positive values of the new interrelationship.

Emotional tonus gives impetus to human motives and drives. If an individual has a strong urge to attain a definite goal but meets resistance from uncontrollable obstacles, he may be moved to engage in behavior that expresses either anger through aggression or fear through submission. Successful achievement usually results in reduced tension and emotional satisfaction. The dull as well as the bright can experience these unfavorable or favorable emotional reactions as they are impelled to action by goal-achieving motivation.

Significant Drives and Urges

Human drives and urges are dynamic forces that exert a potent influence upon the individual's thoughts, emotions, and behavior. The extent to which these drives and urges are gratified or thwarted determines the degree of success and happiness he is likely to enjoy. As a young person is stimulated to action, he attempts so to direct his interests and desires that he may achieve satisfying responses.

Urges Arising from Body Needs. Impulses arising from body needs are experienced daily by everyone. The human being seeks the things that give him a sense of well-being, and avoids those that may cause him pain, embarrassment, or suffering. Certain cravings related to biological conditions, such as the consumption of food, water, or oxygen, are life-sustaining. Yet, the satisfying of these needs begins early to assume social value. For example, in light of his previous experience, a man eats three times a day, he prefers food prepared as his mother prepared it, or he likes or dislikes certain foods.

Social custom influences the way in which many body needs are satisfied. There are wide differences among cultural groups and variations within any one community, especially a national state or a large city, in degree of social acceptability of (1) the amount and style of clothing worn as protection, (2) the kind of structures utilized for shelter, (3) the number of hours and specific hours of the day given to needed sleep, and (4) the amount of daily or weekly time devoted to recreational activity, as well as the kind of activity.

The developing child's or adolescent's means of satisfying his body needs is controlled, for the most part, by home conditions and adult example. The adolescent, especially, is extremely sensitive, however, to peer approval or disapproval of the social aspects of body need fulfillment. Of particular concern to a young person, sometimes with strong emotional concomitants, are the style and monetary value of his clothes, and the social adequacy of his home and its furnishings.

Urges Associated with Social Experiences. Some behavior impulses are rooted in social relationships, thereby being both personal and social in nature. Important urges, drives, or behavior motivators usually experienced in social settings include the urge for success, the mastery drive, the urge for recognition and approval, the urge for security, the urge for adventure, and the sex urge, which is both biological and social.

Success versus Failure. The success motive is a powerful stimulator of continued performance in a satisfying activity on any age level and in every area of activity. Failure to perform adequately in terms of expected results is likely to lead to discouragement and further failure. Actual or expected failure can result in cessation of an activity, even though some degree of success might be earned if the activity were continued.

The effect of success or of failure on an individual's level of aspiration is associated with his former successful or failing experiences, or results from expectation concerning the relative ease or difficulty of an activity in which he is about to participate. For example, a high school junior, A, is scheduled for a course in physics. He is a bright student and has earned success in general science and chemistry. He starts the study of physics with confidence and he earns success in it. Both past successful experience and expectation that the course will be easy motivate him to perform well. His success may raise his educational and vocational levels of aspiration toward election of science as his college major, with an accompanying ambition to become a research scientist or to teach science. Whether the student achieves either ambition depends upon the degree of satisfying success he experiences in science on the college level.

High school junior B is pressured into electing physics, in spite of the fact that in his previous science courses his achievement was barely adequate and the subjects were disliked by him. Since he approaches the study of physics with inadequate preparation and a fear of it, he is likely to fail even though he is a hard worker. If he can be motivated by his teacher to review the background study material in which he had failed earlier and to overcome his dislike of the subject, he probably will begin to perform more successfully. The accompanying feelings of satisfaction may help him continue successfully. Student C, also a conscientious student, is warned by his friends who had not succeeded in physics, against attempting it. Consequently, he elects a supposedly easier subject, even though he had planned to major in science. So strong have become his expectations of unsuccessful achievement in physics that he avoids the possibility of failure. Yet he might have succeeded in the subject if he had not been motivated by his friends to avoid it.

Although the urge to succeed or to avoid failure is a fundamental force in every aspect of an individual's life, it is particularly applicable to school learning. The mentally superior learner usually experiences the satisfaction of successful school achievement. Hence he constantly raises his levels of aspiration. The mentally slow pupil, especially in competition with brighter classmates, is likely to experience failure and accompanying feelings of dissatisfaction that can induce severe emotional strain.

A teacher's goal should be to motivate each of his pupils to experience satisfying learning success within the limits of learning capacity. This is a difficult task for the teacher of a class in which there are extreme differences in degree of learning readiness. Moreover, even with more homogeneously grouped pupils, rarely can successful learning result from a teacher's attempt to motivate improved performance through threats of failure. Rather can better learning effort and achievement result if the teacher, recognizing the motivating force of the success urge, encourage his pupils toward working, within the limits of their abilities, toward successful learning achievement.

An important psychological factor in the functioning of the urge to succeed or to avoid failure has educational significance. A learner's feelings of satisfaction or annoyance attached to his degree of success usually are aroused by the kind and amount of approval or disapproval he receives from his teacher and the effect upon him of the adult's attitudes toward him. If he believes that the teacher is not a good judge of pupil performance or is prejudiced for or against himself, any evaluation of his work by that teacher has little or no influence over future performance. Moreover, to function adequately in the life of a younger or older person, the urge to succeed or to avoid failure must be aimed at practicable activities so that the individual himself can evaluate objectively and accurately whether he has attained his goal.

Mastery. According to some schools of psychological thought, the drive toward mastery is a primary urge. A human being seeks to attract the attention of others to himself. He also wants to impress them with his superioriy in one or another aspect of behavior or to gain control of objects or persons in his environment. The mastery drive is associated closely with the success urge. A learner, for example, is willing to devote time and energy in memorizing learning materials, solving a difficult problem, or practicing a skill until he has succeeded in gaining self-satisfying and teacher-approved mastery of the learning task.

Inherent in successful constructive leadership is the ability to gain mastery over destructive impulses displayed by members of the group. Discipline, as related to pupils' behavior, depends upon the teacher's power to achieve direct or indirect mastery of the whole classroom situation. The concept of self-discipline implies self-mastery of personally and socially determined behavior impulses. (See Chapter 22.)

People differ greatly in relation to desire for mastery, both in strength of drive and functional value. Some individuals are willing to submit to unsatisfying elements of a situation or to disliked control of their activities by others. Other persons are more actively aggressive in their attitudes toward disliked conditions or situations. They are impelled to gain mastery over that which is unsatisfying, sometimes regardless of the methods utilized to attain their goal.

The mastery drive may be so strong in an unsuccessful school learner that he attempts to master the classroom situation through whatever means may seem to be success-achieving or within his ability limits. He becomes the class bully, interrupts class discussions by asking irrelevant questions, makes queer sounds or engages in similar noncooperative behavior, or he flatters or otherwise "apple polishes" the teacher. Activities such as these seem to be mere attention-getting devices, but in many instances they are motivated by a need to control or master the situation. Overt behavior manifestations of the mastery drive may be personally and socially beneficial or extremely detrimental.

The behavior-directing influence of the desire for mastery begins early in life. By discovering a child's special potentialities or talents as soon and as accurately as possible, parents and teachers can help him direct his energy and interest toward satisfying, successful learning mastery in the area of his particular ability. It can be noted in this connection that even the mentally dull child usually can be taught to gain adequate mastery in nonintellectual areas of activity, thereby experiencing satisfying success.

Recognition and Approval. Little need be said concerning the human desire to receive social recognition of achievements as well as approval of general behavior and expressed attitudes. The kind of social interrelationships experienced by an individual is associated closely with the degree of other persons' responsiveness to him and his activities. When one completes a piece of work, satisfaction in its completion is increased by the fact that it is admired by others. Moreover, an individual constantly, often quietly, is devising ways and means to have his personal qualities recognized and his successes approved.

Good social living is characterized by extending to others the kind of approval desired by them for work well done. For an accomplishment that has social significance or that represents a sacrifice of a personal ambition for the welfare of others to be accepted without any apparent recognition of its value or deserved commendation is an extremely discouraging experience. At the same time, for praise to be effective it must be based upon careful evaluation and given with sincerity.

Since adult approval usually is sought eagerly by children, tactful, emotion-free disapproval is one of the most effective techniques for the treatment of socially unacceptable child behavior. Neither approval nor disapproval needs to be expressed verbally. A child or even an older person is quick to recognize approving or disapproving attitudes of others (especially parents and teachers) as these attitudes are expressed by means of facial expression or body movements.

Adventure. Curiosity is a characteristic human trait. The kind of activity in which an individual engages to express his spirit of adventure is limited by various factors: respect for social and spiritual values, legal restrictions, and personal welfare.

Persistent urges to attain complex, sometimes far-reaching goals constantly commands the attention of scientists and other researchers. To explore, discover, or invent satisfies the urge to adventure into the new and the different, as well as the desire for social approval. Many children are driven by their curiosity or urge for adventure to seek satisfactions that take them beyond their limited experiential environment. The satisfying of children's curiosity about the unknown can be a strong motivating force in learning that challenges a teacher's imagination and ingenuity.

The planners of radio, television, and motion picture programs, comic strips, and magazines intended for consumption by young people recognize the commercial value of stimulating youthful interest in adventure. The emotional reactions experienced by young people as they satisfy their spirit of adventure vicariously through these media are psychological factors that need to be considered seriously by parents, teachers, and others concerned with child welfare. The experiencing of mild emotional excitement by children in the satisfaction of this urge is healthful. Extremely exciting programs, however, can lead to nightmares or to stimulation of unfavorable impulses to enact vicariously learned dangerous exploits in their own play activities. They are detrimental to children's emotional and social development, and may result in physical damage to themselves or others.

Security. An individual has a strong desire to be secure in the affection of another. A lonely person is an emotionally insecure person. The infant or young child seeks the love and protection of his parents. A learner of any age needs the security that is gained through teacher approval of him and his achievement. The adolescent wants to have security in the kowledge that he is an accepted member of a peer group. Job security, both financial and personal-social, is basic to adequate job success and satisfaction. The experiencing of security adds zest to life and improves efficiency. The insecure person is likely eventually to face the loss of friends, inefficiency on the job, and perhaps emotional disruption.

The individual who feels secure in his home, in his work, in his social relationships, and in his ability to cope with problem situations develops attitudes of confidence that usually enable him to progress successfully in whatever he undertakes. So strong is the urge for security that many workers prefer to work on a salary basis rather than chance the risk of failure in a private business venture. Because of the confidence in future security it engenders, the Social Security System has a calming effect upon individuals as they approach old age.

Sex Drive. The sex drive is a powerful and biologically important urge. Its biological function is to perpetuate the species. The drive functions so strongly in most individuals that sexual activity is not limited in its purpose to the production of progeny. An individual's sex-stimulated desire may cause him to be promiscuous in the satisfaction of the urge, in spite of social disapproval or the possibility of contracting a venereal disease.

The human sex drive receives continuous stimulation from factors within and outside himself. Human beings have the capacity for thought and feeling and are exposed to the emotional stimuli of a sexual nature that are inherent in romantic literature, vocal music, pictorial art, and various media of entertainment. In addition, information concerning materials dealing with sex are readily available. Many young people no longer are restrained by traditional taboos from discussing sex or engaging in sexually satisfying experimentation.

Although sexual maturity is not reached until the later years of childhood or the early teen years, psychosexual development begins in very early childhood. Environmental influences during the prepubescent years of growing up and maturing therefore should be such that the child is helped gradually to form wholesome mental, emotional, and social attitudes toward sex and sexual behavior. The child develops his basic love patterns through his early experiences in family living. In the home, he can build the kind of attitudes and behavior practices that later will help him in situations in which the sex urge needs to be curbed.

If the sex impulse is so conditioned that socially acceptable self-control becomes habitual, psychosexual behavior has social value, especially in adolescent boy-girl relationships that lead eventually to mate selection. In spite of Kinsey's conclusions, based upon a relatively small cross-sectional sampling, that premarital sex experiences and masturbation are widespread among both sexes, psychologists, sociologists, and educators are agreed that young people can be helped to understand the personal and social advantages of sexual self-control and chastity.

The Formation of Attitudes

The affective qualities of human experience are the substance out of which emerge specific attitudes. These attitudes are associated intimately with an individual's needs and wants; they condition the way he thinks or behaves in his various life situations. Gradually he becomes known by his expressed attitudes. Inner reactions of approval or disapproval accompany each experience. The feeling tones are the elements of which attitudes are constructed. They help determine whether the individual is friendly or unfriendly, or tolerant or intolerant.

Nature and Meaning of Attitude. An attitude grows out of an individual's sensitivity to a situation and his emotional reaction to it. The readiness, inclination, or tendency to respond to inner or external stimuli in accordance with an earlier experience represents the dynamic aspect of attitude.

Attitudes are subjective and relate to self. One individual is affected in one way by specific stimuli; another responds differently to the same stimuli. Each is concerned about the things that are of special interest to him and that affect him directly. Attitudes become so habitual that an individual may not be aware of his attitude toward one or another situation or condition. He may not understand what causes him to respond as he does toward another person or group of people in a particular situation.

Attitude Patterning. Since an element of acceptance or avoidance is present in any attitude, the reaction of the individual in the situation is of paramount importance in attitude formation. What are the factors that influence acceptance of an object or person? When you ride in an automobile, have you a preference between front or back seat? Do you prefer to drive rather than ride? In arriving at your preference, your likes and dislikes are influenced by your past experiences. If a complete analysis could be made of the causes of your specific attitudes it would be found that each is rooted in basic experiences, associated with pleasantness or unpleasantness.

Attitudes are built on previous attitudes. An individual tends to link meanings in broad systems and to generalize many of his attitudes. For example, he tends to generalize his likes and dislikes. A dislike of one food may be transferred to a dislike for other similar foods. A dislike of several individuals in a racial or religious group may create an attitude of dislike toward the entire racial or religious group. Parents, teachers, and other group leaders have a responsibility to help the learner avoid unreasonable and incorrect generalized attitudes.

Imitation and suggestion are potent molders of attitudes. The child is sensitive to the attitudes of his parents, his teachers, and his playmates; he imitates, consciously or unconsciously, the likes and dislikes of those about him. A young person's developing religious attitudes and political interests reflect the power over him of the attitudes displayed by adults in his immediate environment. Since many of the attitudes of children and adolescents are formed through imitation, it is extremely important that good examples of socially acceptable attitudes be set for them by the adults with whom they associate—parents and other relatives, teachers, employers, government officials, and other community leaders.

Attitudes reveal themselves in situations in which an individual's interests are involved. For example, adolescents want to assert an attitude of independence and a release from adult control which they had accepted earlier. In their attempts to display attitudes of independence, their flaunting of authority sometimes is misinterpreted as a form of anarchy. Usually an adolescent's apparent refusal to cooperate with his elders can be attributed to his insecurity or to his self-protecting desire not to "lose face" with his peers.

Teen-agers sometimes are overaggressive in their behavior. They become demanding in the fulfillment of their desires. Extreme selfishness, that may have developed earlier, now becomes a dominant expression of attitudes that interfere with their social acceptance. In general, however, adolescents' attitudes are forward looking. Young people are eager to reform the world and believe they can do this immediately. They become impatient when adults seem to place obstacles in their way that delay progress toward goal-attainment.

Power of Attitudes. Attitudes give mental set to experience. The functioning of readiness is especially observable in conflict situations. The more intense the desire, the stronger will be the attitude toward its fulfillment. Favorable attitudes toward one's work, associates, parents, authority, or environmental conditions predispose toward social acceptance and successful achievement.

Attitudes exert a great influence upon a child, an adolescent, or an adult. In his day-by-day activities, each attitude is influenced by the behavior or opinions of other people. An individual's thoughts, interests, and emotions are stimulated continuously by others in the home, school, and place of work, or by books, magazines, newspapers, radio, television, and motion pictures. Each one of these stimulators exerts its impact upon an individual's attitudes and behavior. Hence, consciously or unconsciously, he constantly is forming attitudes of one kind or another that become potent behavior motivators.

An individual's social status is determined in large part by his attitude toward others and theirs toward him. Hence a child should be encouraged to be concerned about the welfare of his friends and associates. When he has learned to forget self and to focus on service to others he has achieved mature social attitudes.

Importance of Interest

Interests and attitudes have much in common. An interest, like an attitude, is personal. The kind and amount of an individual's interest in an object, situation, another individual, or a group represent a personal experience that may differ markedly from that of other people. A strong interest that has resulted in successful achievement in a particular situation may become the basis of a pleasant attitude toward the situation. Likewise, a powerful attitude may give rise to an equally strong interest. Lack of success in the satisfaction of an interest may be accompanied by a destructively critical attitude toward the entire individual.

Significance of Interest. Interest can be interpreted from either of two viewpoints: (1) as cause—the motivating force that impels one to attend to one person, situation, or activity rather than to another, or (2) as result—the affective experience that is stimulated by the presence of a person or object, or by participation in an activity. A child prefers to play with one toy rather than another. In school, he enjoys one subject more than others. An individual's interests affect his choice of reading material, or of radio, television, and motion picture programs. In fact, much of one's activity is based upon the interest factor. The motivating force for selected behavior may be inherent in the activity itself, or it may result from cumulative experiences in the activity.

If a child wants to continue an activity after he has devoted considerable time to it, there is evidence of interest in the particular situation. If an individual wants to meet an appointment, he will not let a severe rainstorm deter him from starting. A person may spend much time and expend considerable energy in the attempted solution of a problem, the search for a lost ball, or the building of a radio set. If a child enjoys his play with his associates he dislikes to leave it when his mother calls him to come to lunch or to do a chore for her. That which causes an individual to want to continue what he is doing and or to decide between two activities depends upon the amount of interest involved.

Interests constantly undergo change. From early years, an individual's interests are affected by his physical condition, his mental and emotional status, and his changing social environment. Interests are fleeting at first but by the end of adolescence, many of them become relatively fixed. Moreover, changes in interests follow closely the developing patterns of social behavior.

Children's Interests. During early childhood, both boys and girls are interested in playing with simple toys that are within their reach. Individual differences among children show themselves, however, in the kind of toys selected as well as in the length of time devoted to any one toy. If a group of children are playing in a nursery school or kindergarten, each child tends to be active in his own way, in terms of his interest at the moment.

During the elementary school years, the child's interests broaden to include interest in other people, such as his schoolmates and his teachers. He wants to learn what makes things "tick." He is interested in people, places, and conditions outside his immediate environment. Interest in possession has lessened in so far as he is willing to share his toys, books, or game sets with his peer friends.

During the preadolescent years, children become increasingly interested in exchanging confidences with their "best friend." By listening to young people talk about their daily activities, their favorite radio, television, and motion picture programs, and their liked and disliked school subjects and teachers, adults can learn much concerning older children's differing levels of social development as revealed through the overt expression of their interests and attitudes.

Adolescent Interests. The principal activities of the adolescent center around himself and his social and vocational pursuits. His interests reveal themselves in his daily work and recreational activities. Any interest expressed by him has both personal and social implications and may have a bearing on his eventual vocational choice.

Adolescents usually are extremely interested in their personal appearance, and the latest teen-age grooming and clothing styles. Boys want to look "sharp." In contrast to childhood disinterest in appearance, boys now brush their teeth regularly, take innumerable shower baths, and keep their hair cut and styled in the mode of the moment. When they believe it necessary, trousers are pressed, shoes are polished, and shirts, ties, and socks form a symphony of colors. At other times, they seem to vie with on another in achieving a sloppy but clean appearance.

Adolescent girls follow the same general pattern as boys in their interest in grooming and dress. Cosmetics are applied in abundance, but not always with good taste or proper distribution. Hair styles follow the latest mode. The wearing of costume jewelry is popular, sometimes with bizarre effect. Clothing must suit the occasion, according to teen-age standards. Basic to an adolescent's interest in grooming and dress is the desire to be accepted by peer associates of both sexes.

During early adolescence, group activities and double dates are customary. Later, however, twosome dating is preferred. Even in party situations, inviting couples rather than individual boys and girls is accepted procedure. Boys usually are willing to "go stag" but most girls prefer to stay away from a party rather than go to it with another girl or alone, with the hope that one of the "stag" boys will take her home.

Lack of childhood participation in social, mixed group activities, or real or imagined personal unattractiveness may cause some adolescents to be shy, awkward, or insecure in social situations. By providing opportunities for supervised social dances and parties, many schools are helping young people develop greater self-confidence and become more effective in social situations.

An adolescent's willingness to engage in work activity is

closely related to his interest in the work project. Many individuals, young and older, mistakenly consider the term *work* to be synonymous with drudgery. That is, one works because he must, not because he wants to do so. Play or recreational projects, on the other hand, supposedly represent activities in which one engages because they are interest-arousing. The average adolescent is intensely interested in developing satisfactory social relationships with his peers. Hence it may be difficult for him to become interested in work that, having no immediate personal and social value, is regarded by him to be boring drudgery.

Although some high school students lack the capacity for intensive or difficult study tasks, many instances of mediocre performance or failure in learning achievement are the results of learner disinterest. That is why it is so important that a high school teacher motivate his students to *want* to study.

Unless a boy or girl recognizes the value of a subject in terms of an immediate or a long-range interest, he is likely to regard learning it as a waste of time. The social studies usually are popular, especially if the emphasis is placed upon present-day happenings. Students who want to go directly to work from high school usually are interested in commercial, or so-called vocational subjects. Mathematics and the foreign languages, especially the classical languages, may not arouse interest, even among young people who plan to go to college. They find no practical value in these subjects and elect them only because they are required for college admission.

Study is work, but not drudgery, if a little of the play attitude is introduced to stimulate individual interest in mastering the day-by-day study units. Modern teaching approaches are coming to be based upon this principle.

An adolescent will work industriously to further a vocational interest, especially if he is given reasonable freedom of operation. Doing household chores, for example, may be resented bitterly, but engaging in a part-time job is enjoyed even though the work may be strenuous. In fact, some high school students who do not need extra money insist upon working after school hours. Their interest is stimulated by the fact that the job represents a kind of adventure in adult living. Moreover, if the part-time job is in the field of the adolescent's eventual vocational activities, it can help him recognize his need for continued preparation to become efficient and thereby to achieve desired occupational success. Work experience then becomes a strong motivator of interest in school study as well as a deterrent to engage in delinquent behavior caused by an excess of leisure time and lack of interest in wholesome work or recreational projects.

Interest is an extremely important factor in an adolescent's vocational selection and preparation. Various aspects of vocational selection require the attention of high school personnel. Some parents expect their children to select a vocation in terms of parental interests, even though the young people themselves may prefer something else. The prestige value of certain occupational fields may cause an adolescent's vocational level of aspiration to be higher than his ability to achieve successfully. Some adolescents either have so many work interests that they find it difficult to make a final decision, or have no particular interest and drift from one routine job to another without adequate preparation for any.

Recreational Interests. Most young people's recreational activities include: reading for pleasure; listening to radio broadcasts, or viewing television and motion picture programs; sports, and social activities, such as, dances, parties, picnics, and other group projects. The significance of children's and adolescents' interests in the areas of reading, radio listening, etc., are discussed briefly here. Other recreational and social interests were treated earlier.

Reading Interests. A young child likes to have stories read to him. He usually is as much interested in the way the story is read as he is in the story itself. The reader's facial expression, voice quality, and intonations fascinate the child; he may receive further satisfaction from the fact that he is sitting on the reader's lap. Sometimes the child imitates the reading behavior of his elders; he holds an open book or magazine (sometimes upside down), turns the pages, and mumbles softly to himself as though he were reading.

Children's reading interests vary with age and mental ability. At first, children enjoy having comic books read to them. As soon as they are able to read, and sometimes for many years thereafter, they continue their interest in comics. From about the age of 3 to 8 or later, children are keenly interested in animal stories, fairy tales, and stories about other children.

As children grow older, their interests change to the reading of newspapers, and favorite magazines and books. Boys become interested in popular science magazines or other reading matter that has a practical approach, such as geography, travel, biography, or adventure. Girls may select some of these reading materials but they are more likely to read romantic novels, stories about other people, or poetry. Both boys and girls tend to read magazines found in the home.

Reading interests begun during the later preadolescent years continue through adolescence. However, the magazines and books selected are on a more adult level; earlier interest merely in the plot of a story changes gradually to an analytic interest in the purpose and theme of the story, and the behavior characteristics portrayed; greater differences are found between the reading interests of boys and girls. Although all adolescents tend to read more magazines than books, most girls continue to be interested in romantic fiction of book length, but the interest of boys normally centers in nonfiction magazine articles.

An adolescent who enjoys reading is likely to be catholic in his tastes. At the same time, his reading preferences give evidence of his developing philosophy of life. He reads avidly anything that deals with serious, human problems—personal, economic, political, or social. To his elders, his reading tastes may seem to indicate morbid, fatalistic, or society-destroying tendencies. Actually, however, these reading interests are symptomatic of his struggles to achieve adult status.

Courses in literature on the high school and college levels could help adolescents develop wholesome, optimistic, but realistic attitudes toward life, and encourage them to read good literature. To achieve these purposes, teachers of literature should select the books to be studied in terms of adolescent interests and level of comprehension, and refrain from spending too much class time on a detailed analysis of any one book. Moreover, by arousing student interest in the books studied, teachers can motivate their students to want to read other books written by authors, one or more of whose books were read in school.

Radio and Television Interests. The pattern of changing interest in radio and television programs is somewhat similar to that of reading interests. Since most homes are equipped with one or more radio sets, and an increasing number of homes with television sets, interest in them begins almost as soon as a child is old enough to be aware of their presence. Later they become sources of much enjoyment.

The listening time of the average child for either radio or television is high—from 2 to 4 hours daily, according to some estimates. Programs of action, such as *Disney's World*, *Sesame Street*, *Captain Kangaroo* or *Dr. Dolittle* are sources of great amusement. Any program that involves fairy stories or other make-believe adventure delights the young child. According to some studies, interest in radio and television lessens somewhat during adolescence. Among the twelve interests mentioned in one study, "watching television" was rated as the one in which 15- to 17-year-olds were least interested. One explanation for this is the fact that adolescents want to leave the home for their social and recreational activities. Some young people claim, however, that they can study more effectively while they are listening to radio programs.

Some televised programs are excellent teaching aids. The value of television is so great that the Federal Communication Commission (FCC) has allocated certain channels exclusively for educational use. In addition, some teachers are utilizing appropriate facilities of commercial channels. Learning materials presented in "live" form serve not only to motivate learner interest but also to bring about clearer understanding.

For example, young people can learn about various kinds of skilled vocational activities by viewing televised programs of men and women at work. In connection with the social studies, they can observe, at first hand, many important events, and become acquainted with prominent national and world leaders. There probably are few, if any, learning areas in which learning materials cannot be made more interesting and better understood through the utilization of appropriate, accurately and clearly-presented radio and television programs.

Television in the Classroom. Educators are making more and more use of television in the classroom. The FCC has set aside channels for educational use and the Office of Education sponsors educational programs. Many colleges and school systems are making use of television in the classroom or otherwise. For example, The Midwest Program of Airborne Television Instruction is a flying laboratory that started in 1961 and continues to provide television programs for learners in the elementary and secondary schools in such states as Indiana, Illinois, Kentucky, Ohio, Michigan and Wisconsin.

Contrary to common prediction, interest in television viewing has not adversely affected the sale of books purchased and read by young people. Since the advent of television, the sales of books for juvenile readers has increased by many millions. This tends to refute the idea that the viewing of television will adversely affect the reading interest of children.

CHAPTER 10

INTELLIGENCE AND SPECIAL APTITUDES

Although an individual's behavior and attitudes reflect his needs, wants, urges, and desired interests, their expression and control are inextricably interwoven with the functioning of his mental abilities. The teacher's function is to help his pupils engage in constructive, culturally-accepted, and progressively difficult learning situations. Degree of mental status or *intelligence* and special abilities are the primary though not the only, factors of learning readiness. The prospective teacher therefore should know what intelligence is and how it affects learning progress.

Meaning and Theories of Intelligence

Children as well as adults recognize differences among people in ability to meet situations in which habitual behavior or routine responses are inadequate. According to their relative success or failure in everyday activities, individuals are described variously by their associates as "bright," "quick," "smart," or "dull," "slow," or "stupid."

Usually, a person who applies one of these terms to another is comparing the other's behavior with his own behavior. He is not concerned with the reasons for the other's mode of response. He merely evaluates the other's mental reactions in relationship to himself or to others.

Meaning of Intelligence. Since intelligence is a concept, it is difficult to define. The term usually is applied to those mental activities that are supposed to constitute the higher mental processes. A person's intelligence is evaluated in terms of overt behavior that reflects the functioning of the complex elements comprising mental capacity. Little is known concerning the aspects of potential intelligence. Intelligence is not a substance, a power, or a faculty; it may seem to function in one area of activity, but not in another. Since behavior manifestations are more easily recognized and understood than the mental processes involved, there is a growing trend toward utilizing the term *intelligent behavior* rather than intelligence.

Psychologists disagree about the formulation of an adequate definition of intelligence. Some earlier psychologists stressed the hereditary nature of intelligence, giving little if any consideration to possible environmental effects upon an individual's inherited mental potentialities. Emphasized variously in formulated definitions of intelligence are concepts such as readiness to learn, ability to do abstract thinking, and ability to adapt to novel situations. Speed, accuracy, and adequacy of response also have been stressed. The concept of intelligence as dealing with the higher mental processes includes degree of effectiveness in perception, memory, reasoning, and imagination.

Many definitions of intelligence have been formulated. These include: Binet's interpretation of intelligence as "comprehension, invention, direction, and criticism," and Stern's concept of it as "a general capacity of an individual consciously to adjust his thinking to new requirements." These and other earlier definitions stress the general nature of intelligence, as connoting *mental ability* rather than *mental abilities*. Later attempts to interpret intelligence were based upon promulgated theories that take into account both general and specific aspects of intelligence. Stoddard, for example, interpreted intelligence as "the ability to undertake activities that are characterized by (1) difficulty, (2) complexity, (3) abstractness, (4) economy (speed), (5) adaptiveness to a goal, (6) social value, and (7) the emergence of originals (inventiveness), and to maintain such activities under conditions that demand a concentration of energy and a resistance to emotional forces."[1]

Theories of Intelligence. Various theories have been propounded concerning the structure and organization of intelligence. The three best-known of these are Thorndike's connection theory, Spearman's two-factor theory, and its manifestations, and Thurstone's Primary Mental Abilities.

Connectionism. According to Thorndike's theory, the bases of intelligence are neural connections between stimulus and response that underlie behavior. Intelligence is not general. "Intelligences" that show themselves more or less adequately in behavior are: abstract intelligence, mechanical intelligence, and

[1] G. D. Stoddard, "On the Meaning of Intelligence," *Psychological Review*, **48**:255 (1941).

social intelligence. According to this theory, a person might be able to earn success in abstract learning, but not in social relationships or in mechanical activities. Successful achievement in two or all three of the areas would result from overlapping of the "intelligences," rather than from the functioning of general intelligence.

The influence upon behavior effectiveness of experience, derived interest, and environmental conditions seems to be disregarded in Thorndike's theory. In his later writings, however, Thorndike showed recognitions of the possible influence of environmental factors upon neural connections.

Two-factor Theory. Spearman formulated the statistically derived, two-factor theory of intelligence. Spearman concluded from his studies that "intelligent" behavior is affected by two mental-ability factors—general intelligence (the *g* factor), and specific abilities (*s* factors), the *g* and *s* factors working together as a unit.

The *g* factor is the general power or energy that functions in all mental activity; the *s* factors, sometimes forming a group because of likenesses among them, represent special abilities, such as mathematics, language arts, science, or any other special ability. A strong special ability (large *s* factor) usually is an accompaniment of above-average general ability (large *g* factor), although this parallelism does not always hold. A mediocre or weak general mental ability may be accompanied by a high special ability, such as the possession of a photographic memory by an otherwise mentally average or slow learner.

Primary Mental Abilities. Thurstone based his study of the organization of intelligence upon Spearman's two-factor theory. Through the administration of mental tests, the results of which were treated statistically, Thurstone evolved a multiple-factor theory including thirteen factors. Seven of these, listed by Thurstone as representing the primary mental abilities, are: (1) number facility, (2) memory, (3) ability in verbal relations, (4) ability to visualize space, (5) ability to deduce from presented data, (6) speed of perception, and (7) problem solving.

Thurstone's concentration upon primary abilities would seem to indicate that the concept of a general factor is unnecessary. "Factors" probably are not separate phases of mental activity, to be considered as entities. They are specific behavior manifestations of complex, unified mental functioning.

Discovery of Individual Differences in Intelligence. Individual differences in intelligence cannot be evaluated accurately except as they are displayed in actual behavior. Yet teachers and employers cannot wait until a pupil or worker demonstrates by his performance whether he is able to achieve success in learning mastery or in occupational activity. It becomes necessary, therefore, that an individual's degree of ability be evaluated before he engages in a particular activity.

Various types of evaluatory techniques have been constructed and are in the process of construction. Many measuring instruments are available especially to help school people discover the relative intelligence status of learners, as well as any specific aptitudes young people may possess. Evaluating techniques are discussed in Chapters 19 and 20.

Factors of Individual Differences in Intelligence

Observed differences among people in intelligent behavior have stimulated many attempts to discover the reasons for the differences. Forms of explanation include superstition, psuedoscientific beliefs, and conclusions based upon more or less valid scientific research. Systems evolved for the interpretation of man's behavior in terms of astrology, numerology, graphology, or palmistry have been discarded except by the credulous few. Pseudoscientific attempts to determine intelligence, according to supposed physiological criteria, including phrenology and physiognomy, also have lost the influence they once held.

There are factors of possible intelligence differences that are being explored scientifically. Tentative conclusions have been reached concerning them. The relationship that exists between physical growth and mental maturation was discussed in Chapter 4, including the degree of parallelism between body structure and mental ability. Other corrolates are discussed here, briefly. It must be kept in mind that, for the most part, the differences discussed are based upon the results of intelligence tests and observed behavior. Factors other than intelligence may account for some of the differences.

Heredity and Environment. Little need be said about the relative significance in human development of inherited potentiality and environmental influence. Studies have shown that twins reared apart tend to perform differently. Children of low socioeconomic status may test low. If these same children were exposed to better living conditions, they might perform on a higher intelligence level. Great improvement could not be expected, however. Although a mentally retarded child probably could not be changed to one of superior intelligence, a family's cultural background and socioeconomic status are inducers of differences in intellectual abilities.

Age. Growth in intelligence can continue through the early twenties. It has been found that the more intelligent person has a more rapid rate of mental growth and continues to develop longer than does the mentally less able. Although an adult has no more potential intelligence than he possessed as an adolescent or young adult, continuing experience in activities requiring mental activity may cause his behavior to seem to be as intelligent as, if not more so than it was during the earlier years.

Sex. Traditionally, boys were supposed to be more intelligent than girls. This belief still holds among some lay people, in spite of the fact that on the elementary and secondary school levels girls tend to earn higher marks than boys. The results of research appear to indicate that there are no significant differences between the sexes. On the average, girls seem to show a slight superiority in tests of language usage, memory, and aesthetic appreciation. Boys excel somewhat in ability to detect similarities and to reason.

There are more differences among the members of either sex than between the sexes. Since differences in demonstrated intelligence are caused partly by environmental conditions, these differences can be rooted in early home influences. Differences between the sexes in the mastery of certain school subjects may be the outgrowth of cultural attitudes toward the relative educational needs and capacities of boys and girls.

Race and Nationality. Contrary to common beliefs concerning racial or national superiority and inferiority, studies of racial and national differences have yielded data that would seem to indicate that differentiation within a race or a national group probably is greater than between races or nationalities. Experiential background, cultural heritage, and educational opportunities exercise a potent influence upon the extent to which any individual's potential abilities are exhibited in intelligent behavior.

Specific Abilities and Aptitudes

It is an observable fact that some persons appear to be more adept in a particular area of activity than are other persons. Every individual probably can perform better in one field than he can in others. Adequate techniques of discovering ability have not yet been perfected. That people vary in their aptitudes is an accepted fact, however.

Meaning and Function of Aptitude. An aptitude can be interpreted as a quality which is possessed by all persons in differing degrees. It also is regarded as superiority in a limited area of performance, such as mechanics, music, or mathematics. An aptitude can be defined as a characteristic or quality which is one aspect of an individual's total personality pattern.

An aptitude (talent) or a special ability, determined by demonstrated superior performance or from the results of prognostic tests, represents an existing potentiality predictive of the extent to which, with appropriate training, good or superior performance can be expected to result in the future. Hence a special talent represents a present state of readiness for appropriate development.

Various Kinds of Aptitudes and Abilities. Reference has been made to Thorndike's "intelligences": abstract, social, and mechanical. There are apparent differences among persons in the extent to which they are scholarly, mechanically minded, or socially inclined. These terms are relatively vague and represent combinations of complex mental processes that cannot be analyzed easily. That the differences in abilities thus characterized represent inherent specializations of neural function may or may not be a fact.

To be successful in the learning of abstract material necessitates ability to find relationships among numbers, words, and other symbols. Motor, mechanical, or concrete learning includes gaining skill in dealing with objects and handling one's body, although mastery of the higher mechanical skills may depend upon ability to gain insight into some abstractions. The socially adaptable person tends to respond to other people in such a way that he can work well with them. Other learnings may be needed to effect desirable intersocial relations. For example, to become a successful teacher, a person must be able to work with abstractions and at the same time appreciate social values. According to the subject or area of his teaching, he also may be required to possess mechanical competence.

Although successful achievement may be more evident in one area than in another, there may be a question as to whether the difference can be explained completely in terms of native endowment. Early experiences, derived interests, and concentrated study or practice may be influencing factors. A similar situation exists in the case of a special aptitude in music, representative art, mathematics, the sciences, fluency in writing or speaking, or any other field of superior performance.

Psychologists differ concerning the extent to which observable talents are inherited or learned. Caruso, the great operatic star, was found to possess a vocal mechanism and throat formation that were responsible, in part, for the clearness and power of his singing. Other factors were important, of course—sense of rhythm, tone discrimination, and the like.

All the demonstrated differences between a talented and a mediocre performer probably represent some differences in potentiality plus the results of training. A person's decision to prepare for a special field of work probably is conditioned by his interest, his demonstrated intelligence, his specific aptitude (if this has been discovered), the kind and extent of training required, and available opportunities.

Techniques for discovering early signs of a special ability have not yet been perfected. It is possible, therefore, that a young person may possess a special talent that is not recognized as such by himself, his parents, or his teachers. He may prepare himself for one vocation, and as an adult accidently discover that he is talented in another. If he is responsible for the financial welfare of others, the special talent becomes an avocational activity only, otherwise the individual may leave his present occupational work and prepare himself for the field of specialization.

Interest in a special form of activity, especially during the early years, may or may not indicate unusual talent. Some parents regard their child's displayed interests as predictive of the possession of a special talent. The young child "drums" on the piano; a schoolboy spends many hours at home "playing" with his father's tools or experimenting with a chemistry set; a girl is much interested in dramatics—play acting at home and participating in school productions; a boy or a girl joins a church choir. Any of these activities may be symptomatic of a special ability. Children's vocational interests are fleeting, however. They may result from temporary admiration of individuals who have earned success in one or another field, or from pleasant experiences associated with the fulfillment of their immediate needs or wants. Youthful interests also may reflect parental ambitions.

If the premise is accepted that all people possess special abilities in differing degrees, it is the responsibility of school people to discover those pupils who possess superior potentiality in any one area and then encourage them to engage in whatever training is needed to develop the potential ability. To the present, for example, perfume and tea testing, and similar vocational activities related to favorable sensitivity thresholds are entered accidently. A school superintendent discovered, late in life, that he possessed exceptional auditory acuity. Whether his vocational choice would have been different had he discovered this special ability early in life cannot be known now. More refined measuring instruments are needed to evaluate innate abilities, so that parents and school counselors can help talented young people make their vocational choices with greater assurance. Then, if they are able and willing to submit to appropriate training, they may achieve satisfying success in a field of activity for participation in which they possess a better than average aptitude.

The intellectually gifted learner requires an enriched learning environment that is conducive to exploration and originality. This environment should emphasize quality rather than quantity in order to add depth and scope to learning, and thus provide opportunities for reflective thinking, problem solving and creative thinking.

An enriched learning environment will permit the talented to progress as rapidly as he is able to master the concepts and skills needed. A variety of materials and experiences should be provided that will stimulate the individual to explore many fields of knowledge, encourage him to try new ways to thinking and to be concerned with critical analysis. An enriched environment also will enable the individual to develop ideals, attitudes and appreciations of social responsibility. It should make possible the development of self-knowledge and a realistic understanding of his abilities and limitations in light of set goals.

The gifted individual should be provided with opportunities for doing independent work, to plan and organize, to develop initiative, and to acquire study habits that focus on self-direction. He should be given a program that will enable him to appreciate and understand the heritage from the past without being shackled by it, and become independent in judgment, evolve new ideas, concepts, and relationships from past experiences, exercise intellectual control, become sensitive to quality and be able to discriminate between the essential and the incidental.

CHAPTER 11

PERSONALITY FORMATION

The term *personality* often is used loosely by laymen to identify a superficial characteristic that is admired, liked, or respected, or disliked, disapproved, or held in contempt. Lay evaluation of personality is replete with descriptive adjectives such as attractive or repulsive, cheerful or grouchy, pleasant or annoying, adjusted or maladjusted, good or bad, and similar differentiating antonyms. Some people go so far as to claim that an acquaintance "has no personality." Others refer to personality as though it were synonymous with the person or individual himself, such as, "he is an interesting personality."

The Dynamic Nature of Personality

Popular characterization of personality represents no more than the effect upon the evaluator of the overt behavior or attitude of the person described. In spite of the general interest displayed by most individuals in the "personalities" of their associates, little thought is given by them to the fundamental bases of the personality differences which they observe and are quick to evaluate.

Individual ideals, group standards, or personal biases or prejudices may influence lay attitudes toward displayed personality characteristics. For example, it often is difficult for parents (especially mothers) to be objective regarding the behavior manifestations of the kind of personality their children possess. It is equally difficult for an individual to view his own personality accurately and impartially. According to his ideal of a "good" personality, he may judge his own personality pattern as superior or inferior, with accompanying appropriate attitudes toward the personality manifestations of other people with whom he associates, or about whom he hears or reads.

It is extremely important that teachers refrain from making snap judgments concerning the personalities of their pupils according to preconceived notions concerning desirable or undesirable pupil characteristics. Anyone involved in working with children and young people—parent, teacher, or religious or community leader—needs to be able to interpret personality: its meaning, formation, and relation to human development as well as the factors that condition its pattern. With this background of information, a teacher's understanding of and attitudes toward the personality patterns of his pupils should induce a better relationship between his own self and the other selves with whom he is interacting.

Concept of Self. Egoism, egotism, selfhood, self-realization, self-assertion, self-reproach, self-dependence, and self-preservation are common terms. Implicit in the connotation of these terms is the concept, as expressed by one psychologist, of the "whole human being in action." The self can be interpreted roughly as the more or less objective awarenesss, at any age, of one's needs, interests, attitudes, and overt behavior, in relation to one's physical and social environment.

The various aspects of the self cannot be measured exactly. Yet they are modifiable as they are affected by interactions among themselves and with the various aspects of other people's selves. The newborn infant appears to have no concept of himself in relation to others. Gradually, self-awareness develops, beginning with self-assertion as a relatively vague and generalized urge to fulfill simple physical needs. With increasing growth and experience, his needs enlarge to include satisfying relations with objects and persons in his immediate environment. Continuing interactions between physical and social awareness result in a developing consciousness of the self in a world of selves.

During the later developing years and through adulthood, an individual constantly reacts to the impact upon himself of forces inherent in social customs, rules, regulations, and standards. To some extent, at least, he learns to evaluate himself and his self-satisfying behavior tendencies according to socially accepted behavior patterns. Young people reared in our culture characteristically are egocentric. Whatever controls they are able to exercise over their self-satisfying desires are the resultants of learning experiences during the formative years.

The conscience or, according to Freud, the *superego* (ideal self) is considered to be a self-restraining attribute of personality that controls too great display of self-centered or selfish behavior. Modification of a child's self-centeredness is one of the primary responsibilities of the teacher. Through precept and example, the teacher attempts to help a young person develop a constructive awareness of the rights of others and of his own responsibilities.

Meaning of Personality. The term *personality* eludes categorical definition. Psychologists differ in their points of view concerning the meaning of personality. Some stress its stimulus or social value—the effect of the total personality on other people. To other psychologists, personality represents the total response pattern, the "characteristic style of living." One cannot disregard the affective response aspects of personality, but of paramount importance to those who attempt to help young people develop a "good" personality is its third aspect—the *underlying causes* of personal behavior and its effect upon other people.

The adjustive and adaptive nature of personality is stressed by many psychologists in their attempts to construct a workable definition. For example, Gordon W. Allport defines personality as "the dynamic organization within the individual of those psychological systems that determine his unique adjustments to his environment."[1] A similar viewpoint is expressed by H. C. Link, a psychologist interested in personality measurement. In Link's concept of personality is implied the belief that a person learns "to convert his energies into habits and skills which interest and serve other people."[2]

The question then becomes one of discovering the causative factors of personal behavior to the extent that it reveals differences in social adaptability. The biosocial basis of personality differences is defined by Cameron to be "the dynamic organization of interlocking behavior systems that each of us develops through learning processes as he grows from a biological newborn to a biosocial adult in an environment of other individuals and cultural products."[3]

Personality as Functional Integration. Many investigations concerning personality functioning have resulted in the promulgation of certain conclusions implicit in typical definitions. The newborn child is mainly a physical organism; his personality then continues to be shaped and reshaped through his continuous interaction with the elements of his social environment.

---

[1] G. W. Allport, *Personality: A Psychological Interpretation,* Henry Holt and Company, Inc., New York, 1937, p. 18.

[2] H. C. Link, *Inventory of Interests and Activities,* Psychological Corporation, New York, 1938.

[3] N. Cameron, *The Psychology of Behavior Disorders,* Houghton Mifflin Company, Boston, 1947, p. 16.

The personality of each individual is unique in that it differs from every other person's. Personality is structured or patterned, revealing habitual consistencies of behavior that can be recognized by others. Personality changes according to its own functioning, its present functioning being built upon its history, and its future functioning reflecting what has gone before in the total action pattern.

An individual's personality, as expressed in his behavior at any growth or maturational stage and in any situation, is dynamic; it functions as inner motivation toward the satisfaction of his personal and social needs, wants, interests, and ambitions. It probably is correct to refer to the development of personality as though one's personality were a specific aspect of human nature. The human being grows and matures physically, mentally, and emotionally. During their maturational progress, potential tendencies, through interaction with environmental situations and conditions, display themselves in forms of inner and overt behavior appropriate to the particular developmental stage through which the individual is proceeding.

The interdependent activities of the various aspects of developing human nature serve as the functional bases of personality formation. Personality itself, however, represents more than a mere combination of the interacting components of human nature. Personality should be regarded as the process of functional integration that constantly is taking place. An individual's personality, therefore, is a complex, integrative function involving ways in which and the extent to which he himself as well as others are affected by his physical appearance, his intellectual status, his emotional patterns, his attitudes toward people and things, and his day-by-day responses to environmental situations and conditions. Stated briefly, *personality is an abstract generalization, or concept, connoting the qualitative nature of development and the quantitative influence of integration upon the total behavior pattern.*

Significance of Personality Traits

The concept of personality as an integrated functional pattern of individual behavior is a general framework or *Gestalt* for the many personality characteristics whose functionings are interrelated. Differences in personality usually are specific. For example, one man is more interested in people than another; some people are more introverted than others.

Meaning of Trait. Traits are individual behavior qualities that do not function separately but interact with some consistency. Traits are relatively permament and distinctive modes of behavior. Their functioning can be modified in so far as their habitual manifestations receive social disapproval or fail to satisfy personal wants or interests.

In the abstract, there are thousands of traits. To say that a person possesses a trait, such as laziness, quickness in action, lack of emotional control, or any other specific, observable behavior characteristic describes a trait tendency but does not explain it. It is important that a teacher recognize the functioning in any one of his pupils of a particular trait or group of traits. If the trait behavior seems to require modification or change, it is the responsibility of a teacher or counselor to try to discover the inherent motivations or the environmental conditions that cause the display of the trait in its existing form.

Although an individual's personality is more than a combination of his many characteristics and traits, one trait may be so dominant in behavior functioning that other traits appear to be less significant. The dominance of the one affects not only the functioning of other specific traits but may seem to alter the total personality pattern.

Functioning Aspects of Traits. Trait differences are quantitative rather than qualitative. Any trait of an individual differs from the same trait in another person in that one person gives evidence of the possession of it in greater amount than the other. The "amount" is relative in terms of the situation that stimulates its functioning. A person's display of cooperativeness, for example, is conditioned by his understanding of what constitutes cooperation in the situation, his ability to be cooperative, and the relative value to him and to others of his cooperation. Thus interpreted, a trait can be viewed as a social attitude.

It is possible to differentiate between the traits that are fundamental or deep-rooted and those that are more superficial, in so far as the latter are environmentally stimulated manifestations of the more fundamental behavior motivators. Reduction of various trait dimensions (trait analysis) has resulted in the production of lists of basic or primary traits. Cattell, Guilford, and Thurstone, among other psychologists, have presented such lists. According to Thurstone, seven "primary" trait factors can be identified: a pressure for activity, masculinity-femininity, impulsiveness, dominance, emotional stability, sociability, and reflectiveness.

Factor analysis has some value since it can provide a means of identifying basic personality trends. A so-called basic trait is itself complex, however, and may not explain adequately the subtle personality interactions that motivate behavior in differing situations and under varying conditions. Moreover, psychologists are becoming increasingly concerned about an individual's total reaction pattern, as representative of personality differences among people. This point is discussed further in the treatment of personality evaluation in Chapter 20.

Explanation of Personality

Personality is being explained by some through the use of pseudoscientific techniques and by others through the use of more scientific theories.

Pseudoscientific Explanations. Through the years a number of pseudoscientific approaches have been used to interpret personality. Included among them are: phrenology, astrology, numerology, physiognomy, graphology and palmistry. A special procedure has been prepared to indicate certain behavior traits, physical characteristics, lines of demarcation, or general tendencies believed to be associated with specific types of personality. The underlying ideas for the respective forms of analysis are briefly presented.

In *phrenology* it is assumed that an individual's personality traits are located in definite areas of the brain. For example, such traits as love, sympathy, musical ability or honesty are present in specific areas. The extent of the possession of a trait is supposed to depend upon the degree of development of the brain area in control of the trait.

In *astrology* it is believed that the month and day of a person's birth, place him under the influence of a particular sign of the zodiac. A horoscope is used to describe the probable influence of the appropriate sign of the individual. The specific date of birth carries with it certain characteristics that apply. All predicted horoscopes are evolved from elaborate systems that are based on such data as the year, the day of the week and hour of the individual's birth.

In *numerology* numbers such as *three* or *seven* are considered mystic and have their roots in religious beliefs or rituals. However, the number *thirteen* is considered to be unlucky and to be avoided. Yet, it has been used constantly with no ill luck for most people. There is no available scientific evidence that shows a connection between number significance and occurrence of events.

In *palmistry* the general disposition of a person is implicit in the description of his particular kind of hand. For example, the lines of the palm include the line of the heart, the line of fate, the line of health, the line of marriage, the lines of children as well as other minor lines.

Theories of Personality. There are certain theories of personality types that are acceptable to psychologists, psychiatrists and others who are involved with the problems of personality adjustment. These include the *four temperaments; physical types; somatotypes; endocrine types; sociological types; extrovert*, *ambivert*, *introvert types;* and *psychoanalytic types.*

The *four temperaments* include the *sanguine*—quick and gay; the *choleric*—easily angered; the *melancholic*—pessimistic; and *phlegmatic*—slow, unexcitable.

When classified as *somatotypes* all individuals are *endomorphic*—body soft and round with massive digestive viscera; *mesomorphic*—muscular and bony with heavy physique and thick skin; or *ectomorphic*—fragile and sensitive to exposure.

Endocrine types include pathological—explosive; *hyperthyroid*—over ambitious, domineering; *hypothroid*—lazy, intellectually dull; *pituitary*—good humored, patient; *gonads* (*hyper-active*)—very aggressive; *gonads* (*hypo-active*)—interested in art, literature, music.

The *sociological types* include *theoretical*—scientific, economic, business like; *esthetic*—sensuous; *social*—interested in others; *political*—wants power over others; *religious*—pietistic or missionary.

Among the *introvert, ambivert and extrovert* the *introvert* is sensitive and shy; the *extrovert* is less subjective and directs his thinking toward others. Some individuals exhibit characteristics of both the introvert and the extrovert and are classified as *ambiverts.*

The *psychoanalytic types* represent abnormal rather than normal adjustment. They are the *anal-erotic type*—obsessions related to traits as obstinancy; the *oral-erotic type*—can be an active "biting" type or a passive "sucking" type. The *genital type* is (1) the *phallic type*—exhibitionism, boasting, or (2) *normal development of genital-sexual maturity*—individuals who have achieved a desirable balance between ambition and restraint, and dependence and independence.

PART IV

THE PSYCHOLOGY OF LEARNING

CHAPTER 12

NATURE AND SCOPE OF LEARNING

One of the major fields of psychological and educational inquiry has been and continues to be centered around the learning process. As a result of their study of human development and human behavior, psychologists promulgate theories concerning the nature of learning. In their evolving curriculums, experimentally established teaching-learning procedures, and differentiating evaluation of learner progress, educators give direction to the propounded theories. Modern educational objectives and extent of progress in learning achievement reflect the application by educational psychologists to school procedures of now extant well-formulated but still controversial learning theories and their practical implications.

The Nature of Learning

Success in teaching depends upon the teacher's understanding of the *why, what,* and *how* of learning activities. He needs to know the value to learners of the content of his teaching, the differing abilities among learners, and the most effective ways in which successful achievement can be attained.

Meaning of Learning. The experiencing of change is inherent in the concept of learning. Since change in behavior implies that learning either is taking place or has taken place, the term learning can be interpreted as referring to either (1) the process involved while the changes are taking place, or (2) the actual changes that are produced as a result of the functioning of the learning process.

Learning is characterized by inner as well as overt activity. Viewed as a *process,* learning occurs as the learner observes, talks with others, reads, or works mentally with a situation or problem. Considered as *product,* learning includes the total of changes resulting from all the interactions between an adequate, maturing organism and appropriate environmental stimuli.

Various Aspects of Learning. The acquisition of motor skill and factual knowledge, and the formation of attitudinal and behavioral habits represent various aspects of learning. The progressive changes taking place in any area of learning involve complex interactions among the various learning aspects as the learner attempts to satisfy immediate interests or to attain more remote goals.

Any learning that takes place effects a change that can be expected to be more or less permanent. This change may be simple or it may encompass the mastery of a complicated performance or the solution of a complex problem. Much of an individual's learning is engaged in consciously, and the learning outcomes are recognized. Yet during his daily activities he may acquire many habits of thinking or acting, without awareness of the changes that are occurring.

An individual learns through the utilization of various responses to learning stimulations. Something is learned in every situation experienced by the individual. The nature and extent of the learning are affected by the situation, the readiness of the learner, the kind and nature of his responses, and his reaction to success or thwarting. Learning also is affected by the learner's interpretation of an experience in relation to himself. As the individual directs his attention to new or novel factors of the situation, relates them to past experiences, and evaluates them in terms of anticipated responses, he gives meaning and significance to his experiences.

The kind of learning that takes place depends upon the learning approach and purpose. To illustrate, much of the learning engaged in by older children and adolescents deals with the mastery of subject matter. Although increasing skill in reading and in verbal reproduction is essential to progress in learning to work with ideas (abstract thinking), school study requires that the learner gradually acquire basic knowledge as a background for more complex learning tasks.

An individual can demonstrate that he has learned when and if he (1) can repeat learning content verbatim, or (2) can show that he has gained new ideas from material which he has studied. The former is called rote learning or the ability to repeat material correctly even though it may not be understood. The second method involves an analysis and a comparison of ideas that results in the achieving of new meanings. In effect, there are three major levels of abstract learning: (1) to memorize material with little or no understanding, (2) to gain simple concepts, and (3) to discover and to understand relationships among learning materials that require keen insight and rich background experience. Learning to think and concomitant learnings are discussed in detail in the chapters that follow.

The Learning Process

Learning or change in behavior, resulting from responses to motivating stimuli, implies that the learner is different from what he had been previous to the learning. As commonly conceived, learning means improvement. The improvement may or may not have positive value. An individual can learn to improve or strengthen inadequacies as well as adequacies. For example, the penmanship of John M., a high school graduate, is regarded as fairly legible, but his copious, rapid note-taking in his college classes may bring about changes in his handwriting habits that cause it to be almost illegible. Changes have taken place in his penmanship "behavior" that reduce his adequacy in written communication. Bad, not good habits, have been developed.

Informal versus Formal Learning. Informal learning represents the changes in behavior that accompany stimulation by and response to the many environmental elements that are experienced daily. In formal learning, generally referred to as school learning, situations are organized according to definitely formulated objectives that reflect the kind and amounts of learning that a particular society believes should be provided for its citizens, young and older. Certain fundamental learnings are intended for all young people. Other learnings are specific in terms of learner ability and interest, and the special needs of society.

Much of one's informal learning consists of the formation of habit patterns that result directly from responses in social situations. Imitation of socially acceptable behavior and habitual conformity to group regulations and standards are likely to earn social approval. Hence a person of any age tends so to adapt his behavior in terms of existing requirements that he experiences satisfaction in his everyday relationships with other people.

Learning as Activity. Learning, informal or formal, connotes activity. Informal learning takes place as an individual interacts freely with his home and community associates. Even in the more formal learning situations of the school, there are informal learning concomitants growing out of (1) the learner's sharing of activities with his schoolmates, and (2) his relationships with teachers and other school personnel.

For a child just to be active without purpose has little learning value. In informal learning, the goals may seem to be relatively indefinite and only indirectly recognized by the learner, but the learning itself is aimed at one or another satisfying adaptation.

Formal or school learning represents teacher-guided learner activity. It is the responsibility of the teacher (1) to provide materials beneficial to him through his participation in the learning, (2) to motivate him toward learning activity through which he can achieve a purposeful goal, and (3) to give him reasonable freedom in his learning according to his ability and interest level.

The kinds of learning activity in which young people engage and the degree of purposefulness characteristic of their activities are influenced greatly by adults' attitudes toward educational values and their interpretation of freedom of activity in learning. If parents and teachers regard learning as experiential activity through which the child expresses his urges, desires, or immediate interests freely, with little or no adult direction, some learning will take place. The permissive atmosphere of the learning situation is likely, however, to induce license rather than freedom and possibly to encourage extremely undesirable self-aggrandizing activities. Conversely, too great emphasis upon the achievement of specific, adult-centered learning goals and almost complete adult direction of learner activity also will yield some learning outcomes. The learner, however, is likely to acquire negative attitudes toward the subject matter and the teacher, and regard learning as drudgery. In addition, the inhibition in the classroom of desired freedom of activity can stimulate him to utilize his youthful energy in the performance of out-of-school, uncontrolled, perhaps dangerous acts.

Factors Inherent in Learning. Many factors contribute to the amount and kind of learning that are achieved by any individual. Some are inherent in the individual's activities; others are rooted in the situation and conditions in which the learning takes place. Consciously or unconsciously, the learner wants to achieve an immediate or a long-range goal. His maturational level and/or his previous experiences determine his readiness to change his behavior in a particular situation. The significance to him of the various elements in the situation condition his responses which may or may not bring him desired satisfaction. If he is not successful in his first attempt, whether he continues to change his responses until he has learned how to meet the situation adequately depends upon the strength of his interest in it and his emotional reaction to failure.

Most people constantly are learning new skills or improving those already developed, adding new knowledge, and developing new interests, attitudes, or habits of thought. There is an interrelatedness among all these areas of learning. Learning in one area is facilitated by the influence upon it of learning progress in one or more other learning areas.

It is believed by some psychologists that learning results from the adaptation made by a learner as he responds to the tensions initiated through sensory stimulation. As the individual attempts to relieve this stress he is called upon to adapt or modify his behavior. This change can function only if and when the individual is aware of the need to become active in the situation. Lacking this recognition there is no stress or tension. It cannot be assumed, therefore, that all children or older persons will respond similarly to what appears to be the same situational stimulus. Variability of past experience, of emotional reaction, and of learned habits of response are likely to cause behavior differences in situations such as touching a hot stove, meeting a block in the road when driving, being unavoidably detained in keeping an appointment, or facing an unsurmountable obstacle as one attempts to satisfy an interest or achieve a goal. Adaptation of behavior in stress-stimulating situations (learning) is an individual process.

Differences among young people exercise a potent influence upon the extent of their learning achievement. Their interests, attitudes, social sensitivity, health, and degree of emotional tension affect the nature and extent of their learning. The introduction of a feeling of success or an anticipation toward success, however, can arouse interest in learning and promote positive attitudes that impel learners to do the best they can.

Effect of the Emotions on Learning. Learning progress that concerns material in which the learner is interested usually is accompanied by a mild, pleasurable emotional state. The satisfying pleasure that is derived from participation in successful learning activities tends to stimulate the continuance of learning activity. Although the teacher's overt recognition of successful accomplishment is important, it does not follow that the receiving of extrinsic rewards is the most potent motivator of continued or improved learning.

The effect on a pupil's learning progress of a teacher's rewarding successful work and penalizing carelessness or lack of effort is influenced by the pupil's emotional reactions to the reward or punishment. The desire to win a particular award or honor may be so strong that the learner uses dishonest methods to achieve it. The attaining of too many awards may embarrass a boy or girl because of a belief that desired friendship with less successful classmates will be endangered thereby. A mentally able, but disinterested pupil may plan deliberately to do mediocre or failing work so that he can escape from further participation in the activity.

A bright boy, for example, whose parents, against his wishes, forced him to enroll in an academic high school, proceeded to earn failing marks, with the result that his parents and teachers had him transferred to a vocational school. The intent of the adults was to punish him for his lack of effort, but to the boy the transfer took on the aspects of an award. His original desire was to prepare himself for a trade. Therefore, his interest in the curriculum offerings of the second school motivated him toward successful study achievement.

The learning experience itself as well as learning results has emotional accompaniments. If the study material is too difficult, the learner is likely to become extremely discouraged. The greater the discouragement, the less chance there is that learning progress will improve. In the case of failure, the high school student, especially, either wants to take easier subjects or leave school. Consequently, unless some success is earned in the less demanding subjects, the adolescent becomes so emotionally stirred that he leaves school as soon as the legal age regulations permit. If he is too young to be discharged from school or his parents insist that he remain, he may run away from home in order to escape from the intolerable situation. He finds for himself a simple job in which he hopes to experience less emotional stress. The many high-school drop-outs give evidence of the effects of disruptive emotional reaction on learning.

The emotions are associated with learning activities in other ways. A learner with a good background in a particular learning area may discover that little effort is needed by him to earn success as compared with classmates. Hence lack of challenge induces lack of interest in the subject, contempt for the teacher and the other pupils, and a minimum of study application. If or when this learner fails in a test because of his lack of study, his humiliation may take the form of resentment toward the teacher and dislike of the subject.

Some high school students become involved emotionally in the mastery of learning matter, either because of their great interest in the subject itself or their strong desire to win special approval from a much-admired teacher. Consequently, they devote many hours to study, go beyond teacher requirements or expectation in the preparation of special projects, and deny themselves participation in school or other social activities. Even though ill health and emotional tensions result from overconcern with learning activity, these young people tend to resist the efforts of parents and teachers to effect a more sensible attitude. If they are persuaded to reduce their study activities, they experience equally strong emotional tension caused by their unrealistic fear of failure.

Learning Approaches. Learning can be viewed as vertical or horizontal. If knowledge is added to knowledge in a specific area of learning, if a skill is improved, if an attitude is developed, or if thinking procedures are strengthened, *vertical* learning is considered to have occurred. When a learner widens his learning horizons, achieves competence in new forms of skill, gains new interests, discovers different ways of thinking, and develops different attitudes toward situations or other people, he is engaging in *horizontal* learning.

Whether the learning is vertical or horizontal, something is learned. Although learning approaches differ according to the purpose of the learning and the nature of the learning material, the changes that take place should be relatively permanent. To *understand* is not to *know* or to be able to *do*. This aspect of learning is included in some of the theories of learning discussed later in the chapter.

Intelligent drill is a must for certain learning mastery. Exercise of a learning function to the extent that it is overlearned (practiced beyond the point of immediate recall) for permanent recall purposes is sound procedure in all learning. Drill is helpful at the right time, but the learner should understand what he is learning and why it should be mastered. Activities should be aimed at the attainment of goals that have value for the learner.

Although exercise or practice is basic to good learning, ineffectual or negative learning procedures may result from it. To avoid possible pitfalls, the following approaches to success-achieving practice should operate: (1) the learner should satisfy his learning needs in his practice or he is likely not to apply to out-of-school activities what he has practiced in school, (2) he should practice only correct responses or employ only a correct method of practice, so that satisfaction is ensured by obtaining a correct answer through utilization of accurate procedure, (3) he should use repetition of practice only to the point of achieving adequate understanding and habitual performance, and (4) he should practice only those elements of a learning situation that, through pretesting or the utilization of other prognostic devices, are found to need further practice for effective mastery of the entire learning situation.

The amount of drill or exercise needed for adequate mastery varies with its purpose, degree of difficulty, and learner ability and interest. Learning (overlearning) can take different forms. Verbatim responses often need to become automatic, such as spelling, number combinations, and sometimes scientific or mathematical formulas. Learning for ideas and relationships, or problem solving often can be achieved best by experiencing the learning material in many different situations, each of which provides enrichment or depth. College students preparing to become teachers sometimes complain that their courses in education are repetitive or duplicative. Without their awareness of what is taking place, the seeming duplication represents *overlearning* or learning for permanence of certain principles of teaching and learning to the point that they are applied almost automatically by the teacher in the classroom. Some of the materials of this book that may appear to be repetitive are so presented as to induce overlearning.

Teaching Approaches. The attitudes and methods of the teacher are conditioners of learning. His methods of presenting learning materials so as to motivate the learner to want to succeed are closely associated with the degree of learning that occurs. The learner does not easily absorb ideas presented by the teacher. Learning consists of much more than listening, reading, or taking notes. If the learner is to retain much of what he sees and hears he must do something with the learning material. For best learning, the individual himself, with the help of the teacher, comes to understand and associate ideas. Verbal learning is reinforced by application in actual situations. Both memory and understanding function more efficiently when the learner is encouraged (1) to form new responses or (2) to use newly learned material in the solution of problems that occur in situations different from those in which the material was learned but in which elements of the newly learned materials are present.

Teaching approaches differ in terms of: (1) specific subject or subjects taught, (2) age or readiness level of learners, (3) general educational objectives of schools and school systems, and the more limited objectives of the particular subject, (4) learning interests and goals of pupils, and (5) teaching techniques and methods peculiar to a particular school community.

The personality of the teacher and his attitude toward teaching, of course, are determiners of the ways in which and the extent to which the teaching approaches of one teacher differ from those of another. There are several general approaches, however, that are characteristic of good teaching and successful learning on any school level and in every area of learning: (1) interest is a potent learning motivator, (2) learning implies learner activity, and (3) exercise or practice is basic to effective learning.

Theories of Learning

The learning process is so complex that no one explanation of its functioning is satisfactory. The theories of learning described here represent some of the major attempts to discover what is taking place within an individual when changes in his behavior occur as a result of learning.

Connectionism. During the early part of the twentieth century, Edward L. Thorndike propounded a new hypothesis concerning how individuals learn. His theory begins with the concepts of stimulus and response. He was concerned especially with the *neural bond*—the synaptic connection between the neurons that complete the stimulus-response circuit.

Essentially, Thorndike was interested in the physiological bases of learning. Much of his earlier experimentation dealt with animal learning, although his objective was to explain human learning, especially the child's learning in the classroom. Thorndike emphasized the importance of exercise—he believed that learning depends directly upon the strength of the connection made between the stimulus and the response. Stated in another way, he believed that much practice would stamp in the connection for later use.

According to the connectionism theory, learning consists of

the completion of neural bonds or circuits. An impulse starts at a sense organ already sensitized by external stimuli, moves along the *afferent neuron* to the spinal cord or brain and, after proper connections are made with association neurons, continues its journey over the *efferent neurons* to the appropriate muscles or glands. Thus is set up an intricate pattern of neural bonds through which the impulse, possibly electrical in nature, passes.

The complex physiological activations of the dendrites and axones of neurons constitute the principal elements of the neural system which functions during a stimulus-response reaction. This is better understood by reference to Thorndike's laws of learning. He introduced three primary laws of learning, together with five subsidiary laws or statements which grew out of and were designed to amplify and substantiate his major theses.[1] These primary and subsidiary laws of learning are:

Thorndike's Primary Laws of Learning

1. The Law of Readiness
2. The Law of Exercise
3. The Law of Effect

Thorndike's Subsidiary Laws of Learning

1. Law of Multiple Response
2. Law of Attitude, Disposition or "Set."
3. Law of Partial Activity
4. Law of Assimilation or Analogy
5. Law of Associative Shifting

Law of Readiness. By the law of readiness, Thorndike means:

(1) that when a conduction unit is ready to conduct, conduction by it is satisfying, nothing being done to alter its action; (2) that for a conduction unit ready to conduct not to conduct is annoying, and provokes whatever responses nature provides in connection with that particular annoying lack; (3) that when a conduction unit unready for conduction is forced to conduct, conduction by it is annoying.

Law of Exercise. The law of exercise includes two tendencies:

The law of use. To the situation, "a modifiable connection being made by him between a situation S and a response R," man responds originally, other things being equal, by an increase in the strength of that connection.

The law of disuse. To the situation, "a modifiable connection

[1] From E. L. Thorndike, *Educational Psychology, Briefer Course, Bureau* of Publications, Teachers College, Columbia University, 1914.

not being made by him between a situation S and a response R, during a length of time T," man responds originally, other things being equal, by a decrease in the strength of that connection.

The Law of Effect. In the law of effect it is stated that:

To the situation, "a modifiable connection being made by him between an S and an R and being accompanied or followed by a satisfying state of affairs" man responds, other things being equal, by an increase in the strength of that connection. To a connection similar, save that an *annoying* state of affairs goes with or follows it, man responds, other things being equal, by a decrease in the strength of the connection.

Thorndike constantly tried to improve his explanations of learning. Aware of the fact that in many instances a person at first cannot make the correct response to a new situation, he formulated the *Law of Multiple Response.* Realizing also that a response to a situation depends upon the learner's condition as well as upon the nature of the situation he propounded the *Law of Attitude, Disposition,* or *Set.* The *Law of Partial Activity* is based upon man's ability to choose from among the elements of a situation those which best help him meet his needs. In his attempt to explain the bonds that are used in novel situations, Thorndike suggested that the individual uses those bonds already acquired in similar situations as stated in the *Law of Assimilation or Analogy.* The functioning of this law is the basis of Thorndike's theory of transfer of learning through identical elements. Finally, according to the *Law of Associative Shifting,* sufficient practice in responding in a specific situation makes it possible for the learner to achieve any response of which he is capable that is associated with any situation to which he is sensitive.

Changes in the Law of Exercise and Effect. Later, Thorndike made changes in the laws of exercise and effect by adding new sublaws including *belongingness, impressiveness, polarity, identifiability, availability, and mental systems.*

Learning is encouraged when the elements of a situation are connected. Words that belong together or meaningful materials are more easily learned then nonsense syllables. Thus *belongingness* is an excellent principle that includes the idea of expectancy. The strength or intensity of given stimuli determine *impressiveness. Polarity* refers to the tendency of the individual to relate the objects and concepts of experience that have had common associations in learning. The individual who already has stamped-in certain elements in a situation has the quality of *identifiability* in that learning situation. *Availability* is concerned with the physiological and mental readiness of the S-R bonds to function, and *mental systems* include all those methods by which Thorndike accounts for such factors as intuition and the more diffuse kinds of habit formation.

Importance of Learning as Connectionism. The promulgation of the theory of connectionism marked the beginning of much experimentation that resulted in the propounding of various extant learning theories. In fact, Thorndike has been called the "Father of Educational Psychology."

Since connectionism appeared only to establish hypotheses concerning the physiological aspect of the learning process, many subsequent studies were aimed at the possible discovery of other aspects of the learning process. For a time, Thorndike's hypotheses were discredited by some psychologists. The operation of neural connections still may remain a controversial issue. There can be no doubt, however, concerning the significance of readiness in learning, relation of practice to retention, and the effect on learning progress of satisfaction and annoyance, as well as the modifications of learning implied in Thorndike's subsidiary laws.

Conditioning. By the beginning of the twentieth century, learning was believed to involve interaction between organisms and their environment. Since man was being studied as a biological animal, the force that acted upon the man-animal was considered to be a stimulus, and the resulting behavior was considered to be the response. The theory of conditioning is based on this premise.

Guthrie's Interpretation. According to the theory of conditioning, learning is the forming of habits by means of associating a stronger stimulus with a weaker one, given simultaneously, for the purpose of gaining the same response from the weaker stimulus that was experienced from the stronger stimulus. In this way, adaptations are established within the individual that will affect overt behavior. Since the inner changes are involuntary and serve as stimuli to further action, they are anticipatory adjustments that effect cue reduction in the transfer of response from one stimulus to another.

According to Guthrie, the functioning of this theory can be illustrated by furnishing a learner with a list of numbers to be added or a stanza to be memorized. The addition can be checked for correctness and the degree of retention of the memorized material can be measured.

Pavlov's Experiments. Pavlov conducted extensive experiments with dogs to discover what can be done in the way of transferring the cue stimulus that originally excites a response to another stimulus that will effect the same response. He is widely known for his conditioning of the flow of saliva of a dog. By careful conditioning procedures, he succeeded in inducing a dog's flow of saliva through the ringing of a bell, thereby transferring the stimulus from that of food to that of bell to produce the flow of saliva.

According to Pavlov: (1) desired conditioning can be achieved more quickly under rigidly controlled laboratory conditions than in a classroom situation; (2) the new response to a stimulus tends to be less strong than was the response to the original stimulus, and (3) the mental set of the subject is an important factor of the extent to which conditioning is achieved. The application of the principles of *time, intensity,* and *consistency* is a specific requirement in any attempts to develop conditioned responses either in animal or in man.

Human beings are trained to respond to certain stimuli and to ignore other stimuli that may be present. The city dweller cannot sleep in the country because it is too quiet, until he conditions himself to the lack of noise; the farm boy, unaccustomed to the noise of the city, passes through a conditioning process until he can sleep in spite of interfering stimuli.

School Learning as Conditioning. Certain school subjects are more easily mastered through the process of conditioning than others. Conditioning functions in the learning of a foreign language, as the connections are strengthened between a stimulus (Spanish word) and a response (English word), or vice versa. Automatic and consistent responses to situational stimuli result from conditioning. For example, the learning of penmanship or spelling requires automatic responses rather than those associated with reflective thinking. Hence the efficient learner masters these functions in specific ways. The teacher can help by providing proper stimuli or cues as the learner applies the principles of conditioning in these and similar learning areas. Some psychologists claim that Thorndike's laws of exercise and effect function in the conditioning process, if the results of the conditioning are satisfactory.

Behaviorism (Watson's theory). The behavioristic theory of learning attempts to explain the bases of conditioning. John B. Watson, known as the "Father of Behaviorism," believed in the importance of the environment in the training of children. He was concerned with the behavior of the individual rather than with his consciousness. As a consequence, he tended to disregard heredity and placed emphasis on the stimuli in the environment.

According to Watson, it would be possible to condition an individual in whatever way one wished if he were successful in controlling the environment of the individual from birth onward. He conducted many experiments with very young children to induce fear, to recondition their behavior resulting from fear, or uncondition fear when fear of an object or animal had been learned. As a result of his experiments, Watson concluded that the physical needs of a child should receive careful attention but that his emotional reactions should be disregarded.

The Theory of Gestalt Organization. Max Wertheimer and his students started a new approach to learning in the form of insight. They believed that there is essential unity in nature, and that perception depends upon the mind as well as upon the eye. To them, learning was a matter of insight, since there exists in each natural phenomenon an essential unity which embraces more than the sum of its physical parts. This whole is the *Gestalt* or Configuration.

Meaning of Insight and Gestalt. New forms of percepts, mental images, and ideas arise through the interaction between the individual and his environment. Insight is gained through the activity of the mental functions as an individual attempts to arrive at solutions of problems. The integration that occurs in the course of solution is more important to the development of insight than is the fact that the correct solution was found during the first attempt. Insight is present when (1) the problem is perceived by the individual, (2) the difficulty is understood, and (3) the data for solution are available.

A *Gestalt* pertains to the configuration—the pattern or form according to which a stimulus is perceived and understood. The configuration or Gestalt loses something when it is broken into its component factors. An automobile is more than a collection of parts. A learning situation is more than the apparent elements of which it is composed. The perception of a form, configuration, or Gestalt does not result from an analysis of its parts. Recognition of the meaning of the whole configuration represents an integration of mental functions—*insight.*

For example, the act of appreciating a pictorial production does not imply that each of the various elements of the work (paints, canvas, design) at first receives separate consideration.

To appreciate the work of the artist, the viewer responds to the whole picture. Whether he has sufficient insight to appreciate the meaning of the artist depends upon his degree of maturity; his background of experience, patterned through perception; his imagination, and the integration of his mental processes.

Application of the Gestalt Theory to Learning. According to the Gestalt point of view, as many situations as possible should be learned as functional wholes rather than separated into parts. It may seem almost impossible, however, to apply this theory in some learning areas. When the functional method is used in the teaching of a foreign language, for example, it is difficult to demonstrate to the learner that much day-by-day learning is taking place. Inner changes are occurring, however, that reveal themselves when the whole unit of learning has been completed.

The goal is important in determining what should constitute a whole in learning. The whole globe would be too large for the study of the topography of Mexico, but the whole map of New York City should be in front of a child who is learning about the respective boroughs of that city. Insight is gained in any subject as the individual adds new perceptions to his mental store of knowledge. Certain subjects lend themselves to better understanding through the Gestalt approach than others. Insight is needed for effective work in art, music, literature, science, and any other subject area that include elements of appreciation.

Although the solution of a problem illustrates the functioning of the mental process involved in insight, no problem can be solved unless and until there is understanding of its essential aspects. An individual's general insight into the whole situation and his precision in detail help him in the solution of his problem.

Functionalism. Basically, functionalism is not a theory. It is a learning approach in which are applied the physiological and psychological concepts growing out of early twentieth century progress in child study. Emphasis is placed upon a child's need to adapt himself and his behavior to environmental conditions.

Functionalism and Dynamic Psychology. The psychologist, Robert Woodworth, was an outstanding proponent of functionalism and of the dynamic nature of drives in learning. At first, Woodworth and other functionalists stressed the general organismic aspects of adaptation. Later, because of the human being's conscious functioning as compared to an animal's more direct actions, greater attention was focused on the mental processes.

In the dynamic, functional approach to learning, the working of the mind is considered to be a continuous process; the developing of ideas and other mental activities are necessary components of the learning process. Mind is considered to be the more intellectual phase of an individual's movements in the direction of adaptation. Through his own activity, the learner makes needed changes in his behavior. The way he performs or operates is indicative of the kind or amount of learning he has achieved. According to the operational view of learning, the major criteria of progress are rooted in the behavior functioning of an individual in relation to the influencing factors of his environment. The classroom is the center of individual operation or performance in social interplay. Learning progress can be evaluated according to operational improvement or changes in performance resulting from practice.

Significance of the Functional Approach. The functional aspect of learning has exerted a tremendous influence on American education. Although the operational view of learning does not disregard the learner's inner changes, it does help in the task of evaluating learning outcomes by placing emphasis on observable behavior changes that involve the "whole" learner.

The concept of learning as learner activity, advanced by John Dewey and others, revolutionized teaching approaches and learning processes. Educational objectives and curriculum construction also have been influenced, in that they are pointed toward providing learners with the help of the teacher, to engage in school and classroom activities that have both present and future functional value.

Purposive Learning. Edward Tolman, repudiating the behavioristic theory of learning as propounded by Watson, attempted to find an explanation of learning that was more in accord with Gestaltism and some of the aspects of functionalism.

Meaning of Purposive Learning. Tolman believed that previous explanations of learning presented oversimplified concepts. Hence he advanced the view that learning is purposive. He held that learning interpreted as change in behavior represents no more than the overt manifestation of an inner purpose or a striving toward one or another kind of goal. He emphasizes the reason behind the learning rather than the immediate phenomenon of learning.

Significance of Purposive Learning. According to Tolman, learning is the organization of behavior toward the achievement of a purpose. This purpose is a recognized need which stimulates the individual to engage in appropriate activities so that tensions aroused by the stimulus are reduced as the goal is attained. Intervening variables between purpose stimulation and goal attainment are not disregarded by Tolman. His belief in the goal-directed aspect of life, in terms of well-regulated principles, has educational significance in that meaningful and individual goals can be set up for learning. The social environment provides the materials, thereby stimulating further goal striving. Well-organized practice, with appropriate recognition and encouragement can help the learner gain greater application of the purpose of his learning activities.

Learning as Experience. The principal contribution of John Dewey to education was in the area of problem solving, in which he emphasized the value of learning as experience. He held problem solving to be a means of learning as well as a way of life. To Dewey, learning is a social force and must concern itself with problems encountered in everyday life.

Individual survival is based upon man's ability to solve problems. Hence problems suitable to his maturational level and experience should be provided for the learner to stimulate him to be active. He learns through thinking and doing. To the extent that Dewey believed in the dynamic approach to learning, he was a functionalist. In fact, he earlier was identified with functional psychology.

Doubt about a problem or issue is the beginning of learning. One must perceive difficulties and be aware that they exist in order to be able to do critical thinking. It is only when an individual becomes aware of his problems as problems and undertakes to solve them that he is achieving knowledge. Dewey believed that there should be a specific association between the learner's interests and ambitions and that which is to be learned. He viewed the child as the center of learning. He emphasized the importance of reasoning as the means whereby the learner can achieve social competence.

The Eclectic Approach. The maintaining of a scientific attitude toward education by psychologists and educators requires that they constantly evaluate and re-evaluate experimental studies of learning and evolved theories. They then can make whatever educational application of them that seems desirable. It is likely that no educational psychologist or educator conforms completely to any single theory of learning. In fact, no one theory explains every aspect of learning. The various theories complement one another in that each emphasizes its own specific explanatory approach.

The functional or dynamic approach to learning utilized so much of some of the other theories that there is much to commend it. Much has been gained from the laws of learning formulated by Thorndike; practical application is made of the concept of learning as conditioning. The basic values of Gestalt psychology are evidenced in the increasing utilization of the core curriculum. The eclectic approach to the construction and application of learning principles, emerging from formulated learning theories, represents a realistic attempt to meet the learning needs of children and adolescents.

Programmed Learning. Efficiency in learning is being advanced today through the use of mechanical aids. Considerable study and new developments are being invested in programmed learning. Experimentation has advanced sufficiently to give cause for optimism for favorable results in their use in learning and teaching.

Programmed learning is based on a program of subject matter to be learned. To be effective, the material needs to be properly organized into graded steps of difficulty and in proper sequence so that the most efficient rate of understanding and retention will result. Thus, the programming process becomes an all-important consideration.

Effective programming involves the proper arrangement of learning materials so that the student can profit through the use of a series of steps that have been carefully plotted from the familiar to the new, from the concrete to the abstract, and from facts to concepts. It consists of a mechanical system which makes it possible to learn in the absence of a "live" teacher. The essentials of the system are: a learner, a desirable program and a device to present the program such as a machine or gadget or (special books or cards). However, *it is the program* and not the machine or auxiliary device that is the important consideration in programmed learning.

CHAPTER 13

PERCEPTUAL AND CONCEPTUAL LEARNING

An individual becomes aware of the activities that go on in his world of things and people through the functioning of his sense organs. If the sense organs were not sensitive to the stimuli of the environment it would be impossible for a person to satisfy his needs or to experience interpersonal and intersocial relationships. Sensory responses are the primary media through which the individual learns to know and understand the world and the people in it. The awareness of oneself and the elements of one's environment is called perception.

The Nature of Perception

The form of an individual's behavior in which he utilizes his past experience and his present needs and wishes to interpret the stimuli in his environment constitutes an act of perceiving. The functioning of sense organs and mental activity is needed to complete any perceptual process. Experiential background also is a basic factor of perception. Whatever interpretation is given to sensory stimuli by the perceiver is conditioned by (1) his past experience, (2) his interest in the stimuli at the moment, (3) the sensitivity of his sense organs to the particular stimuli, and (4) the kind and amount of integration that occurs.

Significance of Sense Organs. The sensitive elements of sense organs, such as the eyes, ears, skin, muscles, nose, tongue, and internal organs are receptive to stimuli and have the capacity to discriminate among kinds of stimuli. People constantly test their various sensory experiences. For example, a housewife touches a knife blade to discover whether it is sharp, rather than to judge its sharpness merely by looking at it. While a man is in his garden, he hears a doorbell ring; it sounds like his neighbor's, but he goes to his own front door to see if anyone is there. Each act is an experience in perceiving.

A person is sensitive to size, shape, form, color, heat, cold, roughness, or smoothness, in relation to forces and objects in his environment. The sensitive organs by means of which he becomes aware of these forces, objects, or changes in the world about him are called *receptors.* These receptors are classified, according to their specific function, as *exteroceptors, interoceptors,* and *proprioceptors.*

Exteroceptors. Receptors in the eye, ear, or nose that react to stimuli at a distance, or receptors of touch, temperature, pain, or pressure in the skin that react to objects on the body are called exteroceptors.

Interoceptors. Conditions inside the body that stimulate the alimentary canal, or chemicals that sensitize the taste receptors in the tongue and palate are typical examples of interoceptors.

Proprioceptors. Body organs that are sensitive to the position and movements of the body, such as the receptors found in the vestibule of the inner ear and in the semicircular canals which are sensitive to static position and bodily rotation, and receptors located in the muscles, tendons, and joints which are sensitive to the position and movements of body parts are called proprioceptors.

Sense Discrimination. The power of our sensory equipment to discriminate among various stimuli makes possible one's ability to perceive with clarity. Each sense organ is sensitive to a particular kind of stimulus. The eye, for example, is the primary organ that is receptive to light waves, the ear to sound waves. Further, the difference between a noise and a light, or a pressure on the skin or a pain, usually can be perceived; the difference between an odor and a taste may not be detected easily, since one sensation sometimes interferes with the other. Yet a person can distinguish between a sweet taste and a sour one.

Discrimination is dependent somewhat upon the intensity of the sensory experience. These quantitative differences are detectable. Pressure applied to the skin can be slight at first and barely felt; great increase of pressure is sensed strongly. Visual responses differ with degree of light from darkness to bright light, auditory responses differ with intensity of sound from inaudible to loudness. The transition point or the point at which the intensity of the stimulus is sufficient to activiate the receptor is called the *sensory threshold.* The threshold varies according to the sense organ stimulated, and the physiological condition and the attitude of the person when he is being stimulated. The minimum or absolute threshold for any sense organ differs among individuals.

Sensation and Perception. Sensation is the primary response of the receptor of a sense organ; a "pure" sensation represents no more than the bare quality of experience. Perception is awareness or consciousness of the sensation, including the meaning and interpretation that accompany the experience associated with the process begun by the stimulus. Actually, sensation and perception are not separated in experience. Both are needed to recognize the details that identify stimuli as trees, boats, chairs, structures, human beings, situations, or conditions. The impressions gained are not added one to another; the mind acts upon what it receives as it organizes, integrates, and interprets sensoriperceptual experiences.

Attention and Perception. Among the many stimuli in the environment one tends to become selective and to focus upon a few. Attention-giving includes both body movement and mental activity. A person turns his head to hear (give physical set) or he moves closer or farther away to see; or he becomes mentally set to attend to certain stimuli in the environment. If he expects something to happen, he has a degree of expectancy (mental set) that it will occur. For example, a teacher can phrase a question or emphasize certain words in such manner that the mind set of the pupils is so affected that they miss the significance of the question. To illustrate; which is correct, 7 and 3 *is* 11, or 7 and 3 *are* 11? The listeners invariably attend to grammatical correctness and give little attention to the exactness of the number combination, especially when the question is asked during an English lesson.

Attention is influenced by (1) *intensity* of the stimulus, as a loud noise; (2) *suddenness of change,* as the sudden stopping of the ticking of a clock; (3) *novelty,* as an ultramodern style of automobile; (4) *sharpness of outline,* as contrasting shadows on a bright day compared with those on a dull day, and (5) *relevance to an individual's needs,* as a pitcher of ice water on a hot, dry day versus the same pitcher of ice water on a cold, rainy day.

The printing on the page of a book is organized in part to call attention to points of emphasis. The center headings, the boldface type in the side headings, and the kind and size of type all serve as aids to perception by enabling the individual to attend to what the author wishes emphasized. At times, a word is italicized in the context to help the reader focus on it, thereby ensuring his gaining a correct percept.

Structure and Pattern. A percept is an organized totality rather than the sum total of individual sensory experiences. In perception, an individual first gains a general impression of the outlines of an object or situation and later fills in the details. It is because of the percept's quality of organized totality that it has been called a Gestalt, or configuration, by Wertheimer and his followers.

The "whole" constitutes a framework for the individual parts that comprises its wholeness or Gestalt. A chair is perceived first according to its general outline. Then its unified structural details are observed in order of the perceiver's interest or background of experience. Some of these structural details are: the kind of chair—arm chair or straight chair, or conventional or modernistic; the wood of which it is made, and the covering material (if any); its sturdiness or fragility, its softness or hardness, its comfortableness of contours. Other details, not observed by the layman, would be perceived by the cabinet maker, such as quality of wood stain and polish, and carefulness of workmanship. The perception of any object, person, group of persons, situation, or condition follows this pattern. Sometimes the entire process is completed so quickly that one is not aware of the stages involved.

As an individual adds percept to percept, he enlarges his knowledge and increases his ability to form correct and complete percepts. Yet the pattern of a grouping of objects lends itself to individual interpretation according to the mental set of the observer or the functioning of the imagination.

An array of dots may be nothing more than a jumble to an individual unless he has learned to see relationships among them. One person, glancing at the dots in Figure 2, at once mentally arranges them into definite patterns; another merely sees them as an unorganized group of dots.

One set of dots lends itself to arrangement by almost anyone, while another set may defy patterning except by an individual experienced in dot arrangement. How many groups of dots of 5 can you see in A, and in B? It should be possible for you to see 8 patterns of 5 dots in A. What patterns if any, can you discover among the dots in B?

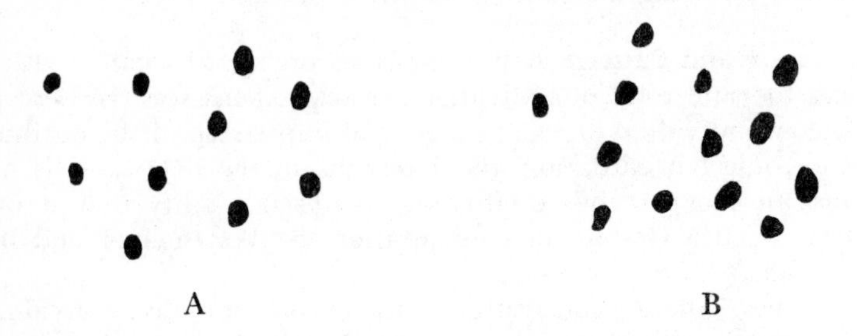

Figure 2. Two Sets of Dots, A and B

To what extent do you fill in the details when enough of the pattern is given to permit the mind to complete the form? For example, a face can be seen even though the lines do not connect.

In the same way, the mind completes percepts to form ideas. If a speaker starts a sentence that has a usual ending, the mind of the listener tends to complete it even though he may not hear all that is said. Waitresses are adept at perceiving what the customer is ordering even if they do not hear every word he says. Sometimes, however, the individual anticipates the speaker's words and consequently misunderstands what he actually says.

Many words can be read corectly in spite of the fact that they are incorectly spelled or even have letters missing. For example, it was reported tht no one had received the book he

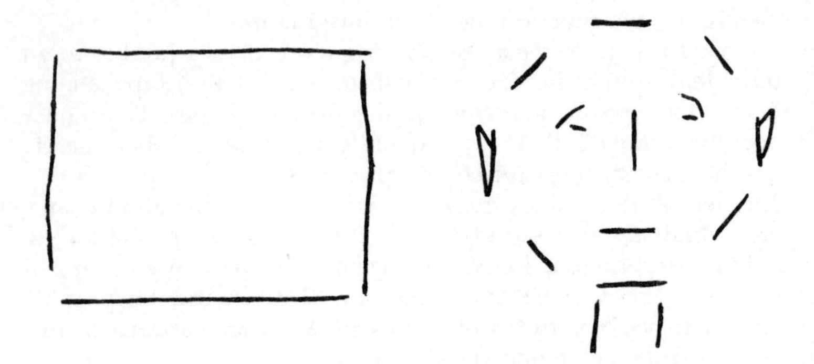

Figure 3. The Mind Fills in the Details

had distributed or that the picture of an autmobile was included in it. A sentance can become quiet meaningful without the inslusion of all the wrods. The mind tends to fill in for these omissions. Did you detect the eight mispelled words in this paragraph?

Individual Differences in Perception. Since there may be variation among individuals in the (1) physical state of the sense organs, (2) interests, (3) past experience, (4) degree of attention, and (5) effect of stimuli, great differences in perception may be experienced by two people as they observe the same phenomenon, such as the performance of a simple experiment in science. The implications of individual differences in perception were suggested in the foregoing discussion of perceptual structure and patterning.

Individuals respond to different details in their environment as they participate in perception of phenomena. There also are many details that are not perceived. This point can be illustrated by the fact that students entered a college building daily for several weeks without observing a hornet's nest that was directly above the door of the building.

Difference in perceptual interpretation is a significant cause of misunderstandings among individuals, especially between adults and children. Parents and teachers sometimes forget that a child's experiential background is extremely meager as compared with an adult's.

Illusions. Perceptions that are distorted for any reason are called *illusions.* The faults, errors, or misinterpretations in perception that result in the formation of illusions are caused by (1) the physical condition of the sensory organ, (2) its sensitivity to stimuli, (3) the ability of the receptor to adapt to a variety of stimuli, (4) the extent of the learning background, (5) the mental expectancy of the individual at the time of the stimulus. Any one or more can contribute to faulty perception, or illusion. In short, illusions result from inadequacies in the sense organs or in the interpretation given to the impulses resulting from the activation of the receptors.

Objects in motion can trick the eye into conveying a mental impression that later can be checked as incorrect. For example, two motionless trains are facing in opposite directions. The train in which you are *not* sitting starts to move, but you get the impression that your train is in motion. Wagon wheels in motion seen through a picket fence appear to be in reverse motion.

A landscape viewed through a picket fence from a vehicle moving at the rate of at least 40 miles an hour becomes clear; the pickets are not recorded in vision unless and until the car slows down to about 20 miles an hour.

Visual illusion is illustrated by the Muller-Lyer Illusion, the Zollner Illusion, and several other figures that trick the eye into reporting as true something that can be checked to be false. The following illustrations are representative of various types of visual illusions.

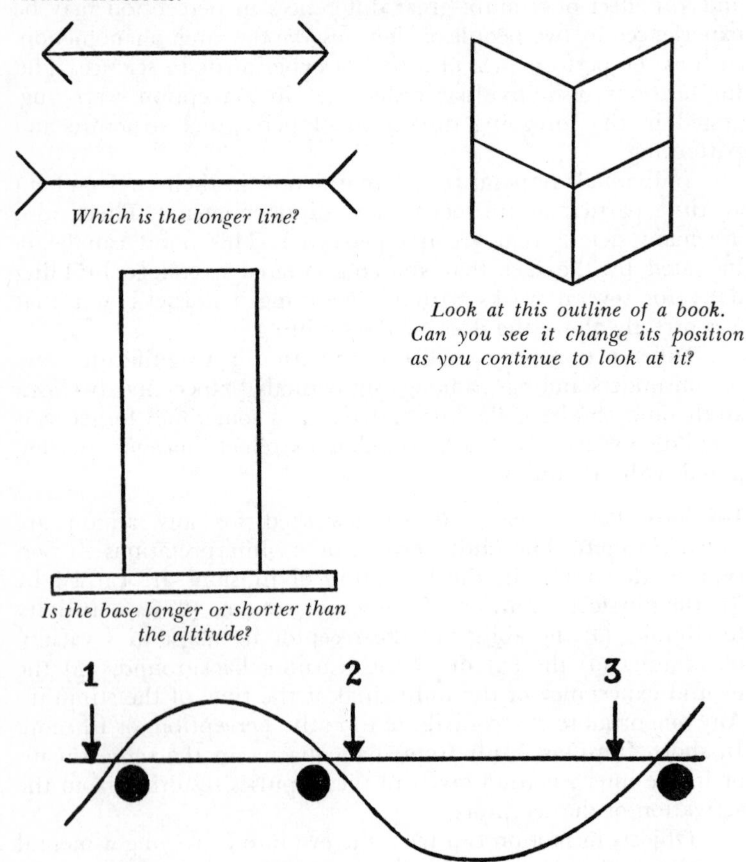

Which is the longer line?
Look at this outline of a book. Can you see it change its position as you continue to look at it?
Is the base longer or shorter than the altitude?
1
2
3
Which arrow is farther from arrow No. 2 — No. 1 or No. 3?

Figure 4. Four Examples of Optical Illusions.

(From Alice Crow and L. D. Crow, *Learning to Live with Others,* D. C. Heath and Company, 1944, p. 160.)

Figure 5.

Floyd C. Dockery, and G. Gorham Lane, *Psychology,* 2d ed., p. 425. (Copyright, 1942, 1950, by Prentice-Hall, Inc., New York. Reproduced by permission of the publisher.)

It can be noticed that in each of these illustrations the eye does not see the phenomena as they are, based largely upon misleading factors in the environment. Fluctuation of attention also can result in obtaining different images from the same picture. Hence, in certain situations, perceptions shift from one pattern to another. Focus your eye on a spot on the ceiling, and after a time observe it appear to move; fixate upon a dim star on a clear night and notice that it seems to appear and to disappear.

The size of objects must be interpreted in terms of the distance from them of the observer. Experience with varying phenomena is required to give correct interpretation to the illusions that inevitably result from comparison of objects at great distances and near at hand. Airplane pilots are trained carefully to cope with these variables in the environment through which they travel.

Accuracy of perception is essential to good mental development and satisfactory learning. As one becomes better acquainted with objects or persons he is able to identify correctly the object or the person by few and, sometimes by a single detail. For example, an individual may be recognized by his footsteps long before he can be seen; he is identified by his facial features, the back of his neck, or the sound of his voice. If a person is seen infrequently, however, some of the details of his appearance need to be observed carefully for recognition.

Preparation, set, or expectancy influences the degree and kind of perception. Effective teachers constantly try to help learners become mentally set to capitalize on all their former experiences for the purpose of understanding what is under consideration at the moment. Learners usually have a great amount of experience but need help to use it in perception formation.

Hallucinations. Another more serious perceptual disorder is known as *hallucination.* Illusions are explainable errors of perception, but hallucinations are false perceptions in which there is no appropriate situation to induce the perception. For a long time it was believed that hallucinations were products of the imagination; now, however, it is believed that a slight sensory element in the mental experience is misinterpreted. There may be some sensory beginning for the individual's perceiving something that is not present. Changed rhythmic action in the body such as heartbeat or breathing may start the reaction which causes the victim to report that he hears "voices" or the "ringing of bells."

The experiencing of an hallucination is uncommon; it usually is confined to persons who are suffering great mental or emotional conflict. The normal individual may experience an hallucination when he is excessively fatigued, critically ill, or greatly grieved by the death of a relative. In the last instance, he may insist that he hears the voice or the footsteps of the dead person, or that the latter appears before him, especially at night. Most hallucinatory experiences of normal persons are associated with night dreams.

Development of Meaning and Concepts

A distinctive attribute of a human being is his ability to think. Environmental concepts result from his ability to communicate with other human beings, thereby influencing their thinking and being influenced by them. Clear thinking and successful living tend to coexist. Those who gain great success in a profession, for example, have learned to utilize their perceptions through direction, interpretation, selection, insight, creation, and criticism. Thereby they have mastered and can apply significant knowledge concerning the nature of the activities involved in the particular profession.

Nature of Concepts. The development of understanding is dependent upon perceptual learning. If learning involved only the forming of percepts from sensed material, mental activity would consist of little more than a continued recognition of the meaning associated with that which is present to the senses. Percepts can be translated into memory images that are the bases of thinking and concept formation.

An object is perceived. Later, in the absence of the object, its image can be recalled. The correctness of the memory image depends upon the completeness and accuracy of the original percept. One memory or mental image is associated with other similar images, resulting from the building up of percepts. The continuing mental process of organizing and reorganizing relationships among the percepts and images induces the formation of a generalized meaning or *concept* of the attributes associated with percepts and images.

The formation of concepts involves thinking. The process of thinking, that can be described as the mental manipulation of memory images, includes imagery, kinesthesia, and symbolization. Words as symbols are basic to perception, although they are not percepts. Experience with a word, however, helps give exactness of meaning as well as variation of meaning. The word *white,* for example, may have many interpretations, depending on the word or ideas with which it is associated. For example, if it is associated with the word *flag,* the term, *white flag,* connotes surrender to persons who, through previous experience, attach this meaning to the term. Similarly, according to previous experience, each combination of the word *white* with another specific word has its own special meaning, such as *white meat, white light, White Sox,* or *white elephant.*

The young learner understands and evaluates his environment in terms of the way it affects him, meets his needs, and fulfills his wishes. As he grows older, he learns through many experiences that various aspects of the environment are related to one another. Hence the child becomes increasingly able to objectify his concepts and to relate them one to another. Thus he develops habits of thinking which become relatively clear and accurate and that enable him to differentiate among specific concepts. A concept, therefore, can be defined as *a generalized meaning that represents relationships in experience.*

Development of Concepts. A concept is more than a percept or memory image. The percepts and images are related to other percepts and images and to the background of experience, resulting in a generalization. For example, a child reared in the country probably knows what a barn is and what a yard is; he also knows that the word *barnyard* applies to the yard of the barn. Yet, he may not understand the meaning of expressions such as, "sweepstakes" or "cellar club" which may be a part of the urban child's vocabulary.

In the development of concepts, the overt behavior of other persons, and situational conditions and experiences are evaluated. For example, one attempts to put meaning into the words spoken by another, or to discover the reason for a person's attitudes or behavior. In order to drive an automobile with safety, the driver must be able to recognize the meaning of an amber light, a sudden shrill of a whistle, an arm or hand signal of another driver, or a road sign, especially if the words on the sign are in a language with which the driver is not acquainted. Through many experiences, an individual arrives at his own interpretations of perceived phenomena. The correctness of his concepts depends upon the nature of his experiences and his skill at generalization.

Language and Concept Formation. Language (combination of word symbols) represents a real situation even though the word symbols are abstractions. Since words are used to identify objects or ideas they should have common meanings to facilitate adequate intercommunication. A child's communication with adults is hampered by his still incomplete interpretation of word symbols. Meanings become more complete as he enlarges his experience with objects, people, and ideas. The learner needs opportunities to have many well-organized experiences with actual phenomena so that eventually his concepts or generalized meanings are rich and correct. He also needs help in the forming of accurate memory images and in the functioning of the thinking process.

There are certain concepts that are basic to the development of socially adequate and personally satisfying behavior patterns. Hence it is important that, during his school days and later, an individual shall accumulate a large number of commonly used concepts that are useful as he adapts himself and his behavior to varying situations. Since concepts are built out of experience, they are acquired through the learner's participation in many forms of purposeful activity: direct experience, reading, exposure to audio-visual learning aids, and classroom discussions by means of which meanings are extended both vertically and horizontally.

Language is the medium through which one individual expresses his ideas (concepts) to another. It is imperative, therefore, that exact meanings be assigned to the words (symbols) that are used to convey ideas. Yet there are many words in the English language, each of which represents several different concepts. The result of such loose concept identification is extremely confusing, especially to a child or to a foreigner attempting to learn the language, unless the intended meaning of the word can be derived from the context of the sentence in which it appears. In oral speech, words such as, I, eye, aye; hear, here; their, there; bare, bear; sea, see; to, too, two, or read, reed, can be interpreted in one of two or more ways except in contextual relationships. The intended meaning of some words is not definite in either oral or written form if they are used out of context. For example:

Turn out the *light.*	The ball is *light.*
The *bark* of the dog.	The *bark* of the tree.
Where did you *hide* the ball?	The *hide* of the steer is tough.
How fast can you *run?*	The man expects to *run* for Congress.

Some word symbols represent many different concepts. The word *light,* for instance, has at least twenty connotations. Terms that comprise separate word symbols are used to identify concepts that have no more than a resemblance to the meaning of each part of the term, e.g., buttercup or jack-in-the-pulpit. A term may be confusing because of the commonly accepted meaning of part of it. For example, the vernacular term *spitting image,* referring to a high degree of resemblance (especially between two persons), might seem ludicrous if the first word were interpreted according to common usage. If one knew, however, that the word *spit* can be used to mean *counterpart,* then the original term, *spit and image* becomes an identification of a particular concept.

Not only children but also adults often are uncertain concerning the conceptual exactitude of words, terms, or phrases common to the English language. Therefore, since a child constantly is groping for correct words and terms to identify his still meager concepts, adults need to use words correctly in his presence. It is extremely important that a teacher explain simply any new words or terms that are introduced into a lesson, to avoid misinterpretation or misuse of them by some or all of the learners.

Modern language is dynamic. Dictionaries are revised periodically to include those new words that continue to be coined for the purpose of identifying changed, expanded, or added concepts, resulting in part from research activities and new inventions. Young people are prone to develop their own language patterns that usually include commonly known words to which meanings are attached that differ from the concepts they are supposed to identify. The actual words or terms coined by young people to express their ideas or feelings change from generation to generation, but their usage reflects the dynamic nature of youthful attempts to be different and to express their individuality overtly by mystifying adults as to what they mean when they employ terms that are understood by their peers but incomprehensible to their elders.

The background of the learner is an important factor of influence on the direction that is followed in concept formation. The mentally slow learner, whose experiences have been meager, cannot grasp easily the relationships that exist between ideas. He usually is deficient in sensory experiences essential to the formation of correct percepts that are basic to his memory images and concepts. The bright learner, on the other hand, usually possesses good sensory equipment, receives clear, correct percepts, and so organizes his images that his concepts are accurate and meaningful. He is able to gain insight into situations and to discover the interrelations of the component parts that elude the mental functioning of the slower learner.

CHAPTER 14

ACQUISITION OF SKILL COMPETENCE

Motor activity of any kind involves responses to external or internal stimuli. Motor ability refers to the kind of bodily movements that are made possible through the coordination of nerve and muscle activity. An individual engages in motor activities to fulfill his physical and psychological needs and to preserve him from danger. Except for required maturation, the functioning of an individual's sensory equipment and his perceptions are basic to, complement, or supplement the development of motor skill.

Development of Motor Control

The patterns of motor development appear to fall into two major categories: primary and secondary. The first includes the gross body movements, such as walking, running, jumping, throwing, swimming, and skating; the second are the controls by the smaller muscles: writing, and using tools and implements that require the coordination of the finer muscles. Most motor skills involve both gross movements and finer muscle coordinations. If motor control is to become proficient, attention needs to be given, during the development of a skill, to accurate perception of a sensory stimuli.

Characteristics of Motor Development. Motor development is closely associated with maturation. Until an individual reaches an appropriate level of muscular maturation he cannot develop to a significant degree his successive motor abilities, such as standing, walking, throwing a ball, and playing tennis. Proper maturation of the finer muscles also must have taken place for the coordination of arm, hand, and fingers that is needed for penmanship. Experiments have shown that learners cannot be forced to achieve progress in the development of a motor activity unless the organism has completed the maturation process in that area.

During an individual's early years, the development of motor skill appears to follow a more or less sequential pattern that is determined by his growth pattern. Motor coordination begins in the head region and moves downward, in a more or less orderly progression, to coordinated foot movements (cephalocaudal trend). Trunk movements precede those of the body extremities (proximodistal trend).

Individual Differences in Motor Development. Competence in motor skill depends not only upon an individual's sensory and perceptual adequacy but also upon the functioning capacity of his muscular coordination. Muscular activation is dependent upon stimuli, internal or external. Accurate perception of stimuli is helpful in the development of skill competence, especially in the finer coordinations.

By the time the infant is 9 or 10 months old he usually can sit without support. At this stage, he is midway between the supine position and walking. The baby next learns to change from a prone to a sitting position, and then back to the prone position. The ability to crawl follows. As soon as he begins to crawl, he may vary his activity by scooting at one time and hitching at another. Later he is stimulated by the sight of objects beyond his reach to pull himself up to a standing position.

The age at which the power to walk develops varies widely among children. However, by the time most children are 15 months of age they are able to walk alone. Such factors as ill health, excessive weight, obvious physical defects, or other abnormal conditions may retard developmental progress in walking. Walking as a motor skill becomes so habituated that an individual may be identified by his characteristic gait.

The development of motor skills to a high degree of perfection often has excellent socializing value. The skilled athlete gains social prestige because of his ability to win. Although the adolescent years sometimes are regarded as the "awkward stage," no adolescent wants to be considered clumsy or inept. Some teenagers spend many hours in practice to perfect a skill in which they are interested, and for superior performance in which they hope to earn well-deserved commendation.

Prehension and Handedness. The development of arm-hand contern. The gross movements of arm lashing, and the reflex hand trol appears to follow a definite but individually different pat-

grasping exhibited during the first few weeks of life may be regarded as the beginnings of those activities which later are to become skilled, manual activities. At first, the infant's grasping reflex is digital. The palmar reflex (grasping with the thumb opposite the forefinger) appears at the age of about 12 months. Once developed, this reflex continues throughout life.

Acquisition of even a simple manual skill seems to be dependent upon sensory acuity—tactual, visual, and kinesthetic. In early infancy, a child's manipulatory movements are awkward and fumbling. There is little coordination between the eye and the hand. About 40 weeks usually are required before a child can be expected to have sufficient eye-hand coordination both to see and to touch a small object placed before him. During the first 6 years, there is a relatively consistent and progressive developing pattern of arm and hand movement. Blocks are manipulated, playthings are handled, and eating and drinking equipment are brought under manual control. Each of these motor activities requires the development of specific motor coordination; many new motor skills are acquired as a result of school learning.

Handedness. The right hand seems to be preferred by most children. At first, the child may appear to favor one hand over the other but, by the third or fourth year, motor habits have been established in one hand or the other. Ambidexterity, evidenced by most children during the first 2 years, sometimes but rarely continues into adult life.

Since the child is born into a world that is more right-handed than left-handed, he is encouraged to develop his right hand. Yet some children, in spite of adults' attempts to encourage right-handedness (either in early childhood or during the first years at school), continue to show greater dexterity in the left hand. It is believed that if a child shows strong tendencies toward left-handedness he should be permitted to remain left-handed, especially if he resists attempts to change handedness.

Handwriting Movements. Development of specific motor skills in handwriting passes through progressive stages. First the child learns to hold a crayon in his hand; by the age of 18 months he can draw a line across a paper. At the age of 2 or 3 years, he begins to scribble. By the time he is 4 years old, he can hold a pencil, and draw a picture of his mental image of a man or a house. For example, Fig. 6 was drawn by a 5-year-old boy and Fig. 7 by a 6-year-old. During this period, the child also is able

Figure 6. A Man as Drawn by a 5-Year-old Boy.

to trace or copy, and to use colored crayon, or to paint with large brush movements.

When or soon after a child enters the first grade he is able to manipulate a pencil for writing. Although he first tends to write with his fingers and wrists, skill in handwriting usually is developed sufficiently by the age of 12 that it becomes the individual's characteristic handwriting for the remainder of his life.

The Bases of Skill Development

The degree of proficiency of motor learning depends upon the development of adequacy of the finer muscular responses.

Figure 7. A Man as Drawn by a 6-Year-old Boy.

Correct motor responses must become automatic for skill proficiency. Long periods of practice are required to increase speed of reaction, develop accuracy of responses, and acquire steadiness or control. Skill development is facilitated if practice is accompanied by a desire to succeed, and confidence that success will be attained.

School Considerations. In many modern elementary and secondary schools, considerable attention is given to the development of muscular coordination. Training in motor skill is afforded in subjects such as penmanship, drawing, shopwork, cooking, sewing, sports of various kinds, and gymnastics. The project approach in academic subjects also provides opportunities for motor learning.

Some schools encourage every pupil to participate in an intramural sports activity. The purpose not only is directed toward development of the body but also toward improvement of muscular coordination. Since effective muscular coordination is achieved through activity, the extent of a learner's skill proficiency is determined by the amount of appropriate practice or overlearning in which he engages.

Importance of Correct Practice. The aim of practice in motor learning, involving the fine muscles, is to habituate correct responses. An individual who wishes to improve a skill not only needs to practice consistently but must be certain that, from the beginning of the learning process, he practices correct responses. Moreover, he is helped or hindered in the development of a motor skill by the muscular habit patterns acquired earlier that are related to the particular skill he is attempting to perfect. For example, earlier habit patterns either aid or interfere with progress in learning to drive an automobile, ride a bicycle, typewrite, sing, or play a musical instrument.

Form in Motor Learning. The simpler skills are mastered by utilizing movements already learned and combining these in a workable pattern. In his learning of a more complex skill, however, the goal of the individual is to develop what is considered to be good *form*. Form refers to the motor coordinations that promote proficiency in a particular skill. Allowance must be made for individual differences, however. What constitutes good form for one person is not necessarily the best form for another. For example, the general standing position at home plate is much the same for all baseball batters. Yet the stance taken by one successful batter is different from that of an equally proficient player. Two equally skilled violinists may hold their bows differently.

Differences in whole body, limb, hand, or finger position or movement are found among superior performers in any skill. During his learning practice, each expert in his field develops a form that is peculiarly his own, such as Ben Hogan's grip of the club that, according to him, was the significant factor of his excellent success in playing golf. The attaining of good form is an important aspect of skill practice. The learner of a skill should be encouraged to imitate known successful procedures, but he needs freedom of selection in developing his own particular form, in so far as thereby he can improve his skill.

Significant Aspects of Skill Mastery

Skill in performance is attained only through direct participation in it by the learner. Ideas gained from sources such as books or teachers assist the learner, but one neither can learn to play pingpong nor become a good dancer without many hours of correct practice. Motor learning is kinesthetic, in that the learner is conscious of his own muscular movements. To master a skill, the learner must be sufficiently interested in it to practice diligently, with accompanying perception of the "feel" of his muscular movements until these become so habituated that certain aspects of performance are automatic.

Importance of Awareness of Goal. In the development of a motor skill the learner should know what the goal is, as well as the kind and amount of activity required to attain it. For example, a person learning to typewrite may set as his eventual goal 40, 60, or more words per minute, depending upon his purpose for learning it. He also must know what different activities are required to learn how, through the touch system, to type perfect copy at the goal-set rate.

If the form to be achieved is known and understood, the individual can make more intelligent refinements in his practice of the skill. He is aided also by knowing the various components of the total learning situation. The greater the learner's understanding is of what he is aiming toward, the more likely he will be to recognize faults and to improve his performance.

Value of Knowledge of Correct Methods. Excellent models that can be observed, analyzed, and understood by the learner usually are helpful aids. The teacher of any skill who himself has mastered it to a superior degree can present model performances for imitation and study purposes. He also is able to establish self-confidence in the beginning learner. If or when a learner develops a mind set of wanting to or of believing that he can develop skill, he is ready to devote sufficient energy and time to profit from instruction given by a skilled and effective teacher.

Teachers of motor skills know that for a beginner to avoid discouragement he must realize that skill perfection cannot be achieved during the initial stages of practice. The learning of penmanship exemplifies the functioning of this principle. Formerly, when the teaching of penmanship consisted of requiring learners on any grade level to imitate perfect copy, handwriting lessons usually included much learner discouragement.

More recently the findings of studies dealing with the development of arm, hand, and finger control resulted in the construction of handwriting scales. The first of these scales presents examples of handwriting that are arranged according to the kind of performance that can be expected at progressive maturational and grade levels By comparing a specimen of a pupil's characteristic handwriting with the appropriate grade samples of the scale, a teacher can evaluate the degree to which the learner has achieved skill in penmanship, adequate for his learning level.

The alert teacher recognizes any incorrect or faulty practice activities, calls them to the attention of the learner and tries to help him overcome this fault. Suggestions offered by a teacher have value only in so far as they can be applied by the learner. Although it is desirable for the teacher of a skill to be a proficient performer, a less skilled person may be more successful in making practical suggestions for improvement to a beginner. A highly skilled person either may have forgotten his beginning difficulties or, because of his superior talent, may never have experienced any. Hence, for either reason, he may find himself unable to analyze the learner's fault sufficiently to discover the cause and suggest pertinent remedial measures. Emotional blocks experienced by the learner that interfere with effective practicing activities can be intensified by a teacher's vague or inept suggestions for changed procedure.

The initial attempts at developing a skill rarely are successful. A learner who is interested and ready to learn may discover that his first or even his tenth practice attempt is inferior to that of others or far below his own expectations. The teacher can do much to encourage him during these usually awkward or clumsy practice trials. It may be that the individual wants to go too far too fast. For example, a child, having some musical talent, may be able to play relatively difficult piano selections "by ear," with no instruction in correct playing techniques such as hand placing, fingering, or timing. At first, his untutored performance may earn for him considerable satisfying praise from his hearers. He soon discovers that he is unable to perform a selection in the way he hears it. The resulting discouragement is not lessened if he is thrown immediately into difficult and tiring scale practicing, fingering, and boring mechanical exercises. If he is helped gradually to improve his playing techniques and is encouraged by his teacher to learn to play simple selections correctly, the accompanying feeling of accomplishment probably will stimulate him to spend many hours in accurate and meaningful practice.

Sufficient and accurate practice of a motor skill results eventually in its becoming automatic and relatively independent of the functioning of the higher mental processes, thereby enabling the individual to direct his attention to other aspects of the learning situation. He can experiment with styling or individualizing his performance. He is free from adherence to conventional patterns of performance; he introduces such innovations as are characteristic of highly artistic or creative, but technically correct, skilled activities.

Need of Consistent Practice. The correct practice that already has been referred to actually means consistent practice. More than mere repetition is required in skill development. The effective development of skill is dependent in part upon attitude. The teacher can help the learner focus on the degree of efficiency to be attained at various stages of practice. The amount of practice and the length of time required to attain a definite goal will vary with individuals and with the habits that were formed before the initial start. The degree of skill attained with a given amount of practice reflects somewhat the abilities and interests of the learner.

Length of Practice Periods. Both the length of practice periods and the length of time between them are significant in motor learning. Motor drill is effective when it is well motivated and properly spaced. The length of practice periods depends partly upon the age and ability of the learner and partly upon the type of skill to be mastered. In general practice periods should be shorter for young children than for older children, adolescents, and adults. The length of the practice periods also varies with the learning stage; in the beginning they should be short and appropriately spaced, but during advanced stages, the individual may be motivated to devote many hours of continuous practice to refine his performance.

A daily practice period of appropriate length usually is productive of skill improvement. In some instances, two relatively short practice periods per day yield better results than one longer daily, or less frequent, period. Although practice periods should not be so long that fatigue or boredom is induced, neither should they be so short that little is accomplished.

When progress in practice is charted on a learning curve a rapid initial spurt is indicated with a leveling off after a number of periods of practice. In fact, during a week or more of conscientious daily practice the curve may show no rise, indicating that a *plateau* has been reached. A subsequent, rapid rise in the curve indicates that during the plateau period learning has been taking place, probably in the form of inner organization that is not evidenced in overt behavior.

Significance of Criticism. Learners vary widely in the consistency of their practice and in the amount of their concentration upon practice material. Normally, progress in skill improvement is likely to be irregular from day to day, in spite of any help that may be given in the form of constructive criticism.

In helping a learner during his early stages of practice, a teacher should direct his suggestions to the correction of gross errors only. The learner needs to become oriented to the general nature of the new practice activities before he is able to concentrate on the development of fineness of response. Hence any adverse criticism of the more subtle practice elements should be avoided. Moreover, at any stage of practice, constructive, encouraging suggestions are superior to those that are negative and derogatory. Praise given by the instructor or by others who know correct procedures acts as a tonic to anyone interested in improving his performance, usually motivating him toward continued and more correct practice.

Significance of Speed and Accuracy. The extent to which speed and accuracy parallel each other in the learning of a skill is an important factor in teaching methodology. Experience has shown that in the teaching of many motor skills both speed and accuracy should be considered together from the start of the training. Accuracy should be given precedence, however, in that it should not be sacrificed to the attaining of great speed. When the importance of both is emphasized by the teacher, they become twin goals for the learner which he strives to reach. Yet, although slow performance does not guarantee accuracy, some skills are so complex that the element of speed is relatively important; the major emphasis should be placed upon careful, painstaking execution that will lead to as near perfect results as are humanly possible to achieve.

Motor learning should begin with learning by "whole" responses, in which attention is given to both speed and accuracy. Part learning may be needed to refine certain responses after the individual has had an opportunity to complete the entire performance and discover his weakness. It is then that he selects various specific aspects of the total skill situation and concentrates on their practice. For example, the golfer plays a game of golf but he practices his drive at one time and his putting at another.

Importance of Guidance. A person who has developed a skill to a high degree of proficiency is relaxed while he is performing. His confidence in his efficiency is basic to his relaxed state. Beginners are advised to relax but, realizing that they are certain to fall short of good performance, they usually tense their muscles in order to make fewer mistakes. The result is that they tend to increase their errors.

Helpful suggestions from one who knows how to perform and how to help others avoid mistakes are superior to the blind trial-error-trial-success procedure that accompanies practice without intelligent guidance in the activity. It often happens that an individual who is being helped by a friend to learn a motor skill is more relaxed than he would be if he were receiving formal instruction from a well-trained but exacting teacher.

Skills once developed require constant practice if the level of proficiency is to be maintained. Pianists and other skilled artists know this from experience. A motor skill, once learned, is never completely lost, however, even though there is a long period of disuse. For example, a 60-year-old man who had not ridden a bicycle in 40 years, mounted one and rode it, without losing his balance or falling.

CHAPTER 15

RETENTION AND EFFECTIVE STUDY

Memory or reproduction of experience is fundamental to all learning, except for manipulatory, trial-error-trial-success activity. Yet even in his manipulation of linked rings to separate them, for example, an individual is likely to apply to the task the memory of any previous experience that is related to the situation. Although skill competence is achieved through exercise, success-attaining practice must be meaningful. During each practice period, the memory of the purpose of the practice experience not only facilitates the practice itself, but rarely can be avoided.

Since the ability to reproduce experience is fundamental to learning progress, one of the most important functions of a teacher is to help learners retain in memory those experiences that are pertinent to his particular learning area. The term *abstract learning* sometimes is applied to learning activity that is concerned primarily with the functioning of the mental processes. The difference between abstract learning and mechanical or social learning is one of degree rather than kind. Much of formal education from at least the middle grades of the elementary schools deals with abstract ideas which then are applied to realistic situations. Successful learning on progressive school levels depends to a great extent upon earlier mastery of abstractions, simple at first and increasing in complexity.

Retention

Retention or the persistence of experience is an outcome of learning. The persistence of "learned" materials and the time needed to relearn them are basic factors of the entire learning process, in that they determine the amount of residual learning after the learning process, as such, supposedly ceases. Retention therefore is closely associated with the nature of the original study of materials to be learned. The effectiveness of study activity is dependent on inherent characteristics of retention and individual study habits.

Ability to recall correctly and quickly that which has been experienced earlier gives evidence of effective learning. Many adults, when they cannot recall things learned at school, believe that their memory is failing and attempt to find ways to improve it. Older persons, especially, are much bothered by the fact that they have forgotten information which at one time they knew well, and that still may be remembered by a contemporary. Differences among their retentive powers result from (1) inherent ability of an individual to remember, and (2) facilitation of retention through effective learning.

Retention and Fixation. Learning for retention requires the ability to *fixate* or to give active concentrated attention to that which is to be learned at the moment. The child or adult who can fixate easily usually is the more able student. If a learner's attention flits from one thing to another, so that he is not able to concentrate on the material to be studied, he probably will retain little. To study when one is emotionally tense or excited is not conducive to good retention. The presence of emotional or environmental distractions interferes with the learner's ability to fixate upon study stimuli.

Effective memorizing includes *fixation, retention, recognition,* and *recall.* A learner retains much learned material that he cannot recall when he needs it. Yet he may be able to recognize and evaluate something that he cannot recall without adequate stimulus aid. A simple cue stimulus usually is sufficient to effect correct recall. This is a common experience. For example, an adult meets a former teacher whom he recognizes, and in terms of his school experiences can evaluate as a person and teacher. Yet he cannot recall the man's name which, of course, he had learned well. If the two enter into conversation, a chance comment by the man may help his former student recall his name and specific experiences with him.

Effective memorizing is aided by (1) a vigorous attack on the material to be learned, (2) spaced practice periods, (3) use of the whole-part-whole method, (4) careful evaluation, and (5) favorable emotional attitudes toward the learning. Retention depends in part upon fixations and in part upon other factors, such as the character of the material to be learned, the use to be made of the learned material, and the age, intelligence level, attitudes, and interests of the learner.

Retention and Forgetting. It is not enough simply to acquire new patterns of response, they must be retained for needed use later. However, forgetting sets in as soon as learning is completed. The rate of forgetting is great at first, tending to slow down until an eventual residuum of retained material is present. The retention of learning is dependent on various factors. Many studies of retention have been conducted. Ebbinghaus, a pioneer in this field of research, investigated the rate of forgetting as applied to the learning of nonsense syllables, such as *otz, uhy, vol, syo,* etc., According to his findings, at least 70 per cent of the nonsense syllables "learned" were forgotten within two days.

Speed of forgetting varies with the nature of the material learned. The rapid rate at which nonsense syllables are forgotten can be explained chiefly by the fact that they represent unrelated learning materials. Meaningful materials usually are retained longer. Although the rate of forgetting continues to be more rapid directly after learning ceases, the curve of forgetting at first does not drop so low as it does for meaningless material, and the loss is not so great. For example, a list of nonsense syllables learned to the extent of *one* correct recall shows no retention at the end of four months, yet a line or a stanza of a poem learned to the extent of one correct repetition may be remembered for a long time.

Learners differ in their capacity to learn and in their interest in learning. Bright, interested, and purposeful learners retain more and forget less quickly than do slower learners or learners who are not interested in learning or recognize no value to themselves of the material they are forced to learn. The amount and rate of forgetting also are affected by the kind of activity in which the learner engages after he completes the learning. Sleep retards forgetting, but interesting experiences unrelated to the learning may interfere with retention.

Teachers know that many of their pupils tend to remember more of their learning material from one school day to another than over a weekend or a longer vacation, especially if the nonschool days have been filled with exciting and much enjoyed social activities. Return to school after a summer vacation often necessitates considerable review of supposedly learned material before new learning projects built upon previous learning can be started.

Retention is facilitated by (1) appropriate motivation, (2) adequate learner experience, (3) intelligent teacher guidance of learning activities, and (4) concentrated, continued study, under favorable conditions, of learning materials that are understood by the learner and in which he is interested. Retention functions successfully when significant learning materials are learned beyond the point of immediate recall, or in other words, are overlearned sufficiently so that they can be remembered by the learner so long as they have value for him.

Effective Study

If it were possible to evaluate the study habits of learners on all school levels, the conclusion reached probably would be that many of these habits are ineffective. Some learners develop success-achieving study habits by chance. To the extent that other factors of learning success are equal, an individual's relative learning adequacy is the result of his voluntary efforts to learn. There are, however, certain principles and conditions of study that, if adhered to by a learner, can improve retention of learned materials.

Meaning of Study. To study is to investigate or to become acquainted with new ideas, facts, or procedures. To direct energy toward the mastery of new material, the solution of problems, or the discovery of relationships is considered to be essential to study.

Much of one's study is concerned with gaining ideas by interpreting the content of printed pages. The purpose or aim of the reader conditions the kind of study approach to be employed. An individual may wish to obtain a general impression of book content or he may be in search of specific data or information. He reads to analyze the meaning of the reading material, to study the style of writing, or to be stimulated emotionally. What the reader learns depends largely upon the nature of his purpose for reading.

General Factors of Study. All learning is self-initiated. The learner must discover for himself how to form associations adequate for the solution of learning problems. A high school student's lack of success in his school work, for example, might be explained in terms of his tendency to daydream rather than to activate himself toward concentrated study. He needs to learn that an attitude of strong desire to become a more effective learner is basic to successful achievement.

Most young people need help in learning to apply sound principles of study. The earlier in his school experiences a learner receives this help, the more likely he is to form study habits that, with needed modifications, will function throughout his school life and possibly later. Secondary school teachers are prone to criticize activity programs on the elementary school level. They claim that the social nature of learning projects and the encouragement of the play attitude deny the child opportunities to engage in individual concentrated mastery of learning materials.

Although there is some justification for such criticisms, the elementary school child is expected to engage in some personal "research" as his contribution to a group project. His teacher, however, may assign him a topic or a phase of the project without informing him concerning what sources to use and how to use them. Consequently, a staff member of the school or a public library has the task of guiding the child's research study, simple as it may be. Hence elementary school teachers as well as those in the higher schools are responsible for guiding young people toward the formation of adequate study habits.

In an increasing number of secondary schools and colleges, attempts are made by the school personnel to teach students how to study or to help them recondition poor habits. Approaches that differ with schools include procedures such as: (1) offering a one-term course, meeting once a week, on "How to Study," (2) devoting certain periods of the first week of the school year, or a part of the pre-entrance counseling week, to the principles of effective study, (3) requiring each subject teacher to utilize a specified number of class periods at the beginning of each term or semester for the preparation by their students under teacher guidance of assigned study units, (4) providing after-school opportunities for pupils demonstrating ineffective study techniques to be given remedial help by a specially trained teacher.

Whatever approach is adopted, there are certain principles and conditions for effective study that should be known, and in so far as is possible, applied by every learner. These suggestions are presented briefly here. It should be noted, however, that if the learner is given freedom to organize his work, he is likely to learn with greater effectiveness than if he is required to follow a definite plan suggested by another. Efficient and effective study usually emanates from the intrinsic motivation of a high degree of interest.

Suggestions for Effective Study

Many suggestions for effective study have been formulated by psychologists and educators. In this discussion, the following aspects of study are emphasized:

1. Need for a study schedule or program.
2. Effect of environmental conditions.
3. Value of background experience and concentration on goal attainment.
4. Influence of mental attitudes.
5. Danger of discouragement during plateau periods.
6. Specific factors of study success.

Need for a Study Schedule or Program. The planning of a study schedule usually is suggested for learners on the secondary and college levels. Efficiency experts are aware of the importance of planning a schedule of work activity for a day, a week, a month, and/or a longer period of time. Probably a better procedure for a student is to think through the activities that he is likely to follow for a day and a week, and then draw up a schedule for their implementation. This schedule can serve as a challenge as well as a guide.

A schedule should provide for flexibility so that a few needed or desired changes can be made without upsetting the entire schedule. A teacher can encourage his pupils to get the schedule habit by helping them prepare a schedule for a month, week-by-week, according to the schedule presented below, with appropriate individual modifications, in terms of necessary activities.

Effect of Environmental Conditions. Environmental conditions, such as room temperature, ventilation, humidity, and lighting may be conducive to study or act as a deterrent. If the student is physically robust and strongly motivated, however, he may be able to complete a great deal of work under adverse conditions. Nevertheless, remedying adverse conditions is likely to improve the effectiveness of study.

A learner may be compelled by circumstances to study under distracting conditions. He must adapt to the presence of factors over which he has no control, including noises either inside or outside his home, sharing the room in which he is studying with other members of a large family, distracting radio and television programs, ringing of telephone or door bells. His studying may

Study Schedule

Time	Monday	Tuesday	Wednesday	Thursday	Friday	Saturday	Sunday	Time
7								7
8								8
9								9
10								10
11								11
12								12
1								1
2								2
3								3
4								4
5								5
6								6
7								7
8								8
9								9
10								10

be interrupted by requests to run errands or help with home chores.

Soft, concentrated lighting, preferably from the left of the reader, helps reduce eye strain. A temperature of approximately 70°F seems to be best for mental work. The air in the room should be neither too damp nor too dry. A straight-backed, comfortable chair is preferable to an easy chair. Some body tension resulting from erect sitting posture seems to favor improvement of thinking. All study materials should be close at hand.

Value of Background Experience and Concentration on Goal Attainment. Richness of background and understanding of study goal are important. The student who has the necessary equipment, in the form of facts and experience, to arrive at solutions of assigned problems is more likely to want to follow through toward the solution of a specific problem than is the one who needs to devote the time and energy in assembling the basic data. A rich background of experience, and the ability to recognize relationships are good study aids.

The achievability of a study goal is a motivating factor. If a study goal seems too far distant, the learner may become discouraged. If the goal is within comparatively easy reach, however, the student is more willing to expend the necessary energy for its achievement. Moreover, if attainment of the goal appears to be so difficult that its achievement seems unlikely, the learner may lose interest in it.

The ability to concentrate on study material is an essential factor of success. Because of the nature of mental activity it is difficult to fixate on a study problem. The constant fluctuation of attention and the new associations that are brought into focus seem to vie with one another in determining to which one will attend. When he becomes distracted, the learner must force the learning problem back into his focus of attention.

Influence of Mental Attitude. Effective study is related closely to a learner's attitude toward the problem or material to be mastered. Pleasant, satisfying attitudes resulting from previous study success impel the learner to continue study activity. Hence a learner is encouraged to apply energy in those learning areas in which success is anticipated; otherwise he may turn away from or avoid it.

Sometimes a young person gives in to worry as he studies or as he thinks about how much he has to study before he can master the material. Worry or anxiety about possible failure usually is aroused by habits of procrastination. If a student delays his study until the last minute, he has cause to wonder whether he can complete his study assignment adequately and punctually. A well-planned study schedule can benefit a last-minute lesson preparer.

Danger of Discouragement during Plateau Periods. As indicated earlier, the plateau on a learning curve indicates that there is a leveling off of the rise in improvement during continued practice. Plateaus are caused by influencing factors, such as (1) reduced interest, fatigue, or boredom; (2) habits that interfere with continued learning; or (3) increasing difficulties encountered in the integration of the learning material or experienced in new, little-understood material. To eliminate or reduce periods of apparently little or no evidence of learning progress, a good principle to follow is, from the start, to form associations as nearly as possible in the order in which they are to function later. Although this method may retard the learner at the beginning or even induce discouragement, it probably will be effective in the long run.

Study Assignments. Reference already has been made to the fact that learning materials should be geared to a student's level of ability and interest. A learner should understand the assignment for home study and have the ability and time to prepare it adequately. Unless the study task is explained sufficiently and the purpose is made clear, the learner is likely to waste time trying to decide just what he should do. If the assigned unit is too difficult for a learner he is likely to do one of three things: (1) try to work at it for a while and then become discouraged and leave it, (2) decide at once that he cannot do it and not attempt it, or (3) if the assignment is solving problems or writing a paper on a given topic, copy the work of another, more able, student.

An assignment such as reading the "next twenty pages" is not an interest arouser. The purpose of home study is supposed to be that of helping the learner fixate the content of class learning and prepare himself for the next day's work. Ideally, then, the assignment should be given at the end of the class period and its relation to what has been done in class made clear. Pressure of time, especially on the secondary school level, causes many teachers to give the assignment at the beginning of the class period, with little or no explanation of its purpose or value. In addition, the background of the assignment may not be completed during the period, leaving a gap between what has been covered in class and what must be done at home. This gap may disturb even the more able, conscientious student. The situation is especially annoying if the assigned work requires an undue amount of study time and the student finds that he must neglect study preparation in other subjects.

Specific Aids to Study Success. Even under the most favorable study conditions, the actual learning that takes place may not be adequate unless the student himself knows how to attack study materials and carry the study process through to successful mastery. A teacher can help his students improve their study habits by bringing to their attention certain psychologically sound study techniques and then encouraging their application.

Reading for Ideas. A unit of reading in a textbook or in several reference books usually is assigned for home study to fulfill a particular purpose, which should be understood by the learner. Purposeful reading requires the mastery of ideas—general and specific.

A good study procedure to follow is: (1) read the entire unit through quickly to discover to what extent the content fulfills the intended purpose and how the material is organized, (2) carefully reread each subunit in sequence, noting the specific ideas included and interpreting them in terms of experiential background, (3) reread again for retention, with the intent not only to fix the ideas but also to recognize, understand, and appreciate the conceptual building-up or integration of the entire content.

The reader may know the meaning of each word in a sentence. Yet he will be able to appreciate the conceptual fineness of the author's presentation of ideas only in so far as he can read into a passage the proper interrelationships among the printed words, according to his own experiential background and power of mental integration.

Use of the Dictionary. Complete understanding and adequate retention of written material necessitates the reader's comprehension of the meaning of all the words included in it. Although the connotation of a word can be guessed from its context in a sentence, it is best to obtain its precise meaning from the dictionary, especially if it is a technical term. The dictionary habit is an excellent learning aid for understanding and retention and in expressing one's own ideas with accuracy and precision.

Utilization of Whole-Part Method. The preceding suggestions for preparing a reading assignment illustrate the utilization of the whole-part method of studying, that is, reading the unit as a whole, then concentrating upon each subunit, concluding with a rereading of the whole. The reader may discover that the ideas contained in one section of the material have not been mastered adequately. This "part" needs further study, but when the ideas in it are learned, it must be placed mentally into its proper place in the whole unit.

There is considerable evidence, resulting from investigation of learning methods, that the "whole" method of approach to verbatim memorization has greater retention value than "part" or piecemeal learning. For example, the traditional method of memorizing a poem was stanza by stanza, beginning with the first stanza and continuing to the second, third, and so on, until the entire poem was committed to memory. During the process of memorization it was customary for the learner to begin each recitation of the poem with the first stanza and continue through the stanza just learned. The result of this technique is evidenced by the fact that many adults can recall the first and perhaps the second stanza of a poem learned at school but have forgotten the remainder of it.

Unless a selection of poetry or prose is extremely long the learner should practice it in its entirety. At first, he may become discouraged because of the many errors he makes. Continued repetitions, however, will give him the "feel" of the whole selection, which he then can recite from beginning to end with confidence. If one section of the selection is more difficult than the others, he can concentrate upon its mastery and then concentrate again on the whole. If the selection to be memorized is too long for complete study and recitation as a total process, it should be divided into meaningful units, each mastered and recited separately. After each of these parts can be repeated correctly, the whole selection should be reviewed and recited.

The value of whole learning lies in the fact that usable associations are formed during the learning process. Piecemeal learning too often is not integrated into the experience patterns in such way as to be functional when the individual wants to make use of it later.

Question Raising. Dewey believed that thinking starts with a doubt or problem. A question, whether raised by the teacher or by the reader himself, can do much to assist the thought process during the reading of any passage. If the reader has something around which to associate his ideas, he is able then to understand what he is reading. The good teacher of reading raises a question that is answered in the printed material before he calls upon the child to read it. By so doing he assists the child to understand what he reads.

The principal purpose of questions at the ends of the chapters or units in a textbook is to give students and teachers focal points around which ideas can be organized during class discussion. If prestudy questions are not given by the teacher as guides in the preparation of home assignments, students as they are reading the assignment should ask themselves the kinds of questions that are likely to be raised by the teacher during the discussion of the material. An alert and successful student often can predict the specific points or areas that the teacher is likely to stress in a test or a final examination. He then prepares carefully to answer expected questions.

Outlining and Taking Notes. The learning process is helped by those teachers who, during a lesson period, place the important points of the discussion on the blackboard. Similarly, students find that home study is facilitated by outlining study material or entering difficult or complex concepts in their notebook. Merely to take notes has little value as a learning procedure. To serve as learning aids the notes must be organized and mastered by the learner as he records them. When outlines or written notations consist of well-organized and carefully selected materials the learner can fill in mentally most of the subordinate details. Readiness for recall is improved when study material is arranged in sequential order in a well-organized outline or set of notes, which the learner reviews from time to time.

Interpretation of Tables and Graphs. Tables and graphs are being used increasingly as learning aids to present pertinent data in concise form. Data presented compactly in the form of a chart, a graph or a table usually can be interpreted more accurately and more quickly than if they were described in words. Yet these aids have value for a learner only if or when he has been trained to interpret them correctly. Without such training, even college students sometimes find it difficult to understand them.

Summarizing, Review, and Overlearning. Summarizing the important aspects of a learning unit helps a student integrate his learning for better retention. The extent to which he succeeds, however, depends upon the ideas he has gained, the interrelationships he has established, and the kind of applications he is able to make. Since forgetting sets in as soon as learning practice is completed, planned reviews of learned materials delay the onset of forgetting and lessen the amount forgotten. Written summarizations, like outlines and notes, serve as excellent media for review and consequent overlearning. Whether overlearning takes place during the original learning experience or occurs as an outcome of review, to learn beyond the point of immediate recall is essential to good retention.

In order to study effectively the student needs to have at his desk all the study aids that he will need to complete the assignment. These materials include pencils, pens and paper, textbooks, reference books, and any other aids that may be useful. The student should provide these aids before he begins to study.

Flash cards can be useful to effective study. The student who prepares study cards for each subject is likely to find them most helpful in the mastery of the subject. He can systemmatize study material by using 3 x 5 index cards. The student looks for an important idea in the learning material and prepares a question to cover it. The question may be an idea or a fact. The question can be placed on the face side of the card and the answer on the reverse side. Drill with the cards until mastery of facts or ideas have been achieved. The index card system is adaptable in a wide range of subjects.

An example of this study approach is given here to suggest how a set of cards can be prepared and how they can be used.

Face of Card	Reverse Side of Card
Who was the first man on the moon? Date?	Neil Armstrong. July 20, 1969

Face of Card	Reverse Side of Card
What is the average length of a newborn boy baby'	Approximately 20.5 inches

Characteristics of Good Study Habits. Reference was made earlier in the chapter to a teacher's responsibility in respect to his pupil's study habits. As learners' study habits are being improved through teacher application, it is good policy for the teacher to present specific study approaches in such form that learners are reminded to utilize them either in classroom learning situations or during assignment preparation.

The following list of suggestions is given by some teachers to their students, either in written form or dictated to them for entry into their notebooks. The implication of each suggestion, of course, should be understood by the learner. Otherwise, it will have no value for him.

1. Study with a definite purpose in mind.
2. Evaluate immediate and remote goals.
3. Provide a definite place for study.
4. Seek physical conditions that are conducive to study.
5. Plan and follow a definite time schedule.
6. Look for the main ideas of reading material.
7. Cultivate the habit of reading rapidly and carefully.
8. Outline the study material.
9. Take brief, well-organized notes.
10. Evaluate the difficulty of the material.
11. Raise significant questions on the material to be learned; then answer them.
12. Study with intent to recall.
13. Give careful attention to all illustrative material.
14. Complete all study assignments.
15. Intersperse active study with rest periods.
16. Employ the "whole" method of learning whenever possible.
17. Concentrate on what you are studying at the time.
18. Shut out emotional distractions.
19. Overlearn sufficiently for delayed recall.
20. Learn to review and to summarize.
21. Be alert to ideas emphasized by the teacher.
22. Reflect on and challenge questionable statements made by authors.
23. Investigate points of view of several authorities.
24. Apply subject matter learned in as many practical situations as possible.
25. Make intelligent use of the dictionary.[1]

[1] L. D. Crow, Alice Crow, and C. E. Skinner, *Psychology in Nursing Practice*, 2d ed. The Macmillan Company, New York, p. 211.

CHAPTER 16

PROBLEM SOLVING AND CREATIVE THINKING

The chief attribute of a human being is his ability to think and reason. His ability to solve problems has helped him extend his average life span as well as enjoy many comforts of living. Organized thinking or problem solving is one of the most important areas of learning.

The Thinking Process

Simple or relatively uncontrolled thinking is characteristic of reverie, daydreaming, and dreaming during sleep. Free association accounts for most of the content of daydreams and night dreams, but both have definite themes that help determine the direction of associations. Thinking that is purposeful, aimed at the solution of a problem, becomes reasoning.

Nature of Thinking. Mental activity fluctuates between daydreaming and reasoning or problem solving. Thinking is an active process that includes the utilization of images, subvocal speech, words, signs, symbols, percepts, and abstract concepts. Abstract thinking enables an individual to think about a problem that goes beyond the immediate present.

Conditions for Thinking. At first the thinking of a child tends to be practical, and is confined to concrete objects. With the acquisition of language he makes great progress in thinking. Later, he assigns causes to phenomena more because of their logical relationships or their effect upon one another than because of their appearance.

Effective thinking is based upon ability, interest, and breadth of experience; it involves proper selectivity among experiences, and well-formed habits. Each individual is dependent upon his own resources for productive thinking. He constantly must reorganize his experiences as he utilizes the respective mental processes that usually are identified with good thinking, i.e., direction, interpretation, selection, insight, creation, and criticism.

Reasoning or Problem Solving

When habitual behavior cannot be used in the solution of a problem the individual must turn to the utilization of those mental processes that are more complicated than free association of experiences and ideas. The thinking then is aimed at the solution of a problem in whole or in part, and it can be designated reasoning or problem solving. According to Dewey, problem solving has three aspects: conception, reasoning, and judgment.

There are five significant steps in reasoning: (1) a felt difficulty, (2) understanding of the problem, (3) classification of data, (4) suggestions of possible solutions (hypotheses), and (5) evaluation and verification. Two major mental processes involved in problem solving are *induction* (using data for generalizing), and *deduction* (making certain inferences from the generalizations), that is, going from the specific to the general (induction), and going from the general to the specific (deduction).

A Felt Difficulty. Reasoning is initiated by situations which cannot be met in a routine manner. A person fulfills many of his daily duties and obligations satisfactorily by following a routine or habitual mode of response, with little need for purposeful thinking. As soon as his habitual modes of response fail him in meeting a situation that may arise he is experiencing a problem and he attempts to solve it through reasoning about it. Reasoning may be initiated by problems such as the functioning of a tubeless tire, starting an automatic washing machine, driving a gear-shift car, reaching a certain city, getting a desired job, and other more or less complex problems. The first condition of problem solving is awareness of a difficulty.

Much of school learning involves the solution of appropriate problems. Unless the problem is associated with the young person's immediate experience, he may not be aware of a problem situation. Hence he needs help to recognize the problem or felt difficulty. A good thought question usually aids in initiating the reasoning process. It motivates the learner to engage in the kind of thinking that may result in the formulation of new opinions or concepts. To be effective, however, the question must be suited to the learner's level of experience and understanding.

Understanding the Problem. When the existence of a problem is recognized, the individual must be able to delimit it, define it, or understand it. He will not be able to solve it unless he knows exactly what the difficulty is. The adequacy of his understanding of it depends upon his ability to recall past experiences that are related to the problem. An accurate, objective understanding of the entire problem situation enables him to isolate those elements of it that do not respond to his habitual mode of reaction. The alert thinker is thereby motivated to employ reasoning in his search for a suitable solution.

The experiential background of understanding determines the direction of an individual's activity as he is impelled to solve his problem. Many illustrations could be cited to describe the behavior of relatively inexperienced children and adults. A mechanical toy refuses to function. The child is aware of the fact that his train stands still on the track, and understands that the difficulty lies in the switch that controls the electric power. Since his understanding of the difficulty is limited by his meager background of experience, he is impelled to seek the help of his father, whose greater understanding of the electric controls enables him to do what is needed to set the train in motion. Similarly, in school learning, a pupil's understanding even of a suitable learning problem may be insufficient. The teacher's function then is to help the learner improve his understanding, so that in the future the learner can meet similar problems more effectively.

Classification of Data. Availability of complete data is essential to the avoidance of erroneous conclusions. The location, evaluation, and organization of the data are basic to the effectiveness of the reasoning process. If an individual does not possess the necessary information to solve a problem, he should continue to study or to investigate until he has enough data for the solution of the difficulty. For an evolved conclusion to be correct, the utilized data must be relevant and accurate.

A trained specialist often arrives at correct judgments quickly because he is fully cognizant of the pertinent facts bearing on the problem. Lay people usually accept decisions made by a person possessing a wealth of knowledge in a special field such as medicine, law, finance, or another knowledge or skill area. Especially is this true if previous judgments made by the person have been correct. Some high school and college students, however, who have learned some facts believe that they have full knowledge concerning a situation. Consequently, much of their reasoning is erroneous, namely, because they are not aware of their lack of complete information relative to the problem to be solved.

The present availability of research materials enables a learner to procure data from many sources. He has access to books, pictures, radio and television programs, specialists in various fields, and numerous other sources of information. The validity of his conclusions depends, therefore, upon the pertinency of his selected data, and the insightful organization or classification of the obtained data, through the functioning of the mental processes.

Evolved Hypotheses. Tentative inferences or preliminary hypotheses accompany the comprehension of the problem. Inferences involve recall of past experience and are limited by what the individual already knows about the situation. For example, if a person were confronted with the problem of forming four equilateral triangles by using only six toothpicks or six match sticks, he probably would manipulate the objects according to the trial-error-trial-success method until he either finds the solution or fails in his attempts. Before each trial, however, he might think of various questions, such as whether the entire match is used to form one side, if it is possible to form four triangles, or what would happen if two match sticks were crossed. Questions concerning possible approaches would continue as thinking aids to the solution until the correct formation is reached, or interest in the problem wanes and the manipulation process ceases. He may attack it again if he is given the cue to think in at least three dimensions.

An understanding of a question to be answered, a goal to be reached, or a particular problem to be solved helps in establishing inferences. For example, the brake light of an automobile stays on when the foot pedal is not pressed down. Although he knows that something is wrong, the untrained person may think that there still is contact with the brake pedal; the trained person, however, knows that after a period of usage a short circuit may develop in the contact unit, necessitating replacement of the unit.

An individual gains insight into the relationships among the data that he has gathered, or that he possesses, through mental activity in which both induction and deduction are employed. He establishes certain inferences or hypotheses and then applies the one that seems to offer a successful solution of the problem. If the first tentative hypothesis is not satisfactory, he continues to utilize his other inferences until he finds the one that seems to fit. If he has not made successful progress after devoting a great deal of time and energy to the problem, he may become so discouraged that he stops working on it. He then attempts to explain his failure in one of several ways: (1) the problem is unsolvable, (2) his basic data are inaccurate, (3) his training background is inadequate, or (4) he does not possess sufficient insight or mental skill to recognize the meaning of the problem and to organize the conceptual relationships.

There is a wide variation in people's ability to formulate adequate hypotheses. This variation is one of the most significant teaching problems. The pupils in an average class differ greatly in relation to the various aspects of problem solving. Included among the area differences are: (1) awareness of the existence of a problem, (2) understanding of its significance, (3) possession of relevant experiential background, (4) willingness to secure pertinent data, (5) insight and power of mental organization of data, (6) ability to formulate hypotheses. First, the teacher is faced with the problem of recognizing these differences. Then, in terms of them, he must formulate questions and present problems in learning in such way that the mentally slow are not discouraged and that, at the same time, the mentally superior are challenged sufficiently.

Evaluation and Verification. As indicated in the foregoing, the final step is to verify the selected hypothesis to discover if it meets the conditions or demands of the problem. Evaluating questions are: Have all the established facts and principles been considered? Is the validity of the involved thinking process satisfactory? What critical evaluation was made during the course of the solution? Were all mental biases eliminated? Although the reasoning of many adults is accompanied by emotional concomitants, children especially tend to see their problems according to predetermined wants or interests.

An individual, young or older, may need to be helped to recognize any personal bias, prejudice, or other limitation in his thinking that interferes with his reaching objective and sound conclusions. Personal bias has no place in scientific procedure. One of the responsibilities of a teacher is to attempt to engender in each of his pupils a constructively scientific attitude toward problems. To do this, the teacher himself must be free from prejudice or any emotional involvement in relation to the content of his thinking. Complete objectivity is a difficult attitude for some teachers to achieve, especially in learning areas, such as literary or other appreciations and the social sciences.

Creative Thinking

Creative thinking is directed toward a goal. In that respect, it is more like reasoning than free mental association or reverie. The distinction between creative thought and reasoning lies in the nature of the goal. Reasoning implies mental organization of known data. Creative thinking is pointed at a new or original outcome. The original outcome may be the result of only one person's creative thinking; the same or similar outcomes may be achieved by two or more individuals, each working independently of the others. The James-Lange theory as an explanation of the emotions is an example in point. Both William James and Carl Lange arrived at identical conclusions without either of them consulting with the other or being aware that the other's thinking was directed toward the same outcome.

Mental Processes Involved in Creative Thinking. Unlike the "building-up" process of reasoning, creative thinking progresses toward its goal in irregular and unpredictable fashion. In spite of its irregularities of procedure, creative thinking appears to include four distinct phases: *preparation, incubation, illumination,* and *revision*. Creative thinking involves experience, association, and expression—the same processes that are utilized in other forms of thinking.

Preparation. Preparation starts as soon as the individual focuses his thoughts on a problem of creation. During this period, materials are assembled by the creator and ideas are formed, often with little evidence of insight into the outcomes of the project. Usually the period of preparation is longer than the individual himself or others realize, although it sometimes is possible for a person to complete an act of creative thinking very quickly.

Incubation. Following the initial state of preparation there is a seemingly inactive period when vague aspects of creative expression are taking form. This is the stage that is characterized by extended plateaus during which nothing seems to be accomplished. An individual may become discouraged by his apparent failure to produce tangible results or by his inability to perceive new relationships.

The incubation period may last for months or even for

years. Some artists, scientists, and inventors report that they often incubate an idea for long periods of complete inactivity. They may give some slight attention to it occasionally, but for the most part tend to forget it. Yet they never lose sight of the fact that they are interested in the idea. Some creative activations, however, come with a flash and must be dealt with at the moment.

Illumination. During an extended period of incubation, insight may come rather suddenly concerning the organization of a central idea, a kind of Gestalt, such as the plan of a poem, the design of a picture, or the general approach to an experiment or an invention. The recognition of relationships that had eluded the individual earlier often appears with amazing suddenness. Although illumination appears to be spontaneous, it is accompanied by intense emotion. An individual who has been thinking about an idea for a long time may display great emotionalism at the culmination of a creative act.

Revision. Once a new idea has emerged, it needs to be refined and put into such form that it can be understood, appreciated, or used by others. The creator of the idea now can relax a little as he assesses the steps of the formative process and perhaps of the total production. Most progress in creative work proceeds step by step. An inventor, for example, is never satisfied with his new achievement. A poet may devote a considerable amount of time and thought in searching for a more colorful or meaningful word than the one he originally used in his poem.

The automobile of today is very different from what it was 50 years ago. In the fields of scientific investigation, exploration and invention, the creative thinking and consequent overt creative production of one man often is the starting point for continued refinement or expansion that reflects the creative thinking of his successors.

The Creative Years. There is no apparent relationship between an individual's age and his power to engage in creative thinking. A young person has fewer bad habits to overcome but the older person has more experience upon which to build. Some creative geniuses such as Keats and Shelley made outstanding creative contributions before the age of 35. Many examples also can be cited of superior creative production at the other end of the age scale. Milton was 50 when he produced *Paradise Lost.* Victor Hugo was past 58 when he wrote *Les Miserables.* Goethe spent the years between the ages of 57 and 82 in creating *Faust.* Some of Wagner's and Beethoven's best musical compositions were created after the age of 45. Scientists, notably Edison and Keyserling, were still inventing during their old age.

A study has been made by Lehman concerning the respective ages at which creative geniuses have made their greatest contributions. After having their productions rated by competent men, Lehman determined the age of the genius when his *best* contribution was made. He ascertained the average number of *best* contributions for each 5-year interval. Although various best contributions were created at ages ranging from the age of 20 to over 80, the ages at which the largest number of best contributions appear to be made in science, invention, and literature are given in Table 1.

THE AGES AT WHICH THE LARGEST NUMBER OF BEST CONTRIBUTIONS ARE MADE IN SCIENCE, INVENTION, AND LITERATURE[1]

Field	*Number of Contributors*	*Number of Contributions*	*Best Years*
Poetry	82	797	26–30
Chemistry	244	993	28–32
Physics	90	141	30–34
Inventions	402	554	31–35
Short Story	220	1396	31–37
Mathematics	163	453	34–38
Literature	101	224	38–42
Astronomy	63	83	43–47

[1] H. C. Lehman, "The Creative Years in Science and Literature," *The Scientific Monthly,* Vol. 43, 1936, p. 162. Reprinted by permission of the author and the journal.

CHAPTER 17

PSYCHOLOGY OF SPECIFIC SUBJECT AREAS

Education is concerned with the learning process in all learning areas. The effectiveness of the learning is determined by the extent to which the individual utilizes his experiences in his daily living. If the information learned becomes functional, he has learned well. Applying the psychology associated with school subjects can help learners develop those knowledges, emotional attitudes, and skills which will enable them to become acceptable members of a group. Application of psychology to the various school subjects in the elementary and high school is discussed briefly, since a complete treatment of each subject would require a separate volume.*

Psychology of Oral and Written Expression

Language is used to communicate with others. The form that the language takes varies with the age of the individual and his ability. The very young child coos, cries, and uses body movements as forms of response. He acquires his early language habits largely through his attempts to imitate the language habits of those about him. The mastery of language is basic to the mastery of learning content and to successful intercommunication.

Success in the acquisition of language is related closely to the capacity of the individual for effective thinking and expression, and to the kind of instruction he receives. Language mastery includes the interpretation of words (symbols) as the individual attempts to acquire thought from the oral expression of others or from the printed page. Ability in comprehension and expression increases as the individual matures in his ability to perceive, and to give attention to language forms and to precision of meaning.

---

* An invaluable compact treatment is available in Dwight W. Allen and Eli Seifman, eds., *The Teacher's Handbook* (Glenview, Illinois: Scott, Foresman, 1971).

Oral Expression. Oral expression begins as soon as the infant is able to make sounds. His early screaming represents emotional reaction more than mental activity. This is followed by the babbling stage, during which the baby attempts to relate to his elders by saying Ma-Ma and Da-Da. With greater maturation, he comes to use words that are related to his wants. At first, only his family can interpret his language. He soon learns to express himself in the language of others in his environment.

By the age of three, the child's vocabulary contains about 900 words. During the next 5 years, the child increases his vocabulary at the rate of approximately 500 words each year. Hence at the age of 5 he uses about 2,000 words, and at the age of 8 uses about 3,500 words. As he improves his ability to use these words in correct sentences in simple conversation, he is enabled to give more meaningful expression to his ideas. Oral language habits are being formed through repeated intercommunication experiences with his close associates. Imitation is employed in the development of speech patterns. Hence his speech patterns develop in accordance with the kind of speech that he hears.

There appears to be a close relationship between the adequacy of an individual's speech patterns and his mental acuity. Slow mental reactions usually are accompanied by slow, hesitant, or inarticulate speech. If slow learners are to understand what they are supposed to learn, the teacher must present simple concepts, in simple, easily understood language or they will not comprehend relationships between the ideas expressed. Rapid learners sometimes think so rapidly that they cannot express themselves clearly. Many so-called speech difficulties such as careless or inaccurate pronounciation and language usage reflect the sloppy speech heard in the home or immediate neighborhood.

Most speech difficulties can be corrected through proper training. There are some speech defects, however, that are deep rooted and have a physical as well as a psychological origin. Those caused by deafness or defective speech organs are difficult to correct. Stammering, stuttering, and inarticulation are associated with emotional tensions, usually resulting from fear-arousing or shock experiences. Emotional relaxation through the removal or amelioration of tension-causing conditions is needed to improve the speech difficulty.

Oral expression serves the child well long before he is able to write. At first, his ability to communicate adequately is limited. Exposure to and imitation of the speech patterns of persons in his immediate environment as he responds to what they say to him cause certain forms of expressions to become habitual. His sentence structure for oral expression gradually becomes set. As his thinking follows certain specific paths, he soon can be identified through the way he expresses himself. He enjoys talking with others and often gives full play to his imagination during his conversations either with his playmates or with elders.

Written Expression. Adequate expression of ideas in written form requires skill in content organization, and mastery of the mechanics of writing. The child has many obstacles to overcome before he can express himself successfully in any of the various kinds of written composition. He must (1) learn to form the characters needed in writing, (2) possess an adequate vocabulary, (3) learn to use correct grammatical construction, and (4) master the elements of form and style, according to the purpose of the writing, such as description, narration, or letter writing. As important as these aspects of written expression, if not more so, are the ideas that constitute the content of written composition.

The child is inducted gradually into the art of good writing. At first he expresses himself in short sentences; then he learns to arrange his sentences into short paragraphs that center around one topic. Considerable practice is needed by most children in learning to write long compositions that include well-organized paragraphs and that present sequential ideas in such a way as to hold the interest of readers.

The content of younger children's compositions usually shows their tendency to imitate. With increasing maturity, greater appreciation of themselves in relation to other persons and enlarging experience, older elementary school children begin to be more creative in their thinking and expression.

Differences between the sexes in writing interests begin to show themselves early. Boys usually want to write about topics that are related to their immediate environment, such as sports of any kind and current happenings. The compositions of girls tend to be less factual, with evidences of greater use of the imagination. Boys and girls differ also in the mechanics of writing; in general, the former use short, terse sentences; the latter are likely to use longer sentences and paragraphs. Moreover, most girls are more careful than boys about grammatical structure, spelling, and penmanship.

A good psychological principle to apply in teaching composition is to encourage creativity, in so far as the imagination is not permitted to distort actual facts. Although young people should be motivated toward spontaneous writing, mechanical corrections must not be disregarded. It is difficult for the inexperienced writer to give equal attention to these two aspects of written composition. Either the composition contains excellent ideas, poorly expressed, or it tends to be mechanically correct but artificial. Individual differences that continue through adulthood probably are as noticeable in this area of learning as in any other, if not more so. Instruction in written composition therefore needs to be geared to the strengths and weaknesses of individual learners.

There has been disagreement among school people concerning the teaching of composition. Formerly, emphasis was placed upon the mechanics of writing, especially during the beginning stages of learning, with the result that some young people developed a correct but relatively stilted form of written expression. More recently, greater recognition has been given to the importance of the content as expressing an individual's thoughts or feelings. Consequently, there has been a trend toward subordinating mechanical accuracy, sometimes logical organization, to the creative aspect, resulting in considerable concern among college instructors over the careless, even illiterate writing of their students.

Spelling. Included among the mechanics of adequate written expression is correct spelling. Probably the most important psychological principle here is that children learn to spell those words for which they will have the greatest use. Although it is good teaching procedure to teach a word when the need arises, there are certain basic words that need to be overlearned to the point that their spelling becomes automatic. Hence basic word lists have been constructed for learners at each stage of their development. One of these lists, Jones's "One Hundred Spelling Demons," includes apparently simple words (many of them consisting of one syllable) that are troublesome even to adults. Other lists have been evolved from studies of young people's progressive writing vocabularies.

Adults as well as young people differ in their attitudes toward the importance of spelling. Some parents and teachers stress the need of a child's learning to spell many words, even those which he probably never will use and the meaning of which he does not know. The present trend, however, is toward teaching spelling words in their contextual relationships. The meaning of a word, as well as its correct spelling, is learned so that it has functional value in the learner's written vocabulary.

There still are people who believe that an extremely bright person should be permitted to be careless about spelling, since his ideas are so prolific that he cannot bother about petty details. Some teachers are willing to excuse the spelling mistakes of their students who demonstrate superiority in solving complex problems. Although many nonintellectual individuals become excellent spellers through the utilization of rote memory, there is no psychological basis for the belief that the intellectually superior cannot or should not learn to spell correctly. The bright profit from being held to rigid standards of correctness in all aspects of learning that have social significance. Moreover, most children can be motivated to develop an attitude of personal pride in and responsibility for learning to spell correctly.

Recognition of the correct spelling of a word can be demonstrated by an individual in any of four ways: (1) detection of correctness when the word is spelled orally by another person, (2) visual perception of correctness of a written word, (3) auditory perception of correctness as he himself vocalizes the spelling of the word, and (4) kinesthetic perception of correctness as he writes or types the word. The last two involve muscular activity. Although a child's learning to spell is helped by hearing another person spell it and seeing it spelled correctly, the correct spelling of a word probably is "fixed" through the formation of a motor and conceptual habit, as the learner practices writing the word in meaningful context.

At one time it was customary to teach spelling rules which were supposed to help learners spell correctly "according to rule." The many exceptions to a rule tend to confuse rather than to aid. Yet some spelling rules may have value if they are applied as needed rather than becoming an end in teaching. In general, however, it has been found that correct spelling patterns are learned best through motor exercise. The length and number of practice periods needed vary with the ability of the learner. Continued drill in spelling words that already are automatic habits is boring and time consuming. Pretests are helpful to both the teacher and the learner to discover those words which require further overlearning. Certain errors in spelling occur so often that consistent and intensive practice is needed to prevent or eliminate them.

Handwriting. The average child begins to scribble and draw before the age of 5. At first, he utilizes large sweeping movements of the hand and arm, together with eye coordination. Because manual dexterity develops slowly, a complex form of skill, such as handwriting, has a slow growth. Penmanship improves with maturation as the child's perceptual powers improve and he acquires greater dexterity in hand, wrist, finger, and arm movement.

Handwriting involves not only correct formation of letters but also joining them into acceptable patterns of words and sentences. Even though a child is not expected to attain the perfection of a model, he should have a model of penmanship available, since imitation plays an important role in its mastery. Handwriting scales help teachers realize that most children cannot imitate a penmanship model exactly until perhaps in the upper grades, after they have had a long period of training and practice.

In some schools and school systems, children of the first two or three grades of the elementary school have been or still are taught manuscript writing and then introduced to cursive writing. This procedure is based upon a belief that the resemblance of manuscript writing to print would make it easier for the child to associate his beginning writing efforts with the letter formations he sees in his readers. There is no conclusive evidence that this approach helps a child's learning process. The transition from manuscript to cursive writing necessitates changing from his already formed motor habits to new muscular patterns.

Regardless of the approach used to start a child's learning to write, some people claim, perhaps rightly, that the handwriting of too many high school and college students is illegible. The cause may be individual carelessness, increasing use of typewriters, or the decreasing attention to continued training beyond the fifth or sixth grade of the elementary schools. In penmanship, as in spelling, continued correct practice is required.

Grammar. Traditionally, learning in the area of oral and written expression on the elementary school level included study of grammatical construction, involving mastery of the rules of syntax, diagrammatic analysis of long, involved sentences, and parsing of the word components of such sentences. Later, studies were conducted to discover the extent to which there is a relationship between the study of grammar and facility in oral and written expression. The findings indicated a negative relationship. It was concluded, therefore, that exposure to correct usage and guided practice in speaking and writing correctly have more value than the actual study of grammar. Hence the principle of learning to do by doing has been applied, resulting in relatively incidental teaching of grammar in many elementary schools, and less on the secondary school level.

Many adults, especially college students and business secretaries, who have received little or no training in grammatical construction, find that, although they recognize structural faults, they are unable to identify the errors. As a result, high school and college teachers, as well as the students themselves, are coming to appreciate the fact that an understanding of basic grammatical construction is valuable. Hence school people on all levels are beginning to include some study of grammar that will have practical application, without returning to former rote memorization of grammatical rules, and detailed analysis and parsing exercises.

The Psychology of Reading

Reading involves the ability of an individual to put meaning into written or printed words in their contextual relationships. The reader's ability to interpret correctly the meanings that supposedly are conveyed by the written words depends upon his conceptual understanding of them in terms of his experiential background and his power of insight.

Reading Readiness. Basic factors of degree of reading readiness are maturational level and extent of interest in reading or felt need to read. It is believed by some psychologists that a child is not ready to begin to read until his mental age is about 6 years. Some children who exhibit little or no interest in reading during their first year in school suddenly begin to read with interest and understanding. Because of differences in reading readiness among elementary school entrants, some educators recommend that formal instruction in reading be deferred until the second grade or later.

Eye Movements. Reading skill is related to eye movement. Studies of eye movements during reading have led to the conclusion that reading is a kind of visual exploration. Reading reactions that can be measured include (1) the span of recognition (number of words recognized in one attention span), (2) rate of recognition (duration of eye fixation), (3) rhythmical progression along the line (regressions per line) during silent reading, and (4) eye-voice span during oral reading (number of letter spaces between the reading material and what is being vocalized by the reader).

During the process of reading the eyes do not move smoothly across a line. As the eyes move across the line they pause for numerous fixations. It is during these pauses that a word or several words are perceived and recognized. The number of fixations per line is determined by such factors as (1) the ability of the individual, (2) his interest in the material and his desire to master it, (3) his familiarity with the material, and (4) its nature and degree of difficulty.

Good readers grasp more words at a single fixation and the eyes move more rapidly over the page than is characteristic of poor readers. Poor readers have more eye regressions, that is, the eyes have a tendency to move backward from the point of fixation instead of going regularly forward. The skilled reader makes fewer fixations of the eyes, has a shorter duration of fixations, and follows a definite reading rhythm more closely.

Comprehension. Both oral and silent reading are to be encouraged during the early grades—oral for comprehension, and silent for speed and comprehension. In general, reading rate and comprehension are closely related. With proper guidance, speed and comprehension increase with the developing years. In order to insure adequate progress, reading material should be graded to the maturity status and interest level of the learner.

Degree of intelligence is a determiner of correctness and ease of reading comprehension. Conceptual relationships are achieved slowly by some mentally inferior learners. Even quick learners may lack the necessary experiences to interpret correctly the words they see. Some learners develop incorrect meanings that tend to persist unless or until they are corrected.

Psychology of Social Studies

In our present society, a reasonable understanding of human relationships and their personal and social implications is becoming increasingly necessary. Since a young child's early social habits usually reflect the cultural mores of his home and immediate neighborhood, he may bring to his elementary school experience many misconceptions of the larger world and the people in it. Even during his school years, exposure to various avenues of news reporting concerning current political, social, economic and welfare problems may intensify a young person's earlier misconceptions or induce new misunderstandings, prejudices, or mental confusion. It is the school's function to help him correct and objectify his thinking.

Objectives. Acquisition of social concepts is one of the objectives of the social studies, including building new concepts as well as reconstruction of those already formed. The purpose of study in this field is aimed at helping the learner toward development of attitudes of cooperation in his relationships with the other members of the society of which he is a part, without regard to race, color, or creed. Included also in the social studies are the geographic settings and the historic backgrounds of present-day social, civic, and economic conditions and happenings.

The social concept to be acquired by elementary school children must be correct but relatively simple and suited to their individual power to comprehend. The fundamental objectives of social studies on the junior and senior high school levels are intensifications and expansions of those operating on the elementary level. Social living takes place on all levels; the form it follows varies with the experiential background of the individual as well as with his ability and willingness to improve his behavior and attitudes as he gains increasing understanding of social living. The high school pupil, for example, generally (1) becomes more sympathetic in his attitude toward people all over the world and less egocentric in his outlook, (2) develops better self-control, (3) gains greater understanding of economic interrelationships and of the significance of contemporary events, (4) learns to understand and to participate in various citizenship activities, and (5) achieves a more realistic appreciation of his responsibilities as well as of his rights in small or large groups.

Social Study Approaches. In the teaching of civic and social responsibility, the local community, cooperating with the school, can provide experiences for the pupils that will help them improve their concepts of community life.* The social environment can be made more meaningful to learners through the use of visual aids, and by trips to museums, botanic gardens, waterfronts, and other places of interest. Television and radio programs, and pictures taken by the students themselves are helpful, as are learner activity programs and projects, such as historic pageants and plays, debates on appropriate issues, school self-government, and group participation in community-sponsored civic or welfare activities.

From early childhood onward, an individual should understand and apply the concept of the democratic rights and re-

* For the relationship with the community and its resources, see Leonard Covello, *The Teacher In The Urban Community* (Totowa, N. J.: Littlefield & Adams, 1970).

sponsibilities of all people. The one-world concept challenges the teacher to present, in proper perspective, significant historical events and existing interrelations of differing peoples. Each societal group has something to contribute to other groups and gives yearly recognition to a notable event in its history. The understanding of human relationships can be furthered through the social studies by apprising learners of the characteristic attributes of each world group.

A high school student may become confused over differences between his own attitudes toward people and social and political issues and those of his teachers, especially his teacher of social studies. It then becomes the responsibility of that teacher to encourage objective, fact-based, and complete discussions on controversial issues, without injecting his own biases into the discussion.

It is characteristic of adolescents to become emotionally aroused over human relationships. One of their dominant motives is to help the underdog and to reform undesirable conditions. It is hard for them to realize that social changes come slowly and are fraught with many problems. They become impatient of the slow progress achieved through social evolution, and may seem to advocate revolution. Alert teachers can capture this youthful enthusiasm and help direct it toward the development of good, democratic citizenship.

Psychology of Mathematics

The concept of measurable quantity is important in its relation to the practical application of scientific and social principles. Since the study of mathematics is concerned with an understanding of numbers and symbols, and of quantitative relationships, learning in mathematics should be associated with the day-by-day experiences of the learner.

Learning Algebra. Algebra involves a system of numbers that sometimes is called "the science of numbers." It represents an extension of the numbers and symbols used in arithmetic, and deals with the general aspects of mathematical processes without reference to the quantitative value of each symbol used. A slightly new language is introduced to the learner as he now is faced with the problem of learning how to deal with signs that represent positive and negative values.

Success in learning algebra is based upon an understanding of the fundamentals in arithmetic. Unless the student who enrolls in algebra is competent in arithmetic he may face failure. At the same time, study of algebra involves so many abstract concepts that the learner must be trained to work with abstractions and algebraic interrelationships. It has been found that pupils with a high degree of intelligence are more likely to succeed in algebra than those with less ability. Studies also have shown that boys are slightly superior to girls in the study of algebra.

Learning Geometry. Since plane geometry is a study of space and space relations, a pupil may be introduced to it before he studies algebra. In fact, this practice is being followed in some places. The mental processes involved in learning geometry include the learner's ability to: (1) master symbols, (2) apply certain principles of logic, and (3) think through geometric problems and hypotheses.

A learner's interest can be aroused by helping him recognize the importance of geometry in his everyday life. For example, he lives in space, and experiences space every moment of the day. The length of a step, the nearness of a car, the height of a tree, or the size of a book is a special relationship to which he reacts almost daily, without much awareness of the fact. In this area of study there is an attempt to bridge the gap between personally experienced space relations and the formalized space situations presented in geometry.

Geometry gives the learner an opportunity to do reflective thinking. Each theorem or exercise makes possible utilization of all the steps of problem solving. There also is value to the student in experience with the principle that no demonstration proves anything beyond the limits set by the assumptions stated.

Psychology of the Natural Sciences

Most young people, especially boys, thrill to wonders of science that have resulted from the utilization of observation by scientists. Simply written but accurate descriptions of current scientific experiments and investigations are read avidly by many boys from the middle elementary school grades through the high school. In fact, some schoolboys are better informed than their elders concerning recent scientific advances in intercommunication facilities, atomic energy, attempts to contact other planets, and similar scientific efforts to discover hitherto unknown natural forces and control them for man's use.

Objectives. The objectives of education in the natural sciences reflect certain significant characteristics of the scientist: (1) his concern with the use of facts that are as free from personal bias as possible, (2) his interest in arriving at conclusions that can be verified by appropriate applications, (3) his belief that through continued inquiry the problems that have baffled man can be solved, and (4) his recognition of the fact that scientific progress must be slow and gradual. The purpose of the study of the natural sciences is to help students not only increase their knowledge and understanding of natural phenomena, but also develop scientific modes of thinking.

Stated briefly, the objectives to be attained by learners in science include development of: (1) a spirit of inquiry, (2) an attitude of independent thinking, (3) an interest in scientific procedure, (4) an attitude of open mindedness, (5) an understanding of fundamental truths, (6) a sensitivity to the forces in one's environment, (7) an appreciation of natural phenomena, and (8) skill in scientific problem solving.

Teaching Approaches. The teaching of the natural sciences can be only as good as the training of the teachers. Some teachers in the elementary schools have an inadequate science background. There are many elementary school children who know considerably more about science than the teachers. Yet the knowledge gained through the reading of magazine articles is piecemeal; the fundamental aspects of scientific inquiry are not fully understood by the readers. Hence the questions raised by these young people during their science periods require that the teacher have the ability to stimulate their thinking in terms of a sound scientific background.

On the high school level, the science teacher usually is a specialist; he is capable of dealing with the scientific problems that emerge from the experiences of the students. Rarely does the teacher need to utilize ingeniously planned techniques to motivate learning interest. With the exception of the mentally superior students, however, best learning results usually are achieved if the practical aspects of the sciences are stressed without sacrificing basic scientific principles. Some teaching approaches that appear to be success motivating are:

1. Provide opportunities for direct observation.
2. Whenever possible, utilize problems based upon life situations.

3. Attempt to develop respect for scientific procedure.
4. Relate scientific applications to other phases of school life.
5. Use visual aids to clarify the connotation of complex concepts.
6. Provide demonstrations that can be understood and observed by all pupils.

Psychology of Foreign Languages

For many years, the purpose of many high school students for studying a foreign language was merely to meet college entrance requirements. Present progress in transportation and communication facilities, combined with the effects of military service abroad, has stimulated a new interest in the mastery of foreign languages. Teaching and learning procedures are changing to meet new learner attitudes toward the languages of other countries.*

Changing Objectives. In the past, teaching emphasis, for the most part, was on vocabulary building, grammatical structure, and reading and translating, with some practice in written composition. Relatively little attention was devoted to the achievement of fluency in oral usage. Although grammatical construction still is taught, one of the chief objectives is to develop skill in comprehending what is said by a native and in speaking the language.

Teaching Approaches. Since practical usage of a foreign language (especially in its oral form) has become a major objective for teaching it, teaching procedures are undergoing considerable modification.

Although the more formal aspects of study are not neglected, there is an attempt to functionalize the learning. If an individual is to make effective use of a foreign language, he must be able to *think in that language,* rather than to think in his own and then translate mentally into the other. This teaching approach is difficult unless the teacher himself is a fluent speaker and writer in the language and is sensitive to the subtle nuances of the language.

By the time a young person reaches the high school, he usually is well grounded in the speech pattern of his own lan-

* See F. Cordasco and L. Roederer, "Modern languages and modern living," in J. S. Roucek, ed., *The Study of Foreign Languages* (New York: Philosophical Library, 1968).

guage. Therefore it may be difficult for him to develop different habits of enunciation, pronunciation, and sentence structure. The student who does not "catch on" to the new forms of speech as readily as some of his classmates may become embarrassed by his faulty speech, especially if the others are permitted to ridicule him. Consequent emotional blocking is likely to interfere with his progress in learning the language, even though he can master the vocabulary of and read materials written in the langauge.

Since children tend to be less self-conscious than adolescents, there is an educational trend toward introducing some foreign language study into the curriculum of the elementary school. The objectives here include mastery of a simple vocabulary and of some correct grammatical structures. The chief purpose of the teaching would be to help the children gain a "feel" for the language and facility in enunciation and pronunciation.

Another functional aspect of teaching a foreign language is to acquaint the learners with the people who habitually speak it. Important areas of study are the mores, customs, and beliefs of these people, a little of their historical background, and their past and present cultural contributions. Utilization of visual and auditory aids that can bring the people and their language into the learning situation is extremely helpful. Where and when it is practicable, students are encouraged to attend dramatic productions in the setting of the country and presented in the language. The art and music of the people also interest learners of the language.

In some schools, language students are encouraged to: (1) attend celebrations or any other program of activities conducted by groups of individuals living in the country of the learners but following traditional customs, and (2) correspond with young people in another country who wish to improve their ability to write in the language of the other. For example, one of the outcomes of World War II was the long-range adoption by the pupils in American schools of young children who were homeless victims of the war. In connection with the project, American high school students began to correspond with their "adopted children" in the others' language, the latter, in turn, responding as well as they could in English. Further, several European secondary schools are teamed with American schools for the purpose of aiding foreign language development through interchange of letters. These practices have psychological value in that the study of a foreign language becomes an interest-arousing and interest-maintaining functional activity, rather than merely a formal, isolated, book-and-classroom-study learning experience.

Psychology of Artistic Expression

Psychologists agree that expression of one's feelings in free, uninhibited creation of more or less recognizable pictorial productions is an effective tension releaser. This principle was applied first in the treatment of emotionally disturbed patients. It now is being utilized in the schools, with mental hygiene implications as well as for the purpose of discovering possible aptitudinal potentiality.

Bases of Self-Expression through Art. A young child enjoys scribbling and drawing pictures of anything that catches his fancy. His random movements represent spontaneous attempts at self-expression. He experiences great delight as he draws "pictures" of his ball, his daddy or mommy, his house and his city, or attempts to copy pictures from his picture book or trace models in a drawing book.

The child may show great disappointment or impatience if or when his elders fail to recognize what he is trying to represent. A small boy, for example, was convinced that his teacher did not know what a horse looks like because she could not identify his drawing as a picture of a horse.

As the child's motor equipment matures, he is enabled through adult encouragement and guidance to refine his attempts at creative expression. What he creates and how he creates it reveal a great deal about his perceptual and conceptual abilities, his degree of muscular coordination, the play of his imagination, and his developed interests. In order to give overt expression to what he experiences, he should be able to observe correctly and remember accurately. He also must recognize line and proportion relationships, be sentitive to color discrimination, and have a "feel" for rhythm.

Some children begin early to display a special talent in art. It is believed that the average person, from early childhood through adolescence, passes through three general stages of interest growth in artistic expression. During the first stage (from about 4 to 9 years old), the child attempts to draw outlines of or represent, through the utilization of paint or similar media, commonly experienced objects or scenes. The second stage (from about 9 to 14 years) is characterized by appreciative interest in objects, people, and scenes of remote places and in adventure. The adolescent stage is marked by the influence of adult interests on the artistic expressions of teen-age boys and girls.

Objectives. The objectives in teaching-learning experiences in art have changed considerably during the recent past, especially on the elementary school level. Earlier objectives tended to stress the formal, mechanical aspects of production, rather than creative self-expression. Learning goals of the past in this area resemble somewhat those of skill development in written composition.

Present-day objectives are pointed toward (1) development of appreciation of a work of art, including pictorial representation, design, construction, architecture, or any other created masterpiece that arouses in the viewer a deep feeling directed not only to the piece of art itself, but also to the meaning attached to it by the viewer, and (2) according to the potential abilities and interests of individual learners, the motivation and guidance of artistic reproduction or creation.

Teaching-Learning Experiences. Although children always have experienced the desire to express themselves freely through drawing, instruction in drawing formerly was almost completely formal. An object or a group of objects, supposedly suited to a class's ability to reproduce, usually was arranged in the front of the room. The pupils were expected to see and to reproduce what they saw. Considerable attention was given by the teacher to the details of form. Pupils "sighted" the model for proportional relationships, marked these on the drawing paper and then attempted to produce an accurate representation of the model. Copying of a more successful classmate's work, with little or no regard to differences in perspective, was not unknown.

A child's impulse to draw freely was limited, for the most part, to the surreptitious drawing of caricatures of the teacher or to idle doodling in notebooks during class work in another subject. Occasionally, an artistically inclined teacher, seeing these informal productions, might recognize the signs of potential ability and encourage further training. In general, however, most "art" periods, sometimes even on the secondary level, represented feeble teaching efforts by a relatively uninterested and untrained teacher, and learner participation in a boring, ineffectual school chore.

The contrast between traditional attitudes and present procedures are so marked that only through a comparison of the new with the old can one appreciate them. Today, beginning in the nursery school and continuing through the college level, creativity is stressed. On the early school levels, children are encouraged to express themselves through gross muscle, large swing appropriate media.

Clay modeling, finger painting, and easel painting with large brushes afford the younger child opportunities for expression without regard for refined detail. Beginnings of appreciative attitudes show themselves as the children view, and comment freely concerning one another's products. During this early stage, the teacher's function is to encourage and commend, and perhaps offer indirect suggestions for improvement.

Free activity is continued through the lower elementary grades. Some refinement of movement takes place as the child gradually learns to work on smaller paper with soft pencils and smaller brushes, and participates in the construction of appropriate objects. Although creative expression should not be crushed, somewhere in his progress through the high school the young person must learn some of the more detailed techniques of production. This poses difficulties for the teacher of art as it does for the teacher of written composition. Study of master pieces in art appreciation classes, combined with actual doing, can help the learner become aware of his faults and attempt to remedy them.

Improved skill and appreciation also can be fostered through participation in art projects that are associated with other learning areas. These include: preparing stage drops and other scenery for school plays and pageants, representing pictorially significant events or drawing maps in the social studies, portraying characters or scenes in the study of literature, and illustrating processes or objects in the natural sciences. Many school projects can be utilized by interested pupils as outlets for the constructive development of ability in pictorial and related artistic expression.

It is believed by some psychologists and art educators that most people have much more ability to express themselves through artistic creation than they know. Earlier, inadequate or wrong learning experiences caused inhibitions that blocked potential abilities to be expressed. It is hoped that the early encouragement of and continuation of free expression may motivate more young people to become interested in this form of self-expression. That some young people possess superior talent is not denied, however. Regardless of the quality of a learner's production, the activities involved afford opportunities for the learner to use excess energy and to release emotional tensions, and for the teacher to discover much about the learner's interests, imaginative powers, and background experiences.

Psychology of Music

Much that has been said about reading, written expression, and art appreciation and expression applies to music. Each culture has developed its own musical forms and preferences and its mode of expression. Hence music merits a place of distinction in the curriculum on all school levels. As one of the appreciation arts it is an important aspect of an individual's experience, both within and outside the school.

Children enjoy music. They like to respond to rhythmic sounds, either in song, in motion, or in appreciation. Interest in musical stimulation continues throughout the life of the individual. With increase in musical education he gradually comes to prefer the musical tones that require greater comprehension for appreciation.

The young child as well as the elementary school child needs to participate in musical expression, especially in singing and dancing. During these years, he should be permitted reasonable freedom of expression. Little attention should be given to teaching him the connotation of technical terms such as pitch, intensity, and tone quality. He should be helped to appreciate good music, since his musical tastes are influenced easily by the kinds of music he hears frequently.

During the later years of childhood and in adolescence, the individual should be helped achieve a mental as well as an emotional appreciation of music. He can be introduced to the mechanics of musical performance and learn how to distinguish between good music and mere sound production. Well-selected phonographic recordings and radio programs are excellent teaching aids, if the learners are helped to understand and appreciate the intended meaning of the musical composition and the techuiques utilized by the composer to express it.

Learning by doing applies to music as to other areas of learning. Many schools encourage pupil participation in school choruses, bands, and orchestras. Organization of junior and senior musical groups provides opportunities for young people to perform according to their maturational level and degree of skill development. Some schools provide individual instruction in instrumental music for those of their pupils who demonstrate a special interest in music and who have superior talent. Like art, self-expression through music serves as an energy user and tension releaser for all young people and many adults.

Psychology of Vocational Subjects

The making of a vocational choice probably is one of the most important problems that confront the adolescent. Although the younger child gives some thought to what he wants to be, his various vocational interests are fleeting. However, by the time an individual reaches the high school, he is expected to select a curriculum that is pointed toward an ultimate vocation. Hence he is faced with the choice of a vocational field, if not a definite vocation.

The new curriculum, with its emphasis upon general education, is helping to defer the need for a final vocational choice. This is to be commended. Although early vocational choices should not be forced, some young people decide upon a vocation early and stay with their choice. Other individuals may not make a final decision until late adolescence or early adulthood. In an increasing number of high schools, opportunities are provided to help adolescents (1) learn about vocations and their requirements, (2) make a decision in terms of personal qualities, and (3) plan toward preparation for occupational activity.

Commercial Activities Formerly the students who were assigned to the commercial curriculum were those who could not succeed in the more academic subjects. That intelligence is needed in the so-called commercial subjects—typewriting, stenography, bookkeeping and accounting, and general business practice—is confirmed by research dealing with requirements for successful achievement in these learning areas. Various curriculums in these areas, therefore, have been constructed to meet the learning needs of bright as well as slower learners.

Typewriting. The typewriter is becoming a household necessity. Hence every pupil in the senior and perhaps the junior high school can benefit from training in typewriting. Development of accuracy is important for all learners, but for those learners who are interested in it as a vocation both speed and accuracy are essential.

Learning to typewrite correctly involves (1) ability to spell correctly, (2) mastery of the keyboard, and (3) development of accuracy and speed in performance. Drill is essential in learning to use a typewriter, but there is a trend toward starting learners with meaningful material rather than with meaningless syllables. Typewriting is a motor skill in which kinesthetic rather than visual sensation is utilized to operate the keyboard. Precision of movement must be observed and a reasonable speed maintained in spite of errors. Appropriately timed music has been found to be helpful in developing speed in typewriting.

Stenography. The mastery of stenography is learning a skill which involves memorizing new symbols for concepts, interpreting their meaning, and using them correctly. The mastery of the stenographic outlines or symbols requires at least normal intelligence and good muscular coordination. For best results, this new language should become as automatic as one's verbal symbolism and number combinations.

The stenographer requires training for accuracy in auditory and visual perception. He must hear correctly what is being dictated, record the material in accurate symbols, and then interpret his notes exactly as he transcribes them. As in typewriting, both speed and accuracy are essential. During the learning process, well-spaced periods of practice are better than long, protracted periods. Correctness of symbol formation should be required of learners at all times.

Psychology of Health and Physical Education

A child's behavior responses in school often reflect his physical condition. Temporary ill health may be the resultant of fear of lesson assignments, of tests and examinations, and of standards of achievement. Helping pupils preserve mental and physical health is a school responsibility. Young people should achieve adequate knowledge and understanding concerning body structure and function, healthful diet, exercise and rest, and the maintaining of emotional balance. Since careful attention to hygienic living is likely to insure good individual adjustment, not only in physical education but in all other subject areas, the principles of good physical and mental hygiene should be applied.

Objectives. Good health habits should be developed in order that good health may be preserved and ill health prevented. Each learner should receive a physical and medical examination at least once each year. Through the practice of health rules, the young person is assured good physical development. Moreover, he and also his close associates are protected from infection and the spread of contagious diseases. Physical education now is the concern of all school people from the early school grades through the high school and college levels. That health and strength result from proper exercise is being accepted as a basic principle of instruction.

School Functions. Increase in industrialization and in concentration of population in urban centers is a promotor of conditions that are detrimental to sound physical and mental health. Hence the need for effective and practical health and physical education is imperative. All teachers, regardless of their subject fields, should exercise precautionary care of the health of their pupils, and be alert to observable symptoms of ill health. In addition, they should encourage pupils to practice good health habits, since many young people know health rules, but disregard them.

One of the means by which good health is maintained is through physical education. Everyone who participates in physical activities desires to improve his proficiency in them. Consequently, he is motivated to apply to his practice the basic psychological principles: (1) correct practice, (2) distribution of practice periods, (3) whole method of practice, and (4) an attitude which impels toward successful achievement.

The play spirit should permeate all activities in the school as well as outside it. School-sponsored play activities should be graded in terms of the age, and sometimes the sex, of the individual pupils. The level of skill proficiency also should be considered. Leaders of school sports need to impress upon their pupils, however, that it is fine to participate in athletic activities for the purpose of winning, but to win should not be the only purpose of the activity. Sportsmanship and fair play should be significant outcomes of participation in physical activities.

Present-day expansion of physical and health education and more stimulating teaching approaches are representative of modern educators' concern with all aspects of child and adolescent development. One could summarize present trends in comparison to traditional procedures in all areas of school learning by listing briefly the objectives, curriculum offerings, and teaching-learning experiences that characterize school programs in physical and health education. The principal requirements of a health program are:

1. Free, guided participation in healthful physical exercise.

2. Achievement of knowledge concerning what constitutes good physical and mental health.

3. Recognition by the school of and care of remedial physical handicaps, and educational provision for the permanently handicapped.

4. Provision of school buildings, equipment, and classroom conditions conducive to preservation of good health and prevention of ill health.

5. Learning activities geared to the learner's abilities, needs and interests.

6. Emphasis upon personal value to and practical application by the learner of content materials of learning.

8. Learning activity, a shared teacher-learner experience.

Other educational applications of psychological principles could be added. This list presents sufficient evidence of the functioning of educational psychology in school procedures. It probably should be noted, however, that learning in any area is *work,* not play, and that "learner interest" connotes long-range interest rather than immediate fancy or whim.

Psychology of Home Economics

The activities included in home economics are of practical value to every individual—man or woman—regardless of the occupational field of either. In our society, the preparation of food and the care of the home and children no longer are considered to be the exclusive responsibility of the wife and mother. Everyone has a shared responsibility.

The objectives of education in home economics include the selection and preparation of food, child care, nursing, home management, family budgeting, home decoration, and clothing design and production. Briefly stated they are to help the learner develop an interest in home making, an attitude of independent thinking on the problems associated with family life, an understanding of human relationships, and skill in dealing with the problems of family living.

Teaching approaches need to be as motivating as possible. The learner should be given opportunities for direct observation and experience. Real situations should be simulated. Respect for careful work for the needs of others should be engendered. Application to real life situations should be made and participation as well as demonstration should be the backbone of the teaching.

CHAPTER 18

INTEGRATION THROUGH TRANSFER

Young children learn with little or no awareness of what or why they are learning; some elementary school and even secondary school pupils participate in school learning because they are forced to do so, but are more interested in certain areas of out-of-school learning. In general, however, as soon as an older child or adolescent understands what it means to be a functioning member of his community he wants to learn whatever he believes will be helpful to him throughout life. He hopes that knowledge and skill acquired in school or in out-of-school activities will be useful to him in his present and future activities and in the solution of any problems he may experience. One goal of the teacher is to provide learning experiences conducive to the learner's development of behavior patterns that can be utilized in out-of-school activities and can be adapted to meet new situations.

The Nature of Transfer

Adaptability of behavior to hitherto unexperienced situations is closely associated with the extent to which learning in one area can function adequately in other areas of school or out-of-school activities.

Meaning of Transfer in Learning. Transfer implies that learning experienced in one situation affects learning or behavior in another. Some things mastered in one learning area can be utilized in other learning areas or in activities outside the learning situation. Some learnings have general application value as, for example, the spelling of commonly used words, simple arithmetical combinations, trained penmanship, vocabulary and language patterns, and other basic knowledge and skills. It is not possible, however, for an individual to acquire, through formal schooling, habit patterns, knowledge, and skills that in their learned form will function adequately in every specific future situation in which he may find himself.

Each new situation confronting the learner contains new elements that challenge him to use his habitual responses in a new way. He must be able not only to remember similar previous experiences but also to discriminate and to select from his experiences those elements that contribute to the formation of a new habit, idea, or skill. The process of carrying over habits of thinking, knowledge, or skills from one learning area to another is called *transfer of learning,* or *transfer of training.*

Positive and Negative Transfer. The transfer process may be either *positive,* that which assists, or *negative,* that which interferes with the acquiring of changed patterns of mental functioning. Although concepts as expressed by verbal symbols must be understood, the symbols themselves, such as words, numbers, and other symbolic representations must be learned and retained in their exact form, or learned by rote through drill or practice. The learning of conceptual relationships, ideas, interpretations, and mental integrations, having psychological connotation, cannot be achieved through rote memorization of their verbal symbols.

By means of the utilization of the logical approach, a learner analyzes and integrates concepts formed through learning experiences. Thereby conceptual understandings are expanded and intensified, resulting in generalizations that then can be applied in situations different from those in which the concepts were developed. It is such positive transfer effect that educators are encouraging through the construction of core curriculums and experiential learning activities.

School people are alert to the learning hazards inherent in the operation of negative transfer in various learning areas. A former skill may interfere with the development of a new skill. Playing golf, for example is believed to interfere with playing baseball. Hence some baseball coaches disapprove team members, playing golf during their leisure time, since the hold and the swing of the club and the stance taken differ from the hold, swing, and stance of a baseball batter. Negative transfer operates also in academic learning. If the study of two foreign languages is started at the same time, such as French and Spanish, considerable interference of one by the other may be experienced in vocabulary, grammatical structure, and other aspects of language mastery.

Theories of Transfer

The demonstrated fact that formal school learning can influence an individual's learning long after it is completed has resulted in the propounding of various theories to explain how transfer takes place. The more widely known theories are described here briefly.

Formal Mental Discipline. Traditional curricula of secondary schools and colleges were based on *faculty psychology,* an explanation of the functioning of the mind that had many adherents during the nineteenth century. According to this theory, the mind consists of faculties or specific, separate mental powers such as memory, reasoning, judgment, the will, facility in mathematics, honesty, ability to learn a language, and the like. Exercise of any one of these faculties, regardless of the nature of the practice, was believed to strengthen it so that it would function adequately in any situation requiring the utilization of the faculty. This theory of learning sometimes referred to as *formal discipline* dominated high school and college curriculums for many years. Its influence is still extant in the form of course offerings in some colleges.

Faculty psychology maintained, for example, that the memory could be strengthened through memorization of long and difficult selections. This or any other exercise of the memory was supposed to develop in the learner the power to remember any type of learning material. Similarly, extensive participation in difficult thinking and reasoning, whatever be the nature of the problem, would enable the individual to succeed in the solution of any difficulty which he might encounter later.

In 1894, the value of strong and effective mental training was stressed in the report of the Committee of Ten on Secondary School Studies, sponsored by the National Education Association. Concerning the development of specific abilities, the committee had this to say, in part, concerning the value of history:

> The principal end of all education is training. In this respect history has a value different from, but in no way inferior to, that of languages, mathematics, and science. The mind is chiefly developed in three ways: by cultivating the powers of discriminating observation; by strengthening the logical faculty of following an argument from point to point; and by improving the process of comparison, that is judgment.
>
> As studies in language and in the natural sciences are best adapted to cultivate the habits of observation; as mathematics is the traditional training of the reasoning faculties; so history and its allied branches

are better adapted than any other studies to promote the invaluable mental power which we call the judgment.[1]

The advocates of mental training through formal discipline claimed that the study of the less abstract subjects exerted little influence on an individual's mental power to solve his immediate problems successfully. They believed that the mastery of a few well-selected formal subjects would prepare a learner for adequate community life. Although faculty psychology and the theory of formal discipline have been discarded, there is a general belief that learning in one situation, no matter what the difficulty of the learning material, can affect the thinking and behavior of an individual in another situation. Consequently, modern educators are advocating that young people be trained to be clear thinkers, to be careful in their mental activities, and to develop constructive attitudes toward themselves and other people. Present attitudes toward transfer effects of learning, however, reflect an emphasis on the total functioning of the mental processes in a given situation.

Identical Elements or Identical Components. Thorndike held that transfer from one situation to another depends on whether the two situations possess identical elements. Later, Woodworth and others, considering the term element to connote a simple, indivisible part of a whole, substituted the term *component* as representing a more complex functional trend. They all believed, however, that learning in one area effects changes in another function only in so far as the two have elements common to both: content, method of procedure, or aim. Thorndike explained his theory of transfer as follows:

> . . . a change in one function alters any other only in so far as the two functions have as factors identical elements. The change in the second function is in amount that due to the change in the elements common to it and the first. The change is simply the necessary result upon the second function of the alteration of those of its factors which were elements of the first function, and so were altered by its training. To take a concrete example, improvement in addition will alter one's ability in multiplication because addition is absolutely identical with a part of multiplication and because certain arithmetical impulses, are in part common to the two functions.[2]

[1] National Education Association, *Report of the Committee of Ten on Secondary School Studies,* American Book Company, New York, 1894, p. 53.

[2] From E. L. Thorndike, *Educational Psychology,* Vol. II, Bureau of Publications, Teachers College, Columbia UUniversity, 1913, pp. 358-359.

According to this theory, a typist who has learned to typewrite on one typewriter having a standard keyboard usually can perform satisfactorily on another standard typewriter built by any manufacturer. However, even one difference in operation between two deviating situations may necessitate reconditioning. For example, an individual who has learned to drive a car having a standard gear shift can drive any make car with a similar gear shift, but he must recondition his gear shifting habits to enable him to operate a car having an automatic gear shift, after which he can handle any automatic gear-shift car. On the other hand, if two learning situations are different except for one important component, after one of them has been learned, the common component facilitates learning of the other. An individual who has learned proper balance in riding a bicycle can apply that skill in his learning to ride a motorcycle.

Theoretically, one task of school people would be to analyze specific learnings to discover their common components and stress these in appropriate learning situations. To some extent, this procedure is practicable, especially in motor skill development. Because of the complex nature of some component functions of the higher mental processes, the identicalness of functioning is so subtle that it defies easy determination. Although the theory of identical components has much educational value, some of the difficulties involved in applying it to all learning experiences have led to promulgation of other explanations for the transfer of learning.

Transfer through Generalization. In his explanation of transfer of learning, Charles H. Judd emphasized the importance of an individual's being able to grasp broad principles for the purpose of making specific applications. Judd believed that the degree of transfer depends upon the ability of the learner to consolidate his experiences in one situation and use them in another. This theory is supported in part by the fact that meaningful material is remembered longer than nonsense syllables.

The individual who understands scientific generalization and who comprehends the significance of a wide range of related principles thereby acquires sufficient insight concerning the applicability of generalizations to make appropriate transfer of them to situations different from those in which his broad concepts were formed originally. The mental processes involved in forming adequate generalizations and then applying them correctly require superior intellectual capacity. Moreover, generalizations are achievable only because of the integrating power of human intelligence as it interacts constantly with accumlated personal and social experience.

The applicability to a particular situation of a generalized principle was demonstrated by Judd through an experiment in which parallel groups of fifth and sixth-grade boys attempted, with darts, to hit a target placed under water. One group was instructed concerning the refraction of light under water; the other group received no such instruction. In the first series of trials, the target was placed 12 inches under the water; in the second, the target was raised to 4 inches under the water. There was no significant difference between the scores of the two groups in the first series of trials. In the second situation, however, the uninstructed group were less successful than the instructed group. The uninstructed boys seemed to become confused because their practice with the target at 12 inches below the surface did not help them in the 4-inch position. The instructed group related rapidly to the new situation. Judd concluded that an understanding of general principles aids in adaptation to new situations.

Transfer through generalization is possible only when conditions are favorable. Unless the body of factual knowledge, the skill competence, or the particular habits and attitudes acquired by an individual in one situation are so systematized and organized that they relate to other situations, they have little transfer value in the solution of his problems. The need for systematization and organization is especially important in the area of attitude and behavior development.

A term such as *honesty, cooperativeness,* or *punctuality* supposedly represents a broad generalization that should be applicable to any situation involving its functioning. Yet a child or even an adult may recognize its relationship to one situation but not to another. To a school child, for example, punctuality may mean arriving at school on time or submitting written assignments when they are due. Although he receives plenty of practice of punctuality in school situations, he may fail to apply what he has learned to out-of-school situations, either during his school life or later. As an adult, he may be notoriously lacking in his application of punctuality to his daily responsibilities. Similarly, honesty can be interpreted to refer only to the stealing of money, and perhaps to the appropriating for oneself of the substantial possessions of another person, but not to the keeping of a borrowed book, umbrella, or pen.

Generalized concepts such as these represent ideals by which behavior is motivated. William Bagley stressed the importance of transfer through the formularization of *ideals*. The significance to a learner of ideal formulation depends upon the extent to which teachers consciously attempt to inculcate an ideal in its broadest connotation, with reasonable assurance that learners understand all its implications in relation to their daily experiences.

The Gestalt Theory of Transfer. This theory, propounded by Max Wertheimer, emphasizes patterns of experiences as media of transfer. The theory represents a fusion of the theory of generalization and the theory of identical elements. The learner (1) responds as an integrated and unified organism to a configuration or pattern, (2) learns to recognize significant elements in the patterns, and (3) as he recognizes common elements in his patterns of experiences, is transferring or transposing them.

The insights developed are the relationships perceived by the individual (in his whole-part interpretations) between his experience and the new situation. The extent to which there is transfer thus depends upon his success in discovering existing relationships that facilitate the adjustment to the new situation or the solution of a complex problem.

Aspects of Transfer

Effective transfer of learning probably is a fundamental teaching-learning goal. School people are concerned with learners' achieving maximal transfer benefits from their formal learning experiences. Through experimentation and other research approaches, educational psychologists continue their efforts to discover transferable relationships between and among respective school subjects, as well as between school learning and out-of-school experiences. Curriculums, teaching procedures, and individual learning experiences are evaluated and reevaluated constantly to increase the functioning of transfer in learning.

The Curriculum. Changing psychological viewpoints concerning the nature of human learning and increasing educational provision for meeting the needs of all learners wield a potent influence upon curriculum construction and implementation. Learning as mental discipline, rooted in the faculty psychologists' concept of mental processes, required construction of rigid curriculums that for the most part have given way to the evolution of relatively flexible, functional curriculums.

Subjects included for their disciplinary value in nineteenth century secondary school and college programs of study, such as Latin, mathematics, and logic still are offered by many schools. In most of these educational institutions, however, they are electives to meet students' special interests rather than required subjects. Yet some present-day American educators encourage the inclusion of Latin in the curriculum as a basis of improved facility in the use of English.

Modern curricular trends are toward integration of learning materials that include aspects of human relationships. For example, significant aspects of former isolated courses in elementary and secondary school history, such as ancient, medieval, English, and others now are combined with related areas in the social studies in which the functional learning approach is stressed. In addition, the twentieth century has witnessed the introduction into college curriculums of courses such as human development, mental hygiene and guidance, aimed at the achievement of greater understanding of personal and social interrelationships.

Not only have the course offerings on all educational levels been expanded, but the learning materials and experiences are becoming more functional. Although a struggle between what sometimes is called the *old* and the *new* still persists, the social and practical aspects of learning experiences are stressed. Curriculum constructors also are attempting to make provision for as many transfer aids as can be utilized by teachers and learners. At the same time, they realize that (1) skill competence results from direct practice, even though transfer components that may be present are helpful, and (2) many specific learning activities cannot be generalized but can be integrated with a learner's previous experiences.

Curriculum content is being geared to meet individual learning needs: physical and mental health and safety; vocational interests and abilities, and home, social, civic, and recreational activities. Learning experiences are becoming more meaningful to the learner, and opportunities for their practical application are increasing. Although specific learning content constantly is expanding, school people are attempting to organize learning materials in such way that learning experiences are integrated according to interrelated, broad-field units, rather than treated as specific and unrelated subjects.

Teaching Approaches. Although some transfer probably accompanies most learning, a teacher cannot assume that it takes place automatically. The concept of learning as functional activity implies integration of experience. The teacher can foster the integrative process by helping his pupils develop an attitude of seeking and discovering relationships. Effective teaching involves constant alertness to transfer possibilities. The teacher's task is made difficult, however, by the fact that his pupils may represent a wide range of mental ability, thus differing markedly in their power to grasp relationships. Since transfer is dependent upon an individual's ability to perceive relationships between situations, the higher his intelligence level is, the better are the possibilities of transfer. The greater the effort to integrate experiences and to associate ideas, the more likely is the learner to gain the insights needed for best transfer.

Regardless of the intelligence level of his pupils, a teacher's purposes or goals are of primary importance in their relationship to the kind and amount of learning transfer experienced by his pupils. If the goal is the memorizing of factual material there will be little transfer; if the goal is the discovery of relationships among learning materials and experiences, the learner will be encouraged to utilize factual information as he thinks through a problem or situation to its logical conclusion.

Excellent aids in the teaching of transfer are suggested here:

1. Have clear-cut objectives. Decide what students should be able to do as a result of their work.
2. Study the course content to find what it contains that is applicable to other school subjects and to out-of-school life.
3. Select instructional materials which are best suited to the job of making relationships apparent.
4. Let students know when to expect transfer, what kinds to expect, and the benefits which it can bring them.
5. Use methods of teaching (e.g., problem solving, discussion, leading questions) which will facilitate transfer.
6. Provide practice in transfer. It is not enough to point out relationships. Pupils should be given practice in finding relationships, on their own. Tests of application, guided discussion, and actual class projects ought to provide this kind of experience.
7. Concentrate on the process of learning as well as upon products. Do not be satisfied with a right answer or solution, but probe to find out why a certain answer was given, and discuss with the class the steps which led to their answers."[3]

[3] G. M. Blair, R. S. Jones, and R. H. Simpson, *Educational Psychology*. The Macmillan Company, New York, 1954, p. 256.

PART V
EVALUATION IN EDUCATION

CHAPTER 19

PRINCIPLES AND TECHNIQUES OF EVALUATION

Evaluation is an important aspect of formal education. With present emphasis upon the learner as an individual has come the need for school people to understand the psychological factors involved and to evaluate or measure learner potentiality and developmental progress. Many different kinds of techniques have been devised during the recent past; others are in the process of construction. A teacher should know what they are and how they can assist him in arriving at sound decisions relative to pupils and their progress.

Nature and Function of Evaluation

Since educational objectives are pointed toward adequate development of the learner's physical, mental, emotional, and social capacities, educators and psychologists are concerned with (1) *measurement* of traits, (2) *appraisal* of behavior, and (3) *evaluation* of achievement.

Meaning of Terms. Although the terms measurement, appraisal, and evaluation often are used interchangeably, their exact connotations differ. Measurement is used to determine quantity or how much of anything. Through *appraisal* an attempt is made to estimate the effect upon an individual of the educational or environmental experiences to which he is exposed. *Evaluation* has a broad meaning, implying more than the measured amount or the appraisal effect of experience upon an individual; through application of appropriate programs of testing, measuring, and other techniques that can be utilized, evaluation represents a continuous process of determining potential attributes, learning readiness and achievement, and behavior changes.

Difficulties of Evaluation. Some aspects of learning can be evaluated easily and with relative accuracy; others seem to defy any attempt to discover the kind or amount of development that has occurred. For example, it is easy to measure how much a child has learned in terms of whether he can reproduce printed material verbatim. It is not a simple matter, however, to discover the extent to which learning in one situation is used functionally in other situations. Elements of uncertainty appear as soon as an attempt is made to evaluate an individual's power to interpret, his ability to apply what he has learned, or his willingness to cooperate.

A teacher knows that each of his pupils should strive to achieve learning success within his ability limits. The teacher's problem is to determine what the individual learning capacity of his pupils is. A similar problem is posed when school people attempt to discover achievable goals of learners at any age level, since individual differences prevent the establishment of standards on the basis of chronological age. What success in achievement is made depends as much upon the evaluator as upon the performer. What constitutes good work for one teacher would not be acceptable to another teacher. The independently reached judgments of two teachers concerning the emotional stability of a child may be widely divergent.

Tools and Techniques of Evaluation

The subjective elements in evaluation require school people or psychologists to utilize instruments that permit obtaining as accurate results as it is possible to achieve. Careful interpretation and recording of data also are essential.

Varieties of Techniques. The classroom test administered by the teacher is a traditional evaluation technique. Its purpose usually is to evaluate the kind and amount of success pupils are achieving in their learning tasks. The appropriateness of the questions formulated by the teacher and the marking standards utilized by him, especially for the older type essay test, determine in large part the adequacy of his evaluation of pupil progress. Classroom tests as teaching and learning aids have their place in formal education. Their form is changing somewhat, however, as is shown in Chapter 20.

Evaluation of a pupil's achievement as measured by classroom tests tells relatively little about him as a person or a learner. It indicates what and how much he apparently has learned in a particular unit of study as his performance on a test is compared with that of his classmates. The mark earned on a teacher-made test of achievement does not give the teacher any information concerning the reasons for the pupil's success or failure, nor does it show, except slightly perhaps, (1) his attitudes, (2) his interests and ambitions, (3) his special abilities, (4) his home background and family relationships, (5) his physical condition, or (6) any other aspect of his total personality except that, for one or another reason, he responded as he did to a particular teacher-made test or tests.

Although progress in subject matter achievement is one of the fundamental educational goals, other objectives are equally important, since the extent of a learner's knowledge mastery and skill competence are not the sole determiners of successful living. Consequently, other adequate techniques need to be devised and utilized as approaches to the evaluation of a younger or older learner's behavior.

Some evaluating tools and techniques of evaluation can be applied by the classroom teacher. A few are utilized best by him because of his close association with his pupils. Other evaluating instruments should be administered by a trained person who is skilled in the methods of administration and in interpretation of resulting data. Still others, especially those that are intended to discover subtle personality attributes, should be used only by psychologists or psychiatrists.

Specific Techniques. There probably is no one evaluating tool or technique that will yield complete data concerning every phase of personality development and adjustment. Consequently, psychologists and educators are employing various approaches in their efforts to know and understand (1) the extent to which and the ways in which individuals differ from one another, (2) the significance of these differences, (3) the causal factors of a difference, and (4) the evaluation of a demonstrated difference as favorable and to be encouraged, or unfavorable and to be remedied.

Some of these evaluating approaches are informal, in that they are utilized to discover a learner's attitudes and behavior patterns as these function in a particular learning situation and in relationships with peer or older associates. Other techniques are more formal. They allow for relatively objective comparisons of the display by an individual or by a small group of individuals of one or more specific personality attributes with large group behavior trends. A formal approach also may represent a more or less complete evaluation of an individual's achievement through utilization of a series of differing tools of measurement and appraisal.

The more widely used formal and informal evaluating tools and techniques are:

1. Standardized tests, scales and inventories
2. Projective techniques
3. Situational tests
4. Observation and anecdotal reports
5. The interview
6. The case history

The remainder of this chapter is devoted to a brief explanation of the purpose and characteristics of each of the six techniques listed. A more detailed treatment of the specific form and usage of each is given in Chapters 20 and 21.

Standardized Tests, Scales, and Inventories

A standardized test, scale, or inventory is utilized as a means of objective comparison between an individual's demonstrated abilities, interests, attitudes, skills, or knowledge and what can be expected of him according to the general tendencies or performances exhibited by others of the same age or developmental level. Hence, to yield accurate data, the measuring instrument must be so constructed that it meets specific conditions.

Conditions of Standardization. Thousands of standardized measuring instruments are on the market. They represent a wide range of differences in standardization. Since the value of a standardized test lies in the extent to which it fulfills certain required conditions, users of these instruments should select only those tests that seem to fulfill the conditions listed below, regardless of other factors, such as relative costs of tests, apparent ease of administration, or time consumed in giving them.

1. Accuracy and objectivity of administration, scoring, and interpretation of results
2. Established norms
3. Validity of test content
4. Reliability of resulting data

Accuracy and Objectivity. Testing material usually is presented in short-form questions or statements. (See Chapter 20.) The subject must know to what he is expected to respond and in what way. The administrator must follow exact procedures in administering the test, scoring responses, and interpreting results. Otherwise, data obtained through its administration by different persons, each employing his own method of procedure, are not comparable. Consequently, a manual of directions, prepared by the constructor of the test, accompanies each set of tests and includes specific instructions concerning method of administration and timing, scoring device, and intepretative significance of test results. These directions must be understood clearly and followed without any deviations.

Norms. The concept of normality has been discussed earlier. The term *norm,* as applied to standardized testing instruments, connotes the level of performance (expressed as a score or other derived symbol) of the greatest number of same-age or grade subjects to whom the test has been administered. For a norm to have meaning, it should have been ascertained through administration of the test to large cross-sectional groups of subjects under the same conditions.

For example, a teacher of a fourth-grade elementary school class can determine whether his pupils are achieving satisfactorily in arithmetic by administering a well-standardized test that includes the arithmetic materials usually taught in the fourth grade. By comparing the score of each of his pupils with the standard norm for the test, he can discover which of them are performing adequately or normally, and which are superior or inferior to the norm, and how much.

Validity. If a test includes the material that should be used to measure success in a particular trait it is said to be a valid test. The test then measures what it is supposed to measure. Hence the items selected for use in the test and the wording of them, to a high degree, determine the validity of the test.

Reliability. A test that yields the same results each time it is administered is considered reliable for the items included. That is, reliability refers to the extent to which or the accuracy with which a test measures what it has been constructed to measure. In short, this means that good tests are both valid and reliable. However, an invalid test may show a high reliability if it yields consistent results.

Classification of Standardized Tests. Tests, scales, and inventories can be classified according to form, function, or administration as:

1. Form
   a. Rate or speed test
   b. Quality or power test
2. Function
   a. Survey test
   b. Diagnostic test
   c. Prognostic test
3. Administration
   a. Individual test
   b. Group test

Since these categories represent three different aspects of tests, a particular test for example, could be (1) a rate or power test, (2) serve any one of the three functions, and (3) be administered individually or in group situations. Classification interrelationships may be understood more clearly as each is explained briefly. It can be noted also that most tests, scales, and inventories are verbal pencil-and-paper tests. Some, especially individual tests, are nonverbal tests of performance.

Rate or Speed Tests. The purpose of these tests is to discover the number of items of uniform difficulty to which answers can be given in a specified time.

Quality or Power Tests. The purpose of these tests is to discover the quality of performance rather than the rate at which the responses are made. The material of these tests is arranged in order of increasing difficulty beginning with relatively simple material and continuing toward the more difficult items. A penmanship or a handwriting scale is an example of a quality test.

Survey Tests. These are standardized tests devised to measure the performance of individuals in a large unit of learning. They usually are group tests designed for the purpose of gaining information relative to the achievement status of classes or groups of students. For example, the progress of one class can be compared with that of another or the progress of one school with that of another school or of other school systems.

Diagnostic Tests. Diagnostic tests are used to discover the learning difficulties of individual learners. For example, after the administration of an arithmetic test, the results can be analyzed to discover general or individual errors. Remedial instruction then can be given to the entire class or individual instruction to those learners who appear to have specific weaknesses.

Prognostic Tests. Essentially, prognostic tests are modified aptitude tests. Through their administration an attempt is made to predict probable success in a particular area of ability.

Individual Tests. An individual test is one that is administered to one subject at a time. Normally, a great amount of training and experience with the test is required to administer an individual test. The validity and reliability of the results of an individual test depend, to a high degree, upon the administrator's attitude toward the testing situation, his rapport with the subject, and his insight as he interprets responses.

Group Tests. Group tests have been so constructed that they can be administered in group situations by teachers under the guidance of a trained tester. Although they can be administered more easily than most individual tests, certain cautionary procedures must be observed: (1) The group should not be so large that some of the subjects cannot hear or see the administrator. (2) Directions contained in the manual must be followed exactly, especially those dealing with the time limits of the entire test or the subtests. (3) The administrator must be certain that every subject stops immediately when the signal is given, and that no subject begins before the starting signal. (4) In large group testing, proctors should not walk among the subjects or engage in conversation, thereby distracting the attention of any subject. (5) The time factor is important. (6) The test papers must be scored correctly, and checked for accuracy of scoring. The scoring of a large number of standardized tests by a busy teacher becomes an irksome chore, encouraging unintended carelessness.

Projective Techniques

New techniques called projective techniques have been introduced for the purpose of evaluating personality. Since it is believed that personality is something more than the sum of all its traits, the problem of its evaluation is a complex one. The paper-and-pencil type of test does not yield adequate appraisal of the subtle interactions inherent in personality formation. Psychologists have constructed forms of evaluation that permit the subject through his free responses to *project* his habitual attitudes, hopes, ideas, aggressions, fears, or worries. Hence they are known as *projective techniques.*

Characteristics of Projective Techniques. Free association is the basic principle of these tests. In the administration of a projective technique the individual is presented with relatively unstructured situations to which he responds freely. Thus he gives overt expression to attitudes and ideas that presumably are representative of his personality pattern.

A variety of projective techniques are available. Included among the better known are (1) the verbal technique or free association test, (2) drawing and painting, (3) play and dramatic approaches, (4) the Rorschach (ink-blot) technique, and (5) pictorial techniques, such as the Thematic Apperception Test (TAT). These personality tests are described and illustrated in the next chapter.

Situational Tests

The primary function of a situational test is to observe the behavior of the subject as he reacts in a situation that appears to resemble an everyday situational experience. One of the earliest of these testing approaches was used by H. Hartshorne and Mark A. May in their Character Education Inquiry. Included among situational tests are the Character Research Projects that are being conducted experimentally by the Laboratory of Psychology of Union College. For example, one of the studies in this project is "Growth toward Attitude Objectives in a Summer Camp as Indicated by Two Sociometric Devices."

Observation and Recording

An individual's overt behavior and expressed attitudes constantly are being evaluated by his associates as they observe him in action. Since an observer may fail to perceive all aspects of the other's behavior or may be prejudiced in his judgments, much of so-called casual observation has little evaluative worth. The classroom teacher continuously evaluates his pupils as he observes them in action.

Value of Teacher Observation. Careful, objective observation of pupil's behavior is basic to a teacher's understanding of what causes them to react as they do. On occasions, a teacher's observation may be controlled by a special purpose, such as to discover a learner's attitude toward a class project, his relationships with his classmates, his responsiveness in class discussion, or his behavior during a test. The purpose of controlled observation also may be directed toward studying group reactions in learning or play situations.

Utilization of Anecdotal Reports. A teacher's daily observations of his pupils are helpful to him, especially at the time they are made. Their worth as a means of evaluation is increased if or when the teacher records in writing any observed incident or behavior reaction that represents a significant deviation from what is considered by him to be normal. A record of displayed behavior is more reliable than memory and can be used by the teacher to give him a better perspective as well as to explain to others the problems of a particular child, or the bases of certain deviant group behavior.

Many incidents happen in a classroom each day to which the alert teacher directs his attention and records, as soon as is practicable, in the form of anecdotal reports. Some teachers believe that they are too busy to be bothered with this kind of activity. Yet a teacher who makes note of the happenings in his classroom often discovers that at times a behavior incident has serious significance in relation to a particular child's personality status.

In an increasing number of schools, the principal, dean, or chairman of guidance encourages teachers to keep anecdotal reports of their observations. Some schools have printed or mimeographed forms for teachers' anecdotal reporting. These forms differ among schools. One kind consists of a card or sheet of paper containing suggestive questions for the teacher to consider as he writes on the form a brief description of his observation and his reason for reporting it.

The form of reporting is relatively unimportant. The value of the record lies in its significance from the point of view of the teacher himself. The report should be brief but succinct; its interpretation should be objective and to the point. One report about a young person may have some value; a series of them, submitted by various teachers, kept in a confidential file, and utilized by a counselor, and/or teacher can provide extremely valuable information concerning the individual's developing personality. For a teacher trainee to obtain practice in careful observation and recording will be helpful to him as a classroom teacher.

The Interview

The interview is a valuable technique for studying personal characteristics. The face-to-face relationship between interviewer and interviewee affords opportunity for each to improve his understanding of the other and to gain insight into the problems of the interviewee. The form and purpose of the interview range from the simple brief information giving or receiving that a teacher experiences constantly before, during, or after class sessions, to the intensive, perhaps protracted interview of the psychologist with an emotionally disturbed patient.

The interview, as utilized by teachers and other school personnel for the purpose of evaluation, is concerned mainly with the study of the interviewee's personal characteristics, his interests and ambitions, and his problems for the solution of which he needs help. Since much of a teacher's time and energy must be devoted to activities involving all his pupils, his opportunities to engage in individual interviews is limited. Yet many teachers who give generously of their time after school hours to talk with individual pupils are enabled thereby to give them considerable help. The function of evaluating a young person's attitudes and behavior rightfully is that of the counselor or teacher-counselor.

The face-to-face relationship in the interview gives rise to the display of various personal characteristics and modes of thinking that often are not revealed in a group situation. Confidence in the other person can be established through the interview. Through tactful questioning and intelligent listening the skilled interviewer can discover qualities that heretofore may have eluded him or others in group situations.

The interview is an important although difficult guidance procedure. It usually serves one or more of the following specific purposes: (1) to give information, (2) to obtain information, (3) to evaluate for educational or occupational purposes, and (4) to help in the resolution of a behavior problem. In the achievement of these purposes, certain principles and procedures are basic.

1. The place of the interview should provide as much privacy as possible.
2. The interviewer should prepare for a scheduled interview.
3. A friendly attitude should permeate and dominate the entire interview.
4. Confidence should be established so as to encourage the interviewee to talk freely.
5. The interviewer should avoid talking excessively.
6. To as great extent as possible, the interview should be unstructured.

7. The interviewee should be assured that what he says is in confidence.

8. The interview should be terminated by the interviewer when either the purpose has been accomplished or some satisfactory progress has been made.

9. The interviewee should believe that he has gained from the experience.

10. The way should be made easy for further interviews when and if needed.

The Case History

The technique of the case history involves a comprehensive study of an individual, including as much accurate data as can be obtained concerning his full life history from birth onward. In education, a relatively simple case report is constructed as an aid in studying and giving therapy to slightly maladjusted children; in psychiatry, the entire life story of a badly maladjusted individual is needed before intensive therapy can be applied.

The ultimate purpose of a case history is to evaluate present behavior in terms of background factors of experience. It is utilized especially in child guidance clinics, hospitals for the mentally ill, and those other organizations concerned with helping mentally or emotionally disturbed persons.

Although there is no standard form to be used in preparing a case history, it should include the following kinds of evaluating data:

Identifying data
Information concerning present activities or status
Symptoms of the problem, conditions, or situations
Examination—physical and health, psychological, and educational
Health and physical history
Family history
School history
Occupational history, if employed
Social history and contacts

Many persons are needed to gather pertinent data. The accumulated data then are arranged and organized by a trained person, preferably a psychiatric social worker. Accurate and complete information is essential if correct diagnosis and treatment are to be implemented. If the client responds to the therapy, a general follow-up program can be planned for him.

CHAPTER 20

EVALUATION OF INTELLIGENCE, PERSONALITY, AND ACHIEVEMENT

The many differences in young people's developmental patterns show themselves in their mental abilities, personality characteristics, and learning achievements. This chapter is concerned with evaluation in each of those areas of individual capacities and development.

Measuring Capacity for Learning

A teacher has greater need to know how to use measuring instruments and how to interpret results than to understand the construction of the tests that have been standardized for use in the measuring of mental ability. The many tests in this area that have continued to be constructed since the beginning of the present century reflect in their changing patterns some of the changing interpretations of intelligence discussed in Chapter 10.

Intelligence Testing. Alfred Binet, a Frenchman, was the first to devise an examination to test the mental capacity of individual children. He was invited by the French authorities to construct a test that would identify those pupils who were sufficiently dull to be regarded as feebleminded.

Individual Intelligence Tests. Binet, with the help of Theophile Simon, devised and published in 1905 an *individual test* which consisted of 30 separate items. The scores were interpreted in terms of mental age. This test was revised in 1908 and again in 1911. The *Binet-Simon Scale of Intelligence* was translated into English by Goddard and used in his work at the institution for the feebleminded at Vineland, New Jersey. The *Stanford Revision of the Binet Scale,* constructed by Lewis M. Terman, was published originally in 1916. The form of the scale now used is the Terman and Merrill 1937 revision. Some of the test materials are verbal, presented orally by the administrator, others are read by the subject, and still others are performance tasks. Items included in the revised Stanford-Binet Scale for a normal 5-year old child are:

Picture Completion: Man
Paper Folding: Triangle
Definitions
Memory for Sentences
Counting Four Objects

Because of the difficulties of administration, scoring, and interpretation, training and practical experience are needed for a person to administer an individual intelligence test. Additional individual tests devised to measure the mental ability of very young children include *Cattell's Test for the Measurement of Intelligence of Infants and Young Children* (for children between the ages of 2 and 30 months), and the *Minnesota Preschool Test* (for children between the ages of 18 months and 6 years.) Much still has to be done to improve the reliability of these tests. Recently constructed individual tests that are gaining recognition, especially in psychological clinics, are the *Wechsler Bellevue Intelligence Scale* (for older children and adolescents), the *Wechsler Intelligence Scale for Children,* and the *Wechsler Adult Intelligence Scale.* The giving of these intelligence tests is too difficult for anyone except trained persons.

Group Intelligence Tests. The need for testing the intelligence of individuals in groups rather than singly arose during the first world War. In an attempt to deal effectively with the large number of conscripted men, two tests were constructed that could be administered to large numbers of individuals at one time. Hence the *Army Alpha Tests* for those conscripted men who could read and write and the *Army Beta Tests* for illiterates and non-English-speaking servicemen were constructed and administered.

At about the same time, several psychologists and educators became interested in the construction of tests that could be used by school people to measure the mental capacities of learners on all age levels. Among the psychologists participating in the early testing movement are Terman, Otis, Haggarty, Thurstone, and Pintner. Since then many new instruments have been developed. Below are listed some widely used intelligence tests, arranged according to age levels.

Pintner-Cunningham Primary Scale—for kindergarten

Otis Group Intelligence Scale—for primary grades

Otis Self-Administering Test of Mental Ability—for upper grades and high school

Terman Group Test of Mental Ability—for high school

Kuhlmann-Anderson Intelligence Test—for all elementary school grades and high school.

Mental Age and Intelligence Quotient. The concept of mental age as introduced by Binet and Simon has value in the interpretation of raw tests scores. An individual's mental age is obtained by interpreting his raw score according to standardized age norms. The mental age of the testee may be lower than, equal to, or higher than his chronological age. Terman carried the relationship between mental and chronological age a step further. By reducing both ages to months, dividing the mental age by the chronological age and multiplying by 100, a ratio is obtained that is called the *intelligence quotient* (IQ). For example, if a boy's mental age (M.A.), as determined by his performance on a valid and reliable test of intelligence, is 126 months and his chronological age (C.A.) is 126 months, his intelligence status is normal for his age, since the mental age and the chronological age are the same, indicating a one to one relationship between the two.

The formula to compute an intelligence quotient is

$$\frac{\text{M.A. (months)}}{\text{C. A. (months)}} \times 100 = \text{IQ}$$

An IQ below 100 represents mental acuity or intelligence below the average; an IQ above 100 indicates better than normal intelligence. The greater the deviation from 100, the more inferior or superior the individual's intelligence status is.

Distribution of Intelligence. The law of chance operates to a remarkably high degree in the distribution of mental ability. According to the evaluation of these abilities the number of individuals who have the lowest ability is equal to the number having the highest ability. Experimental evidence indicates that mental ability is distributed about as follows:

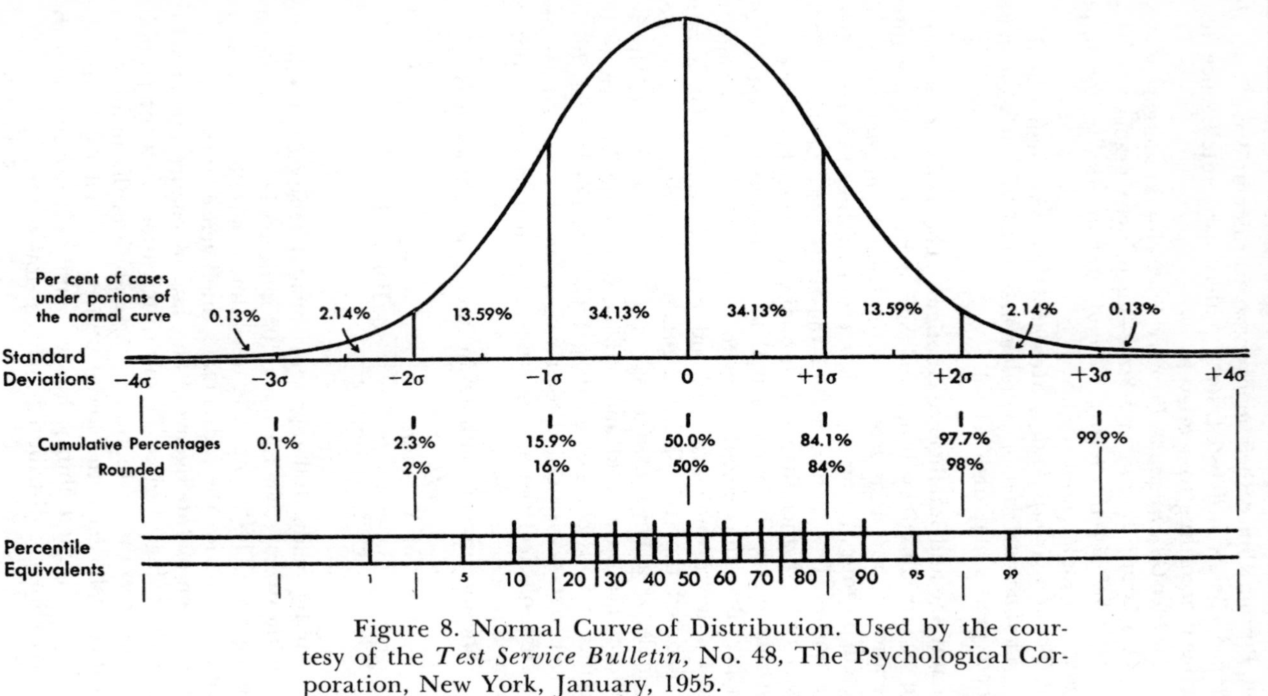

Figure 8. Normal Curve of Distribution. Used by the courtesy of the *Test Service Bulletin*, No. 48, The Psychological Corporation, New York, January, 1955.

Table 2. Distribution of Intelligence Quotients

IQ'S	*Classification*	*Percentage of all persons*
140 and above	Near genius or genius	0.25
130-139	Very superior	0.75
120-129	Superior	6.00
110-119	Above average	13.00
90-109	Normal or average	60.00
80-89	Below average	13.00
70-79	Dull or borderline	6.00
50-69	Feeble-minded: moron	0.75
49 and below	Feebleminded: imbecile, idiot	0.25

The distribution of intelligence in a normal population is illustrated graphically in Figures 8 and 9. Other statistical comparisons, such as standard deviations, cumulative percentages, and percentile equivalents are included in the presentation. If an individual's intelligence status is expressed in terms of percentile equivalence it means that the scores of some individuals are below his percentile. For example, if he is at the 90th percentile he has a score higher than 90 per cent of the individuals who have taken the same test and only 10 per cent have a score higher than his score. See Figure 8.

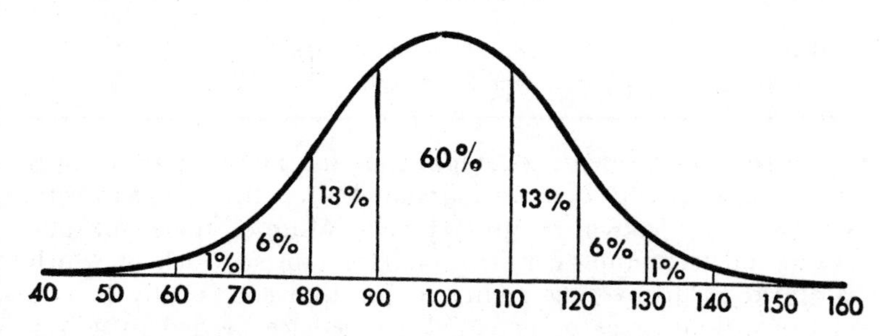

Figure 9. Distribution of Intelligence Quotients.

The Measuring of Special Aptitudes

A good aptitude test should measure most of the factors required for success in the activity or vocational field for which the test is intended. Many tests have been devised to discover the possession of special aptitude. The results yielded by some of them have high predictive value. Because of the many subtle elements associated with special ability in some areas, however, tests constructed to determine possession of the aptitude fail to achieve their purpose completely.

There are available more or less adequate measuring instruments for various areas of potential aptitudes. Tests to measure special academic ability include the psychological examination of the American Council on Education and the *Academic Aptitude Test* (verbal and nonverbal) by Kobal, Wrightstone, and Kunze. To indicate the wide variety of aptitude tests that have been developed, one for each area is listed.

Table 3. Aptitude Tests in Various Areas of Learning

Aptitude	*Test*
Algebra	*Iowa Aptitude Test*
Art	*Meir and Seashore Art Judgment Tests*
Clerical	*Thurstone Clerical Test*
Law	*Yale Legal Aptitude Test*
Mechanical	*Stenquest Assembly Tests of General Mechanical Ability*
Medicine	*Moss Scholastic Aptitude Test for Medical Students*
Music	*Seashore Measure of Musical Ability Tests*
Science	*Stanford Scientific Aptitude Test*

The list represents a sampling of the many aptitude tests that can be used to help an individual assess his ability to earn success in his chosen vocational field. Most of these aptitude evaluating techniques consist of several subtests, each of which is aimed at discovering ability to function successfully in one of the various areas of potential competence needed in a particular field of activity. For example, before a candidate is accepted in a nurse training program, he or she must submit to a battery of tests to discover aptitude for nursing. Since each of the various tests of the battery emphasizes a particular aspect of readiness needed to prepare for the various areas of training, the battery has predictive value.

Another example of "readiness" discovery that has shown high predictive value is the *Crow-Crow Test For High School Entrants,* designed to classify entering high school pupils according to readiness to succeed in study on the secondary school level. The performance of an entrant in each of the four subtests: English, Reading Comprehension, Arithmetic Reasoning and Computation, and General Information, helps his counselor guide him, according to his demonstrated degree of readiness resulting from his previous learning experiences, toward the selection of a curriculum best suited to his abilities.

One point concerning many of these so-called aptitude tests should be noted. One connotation of aptitude presented in Chapter 10 implies that an aptitude is a *special potential ability* that, with training, can lead to exceptional performance. Many of the "aptitude tests" now on the market attempt to determine the chances for future success in a field as indicated by degree of success in related previous experiences. Hence many of these tests are prognostic rather than aptitudinal. One of the exceptions is the *Seashore Measure of Musical Ability Tests,* whereby the subject, supposedly without previous training, gives evidence of his degree of ability to discriminate among differences in pitch, rhythm, tonal quality, time, and other aspects of the many auditory stimuli presented in rapid succession by way of phonograph records. Fatigue or perceptual confusion may interfere with a subject's displaying, through test responses, the extent of his potential aptitude in music, however.

The Evaluation of Personality

The fact that personality is conceived by present-day psychologists to be an integrating and integrated unified, functional whole rather than merely a totality of separate traits has exerted a tremendous influence on the construction of techniques aimed to evaluate personality. Earlier test developers were concerned with the measurement of individual personality traits. Although trait-measuring tests or inventories still are being constructed, increasing attention is being given to attempts at total personality evaluation through utilization of projective techniques.

Tests or scales devised to measure extent of physical, mental, emotional, or social development are in effect, attempts to evaluate personality attributes. In addition, measuring instruments have been constructed for specifically displayed attitudes or characteristics.

Rating Scales and Inventories. Many available rating scales and inventories are intended to measure specific personality traits or human qualities, such as initiative, interest, social adaptibility, honesty, cooperativeness, responsibility, degree of submissiveness or aggressiveness, extent of introversion or extroversion, attitudes toward people, conditions or situations, and similar habituated aspects of personality that affect overt behavior. Some of these rating scales and inventories are intended for utilization by the subject himself for self-appraisal; others serve as guides, especially for teachers and counselors, in the appraisal of the subject's personality traits.

Most personality traits and inventories are questionnaires containing questions or statements, the responses to which usually are in the form of words or numbers. Earlier tests require no more than the underlining, circling or checking of *Yes* or *No*. For example, "Do you like to play alone?" *Yes, No.* Responders found that they could not give a categorical answer including only two choices. As a result, later tests made provision for more exact evaluation, such as, *Yes, ?, No; Always, Sometimes, Never; Always, Often, Usually; Occasionally, Seldom.*

In some tests, numerical designations are used, representing a sliding scale, from a high of 9 (complete possession) through 7, 5, for example, to 1 (very slight possession) or 0 (no apparent evidence). A few of the most recently constructed personality scales and inventories employ ingenious modes of response.

Personality rating implies the functioning of the mental processes for the purpose of comparing an individual's possession of one or more personality traits or attributes with their possession by other members of his group. Regardless of whether (1) the rating is self-appraisal or evaluation of one individual by others, or (2) rating responses allow for fine discrimination, the raters tend to be subjective. Complete objectivity is almost impossible to attain in evaluation that is based upon personal opinion and that deals with the subtle factors of human interrelationships.

Self-Appraisal. The term *improvement* connotes change from one status to another regarded to be more effective or satisfactory. In order to bring about the desired change, the constituent elements of both the original and the improved status must be known and understood. The purpose of personality self-appraisal is to help the individual himself, as well as his teachers or counselors, discover his specific strengths and weaknesses so that his strong or favorable characteristics can continue to function as they have, and his weak or detrimental behavior or attitude qualities can be eliminated or reconditioned.

In the case of children who may not understand the implications of their responses to questions in a self-rating scale or inventory, the evaluation of the responses and the application of needed remedial techniques are the responsibilities of parents, teachers, and counselors. Older adolescents and adults usually have greater insight concerning the significance of their self-appraisal. Hence, if they are interested in improvement, they often can effect needed changes with little or no help from others.

No matter how honest a self-evaluator tries to be concerning himself or how much insight he possesses, he cannot be certain that he is reporting correctly. Personal standards of desirability and extent of understanding one's self in relation to these standards have a potent effect on accuracy of judgment. The functioning of one trait may interfere with the evaluation of another. For example, it has been found that many individuals underrate their strong attributes, either because their standards are extremely high or they are unduly modest. Some self-raters overrate their possession of a socially emphasized quality because they are unwilling to admit their own inferiority or are unable to recognize the kind or extent of their deviation from a desirable standard; others, knowing what the correct responses are supposed to be, answer accordingly, even though the answers do not represent their actual behavior or attitude patterns.

Psychologists and educators recognize the subjective nature of self-appraisal techniques. Consequently they (1) check the accuracy of test responses according to other criteria of evaluation, such as displayed behavior or the judgment of reliable associates, (2) accept the responses as indications of the individual's understanding of the degree of trait possession he *should have,* or (3) so construct the scale or inventory that any discrepancies can be discovered among the responses, showing inadequate self-evaluation.

One of the first self-rating inventories, the *Personal Data Sheet,* was devised by Woodworth in 1917 for use in helping service men adapt themselves to army life. It contained 116 questions (each to be answered by *Yes* or *No*) that dealt with an individual's abnormal fears and obsessions, compulsions, and psychosomatic symptoms as they were related to his experiences. In 1923, the inventory was adapted by Mathews for school use. Subsequently, many adaptations of Woodworth's inventory were published.

In some of the more recent self-rating inventories, the items are classified according to separate categories, each of which yields a trait-evaluating score. The *Bernreuter Personality Inventory* is one of the most elaborate of the categorized inventories. It measures six supposedly separate aspects of personality (by the utilization with the 125 test items of six different keys): neuroticism, self-sufficiency, introversion, dominance, confidence, and sociability. A modification of this inventory by Thurstone is not categorized. Other well-known inventories include the *Allport A-S Reaction Study,* presenting in each question a brief description of a situation which is followed by several possible ways of resolving it according to the responder's tendency to be ascendent or submissive; the *Bell Adjustment Inventory, Student Form,* designed to measure adjustment in four areas: home, health, emotional, and social, the *Pressey X-O Test,* including items dealing with emotionality; Laird's adaptation of Woodworth's inventory for use with college students, providing a graphic rating scale for scoring; and the relatively recent *Heston Personality Adjustment Inventory,* including 6 categories: analytic thinking, sociability, emotional stability, confidence, personal relations, and home satisfactions. These represent only a few of the currently available self-appraising instruments.

Appraisal by Others. Rating scales designed for use by teachers and counselors to evaluate the manifested personality qualities of children, adolescents, and young adults often are so constructed that the various items of the scale can be evaluated a-cording to a device that indicates varying degrees of possession of specified traits. Many of these instruments are constructed by the counseling or teaching staff of the particular school or school system in which the scales are to be used. Hence emphasis is placed upon those aspects of personality that appear to be most significant in the local setting.

Since performance on one or more of these scales often is basic to guidance or counseling approaches, several cautions are necessary.

1. The items should be stated definitely and clearly; all-inclusiveness or vagueness of questions must be avoided.

2. The raters must know enough about the subject to be a competent judge of his characteristics.

Personal bias or prejudice on the part of the rater may invalidate his judgment. The influence of the "halo" effect that might operate if only one person were to evaluate the subject is mitigated by having at least three other teachers or counselors independently rate the pupil's personality. Discrepancies then can be explained in terms of existing relationships between the rater and rated, or serve as an appraiser of rater competence. Brief explanatory anecdotal reports accompanying the rating of the various items of the scale often are helpful to the person utilizing the results.

These personality scales for rating by others emphasize the significance of interpreting an individual's personality as that which is displayed in overt behavior by him to another. In other words, the individual has specific personality qualities to the extent that they affect the rater. Hence adolescents, especially, knowing that they will be rated, attempt to make a good impression on teacher-raters, e.g., the hair is combed, the manner is courteous, the dress is clean, the language is guarded, and the like, in order that a teacher will give them favorable ratings.

Interest Inventories. The interests of an individual may be discovered in a variety of ways: (1) observing his behavior during his recreational activities, such as sports and hobbies, and (2) noting his success or failure in the various areas of his school study. Many deep-seated interests, however, are difficult to discover through observation. Hence the utilization of an inventory consisting of a systematic series of questions may help the counselor to discover the less obvious interests. Although responses on an inventory may not be indicative of habitual or persistent interests, the total performance on it may give evidence of attitudes, understandings, and interests that help the counselor evaluate the subject's personality trends.

Interest inventories that have yielded worthwhile results are:

Kuder Preference Record—Personal
Kuder Preference Record—Vocational
Strong Vocational Interest Blank for (1) *Women,* (2) *Men*
Thurstone Interest Schedule

These and other available inventories are especially valuable if the results of their administration are used in conjunction with data obtained from appropriate aptitude or prognostic tests, and observed behavior.

Projective Techniques in Personality Evaluation

The nature and function of the projective technique were discussed in the preceding chapter. Here are presented in somewhat greater detail some of the approaches that are classified as projective techniques in personality evaluation.

Verbal Techniques. An individual's thoughts, interests, mental associations, and emotional states sometimes can be discovered through the use of "free association tests." The individual may be given a list of words and instructed to respond to each with the first word that enters his mind. The length of time required to respond and the exact response are recorded. A delay in any of the responses may be indicative of a desire to avoid expressing the responses or the subject's habitually slow reaction pattern.

Another form of verbal technique is the sentence completion method in which the individual is given freedom to complete a given sentence in any way he chooses, as for example, My home____________________. His responses to a number of sentence-completion experiences may reveal much concerning the individual's imaginative powers, and social interests and associations.

Drawing and Painting as Techniques of Self-Expression. The interests and attitudes of the young child often are expressed through pictorial art, design, and crafts, including finger painting, easel painting, pencil drawing, and construction. Through these media a child is encouraged to give free expression to his interests and desires. Probably, at some time in his life, an individual possesses an urge to express himself through one or more of these media. The urge is stronger during childhood for most persons, but tends to weakness during later adolescence and adulthood.

Play and Dramatic Techniques. Those activities to which children turn when they are free to do as they want are called play. Personality traits reveal themselves during free play activity, since the individual then is not under the stress of meeting any kind of set requirements. Play therapy in kindergartens and early school grades, as well as in child clinics, is used successfully as a means of releasing the tensions of emotionally disturbed children. School and clinic play rooms are established to discover the personality problems of children during their activity in these rooms as they express their resentments, fears, or aggression through the manipulation of play materials.

Psychodrama is used to study adolescents and adults. Attitudes and feelings are expressed overtly as a subject enacts one or another role on a stage, or in another controlled situation. It sometimes is difficult to evaluate behavior during a psychodramatic performance. The subject's imaginative powers and his ability to "throw" himself into the more or less artificially structured situation affects the validity of conclusions concerning his emotional states.

The Rorschach Technique. In the so-called ink-blot test the subject is asked to respond to each of ten cards containing ink blots which are shown him, one at a time. Five of the blot forms are in shades of black and gray, the five others are in two or more colors.

While the subject is examining an ink-blot from any desired angle, he reports to the examiner what he sees in the whole ink-blot or in any one or more of its segments. The comments made concerning each of the ten cards are recorded by the administrator. Then the examiner again shows each card to the subject and asks him to point out exactly the area or areas representing the various objects or situations reported the first time.

The examiner who administers this test must be skilled in its use. The ink-blot test is difficult to administer and especially difficult to interpret. Although standardized sets of responses are available, the range of possible responses is wide, requiring accurate and insightful interpretation. Errors of judgment can be made even by a highly trained specialist because of these subjective aspects of interpretation. Nevertheless, it is a valuable technique, in that, through his responses and expressed attitude toward the task, the subject gives evidence of his imaginative powers, attention to details, intelligent behavior, attention span, and attitude of interest or boredom.

The Thematic Apperception Test. (TAT). This test consists of twenty cards, nineteen of them representing different situations involving one or more persons, and one blank card. The subject is asked to look at each picture in turn and tell a story about it. After he has reported about each of the nineteen cards, he is asked to imagine a picture on the blank card and tell a story about it. The difficulty of interpreting responses on the TAT is similar to that for the Rorschach. Yet it has value as a means of discovering emotional disturbances among older children, adolescents, and adults.

Evaluation of Learner Achievement

Accurate evaluation of learner achievement is one of the essentials of good teaching-learning procedures. The extent and intensity of knowledge mastery can be measured through utilization of tests constructed by (1) the teacher (teacher-made tests), (2) test experts (standardized tests), or (3) state or local test constructors of uniform examinations as, for example, Regents' Tests in New York State. Regardless of the constructional purpose of an achievement test or examination, to achieve best results it should be administered correctly, and the results should be interpreted objectively and applied with understanding. For the evaluation of pupil achievement, several types of teacher-made tests are used: the essay examination, and the more objective short-form tests, such as true-false, multiple choice, and matchings tests, or some modification of these types. The short-form testing types also are used in standardized tests.

The Essay Examination. In an essay-type test, the learner is asked to describe, compare, discuss, explain, show how, and/or evaluate learned materials. Either one or both of two major problems in regard to essay examinations present themselves: (1) the pupil does not understand the teacher's intended connotation of the question, and (2) the teacher's evaluation of pupils' answers gives evidence of subjectivity and variability of interpretation.

The essay-type question offers the learner an excellent opportunity to organize his thinking and to learn to express his ideas and points of view on paper. It promotes the principle of integration in learning. A significant weakness of essay examinations is that their scoring defies complete objectivity. The same question rated by various competent raters has been known to receive scores that vary as widely as 80 points out of 100. One rater, believing that no credit should be given for the solution of a mathematical problem if one arithmetical error is made, rates an answer 0; another rater, admitting that there should be some penalty for a careless error, gives the answer some credit that may vary from anything above 0 to 90 points out of a possible 100. In either instance, the decision is made according to the rater's philosophy of evaluation at the moment. The same attitude may not hold for the papers of other pupils rated at the same time or the answers of subsequent tests.

Differences in rating standards for an exact science represented by mathematics are even greater in the rating of composition papers or of essay-type questions that deal with opinion or appreciation. Even when model answer papers are prepared to serve as guides to the raters, human subjectivity may interfere with the attempt to objectify the rating process. For example, in a teacher-group rating of history test papers, identified by numbers, a numbered set of model answers was rated a failure by one rater who did not know that it was a model rather than a student's paper.

In spite of its faults, the essay-type question serves a definite educational function and should not be discarded. There is a trend toward formulating essay questions in such way that definite organization of thinking is induced and the correction of the answers is controlled by the requirements of the question. A question of this kind is called a *controlled essay question.*

Objective or Short-Answer Tests. Short-answer tests sometimes are referred to as *new-type tests.* These tests provide for objectivity of scoring to the extent that anyone may apply the answer key of correct responses to the various questions. Although the actual scoring of responses is correct in terms of the key, there may be differences of opinion concerning the accuracy of the key answer as applied to the question. In this case, the subjectivity is attached to the wording of the question. Formulation of objective, clearly stated, and accurate questions is difficult; rating them is simple if the question and the key answer agree.

True-False Questions. The following is a sample of the true-false question approach:

DIRECTIONS: Place a plus sign (+) before each statement that is true or essentially true; place a zero (0) before each statement that is false.

+ 1. Attitudes are important molders of behavior.
0 2. The brain reaches its maximum growth at the age of 10 years.
+ 3. Marking standards vary among teachers and with the same teacher.
0 4. The median is the tenth lowest value in the distribution.
+ 5. A spelling scale is an example of a quality test.

In the construction of a true-false test the number of questions should be sufficient to include all the material to be tested, but unimportant details should not be emphasized. Although some teachers find it difficult to construct adequate true-false tests, the results of well-constructed tests of this type correlate highly with those of essay-type tests that are evaluated objectively.

Multiple-Choice Questions. A multiple-choice or multiple response test question presents four or five responses from which to choose the correct or *best* answer. The following questions taken from an examination in educational psychology illustrate this type:

DIRECTIONS: In the following statements, *draw a line under* the best answer and place its letter in front of the statement.

c 1. The most successful teacher (a) usurps the role of the parent, (b) gives bright pupils special favors, (c) retains leadership and is sympathetic but firm, (d) becomes very friendly with the pupils.

c 2. Bridges found that fear, disgust, and anger arise as emotional experiences as early as the age of (a) 2 months, (b) 3 months, (c) 5 months, (d) 7 months.

d 3. One of the most successful methods of testing the association between terms, names or principles is to use a well-constructed (a) true-false test, (b) multiple-choice test, (c) completion test, (d) matching test.

a 4. In an average group of fifth-grade children, the child who on an intelligence test has attained a percentile rank of 65 is considered to be (a) above normal, (b) below normal, (c) normal, (d) feebleminded.

Matching Questions. Questions of this type usually are arranged in two columns in such way that each item in one column (A) can be associated in meaning with at least one item in the other column (B). For example:

DIRECTIONS: In the margin to the left of each item in Column A, place the number of the term in Column B that is most nearly associated with it.

Column A

- 2 Intelligence quotient
- 1 Ink-blot test
- 7 Personality inventory
- 3 Theory of identical elements
- 11 Gestalt psychology
- 9 Validity
- 8 Reliability
- 10 Theory of behaviorism
- 13 Produced first individual intelligence test
- 12 Score of greatest frequency in a distribution

Column B

1. Projective technique
2. Relationship between mental age and chronological age
3. E. L. Thorndike
4. Charles H. Judd
5. Arnold Gesell
6. John Dewey
7. R. G. Bernreuter
8. Measure of consistency of test results
9. Measures what it purports to measure
10. J. B. Watson
11. Kurt Koffka
12. Mode
13. Alfred Binet
14. Median

Completion Questions. There are several forms of this kind of test. In one, the pupil is asked to supply the word or phrase that has been omitted in a given sentence. For example:

1. The first President of the United States was ________ ________
2. A true-false test is an example of an ________________ type test.
3. Even when ________________ answer papers are prepared to serve as ____________ to the ____________, ____________ subjectivity may interfere with the attempt to ____________ the ____________ process.

It may interest the reader to fill the blanks of item 3, and then compare his responses with the actual sentence on page 253.

Comparisons between Words or Phrases. Another short-form type helps to differentiate between the meaning of two words or phrases on the basis of same meaning (S) or different meaning (D) as follows:

DIRECTIONS: Place an *S* before each of the following pairs of terms that refer to the same thing, and a *D* if they refer to a different thing.

S aptitude–talent
D validity–reliability
S correlation–agreement
S norm–standard
S understanding–insight
D mental age–educational age
D range–mode
D frequency distribution–skewness
D identification–projection
D concept–percept
S reflective thinking–reasoning
S intelligance–mental ability

Advantages of Short Form Tests and Examinations. Short-form questions usually are specific and require direct responses. Hence they are factual, thereby handicapping the pupil who wants to bluff. It is claimed by some teachers that they encourage guessing. However, when the guess is based upon the experience background of the pupil (an intelligent guess), the guess serves a learning function. On the other hand, if the guess is not based upon an evaluation of the question (random guess), it has no learning value and serves no good educational purpose.

The objectivity of the answers helps the student develop a confidence in the results that he does not always have in the scoring results of essay-type papers. Objective tests, especially if several types are employed as subtests in the construction of a test or examination, can be reliable measures of achievement.

Disadvantages of the New-Type Tests. The weaknesses of an objective-type test are inherent in the tests themselves. The questions tend to become unduly factual, dealing with meanings of terms, definitions, and quantitative values. The formulation of questions that meet the requirements of being completely true or false, or that have a best answer, is very difficult. The scoring may be a time saver for the teacher, but this advantage is offset by the time required to construct adequate, objective questions. In addition, a student's approach to his preparation for an examination differs according to whether the test has been announced to be a short-form or an essay type test. For the former, he concentrates on details; his study for the other emphasizes broad-view generalizations or trends.

Standardized Tests of Achievement. Standardized tests have been constructed to evaluate learner achievement in practically every school subject or large learning unit. Standardized tests are available for subjects such as art, English, composition, arithmetic, alegbra, biology, and many other areas of learning. In all, more than 400 achievement tests are listed in the *Fourth Mental Measurements Yearbook,* including those testing instruments that are concerned with measuring achievement in larger units of learning. These tests, designed to give a general overall picture of the pupil's achievement in a variety of skills or areas of knowledge, are called *achievement batteries:* A few examples of widely known achievement batteries are:

Iowa Every-Pupil Tests of Basic Skills—Houghton Mifflin Company, Boston.
The Metropolitan Achievement Tests—Houghton Mifflin Company, Boston.
Municipal Battery Tests, Grades, 3-6, 6-8—World Book Company, Yonkers, N. Y.
Advanced Battery—The Speroffs, 8145 Van Buren Ave., Munster, Ind.
Essential High School Content Battery—The Psychological Corporation, N. Y.

Standardized achievement tests serve several purposes. A comparison can be made between the progress of a pupil or group of pupils with that of other children or older learners in various parts of the country. School people can discover the relative achievement of their learners in any subject at any grade level. Subject supervisors are enabled thereby better to evaluate the effectiveness of teaching and learning procedures. The purposes for administering a standardized test are defeated, however, if a teacher attempts to drill his pupils in the content of a test that is about to be administered.

It should be noted also that the content of standardized achievement tests in any area of learning must be limited to *fundamental* or *common* aspects of the subject. Learning needs and teaching emphases differ with individual school objectives, geographical location, and other factors. Hence a standardized test may not be an appropriate evaluating instrument, especially if standardizing procedures are based upon a small or geographically limited number of cases. For example, identification of the names *Houston* and *Hudson* would differ in difficulty for children living in Texas and New York State, respectively.

Test Questions on the Chapter

Directions: Place a plus sign before each statement that is true, and a zero before each statement that is false.

____ 1. Goddard prepared the first test used to measure the ability of an individual.

____ 2. The testing of intelligence had its origin in the United States.

____ 3. The Wechsler Intelligence Scale for Children is an example of a group test.

____ 4. An IQ above 110 represents better than normal intelligence.

____ 5. If a student is ranked at the 90th percentile of his class it means that only 10 per cent of the class are below him in standing.

____ 6. The Crow-Crow Test for High School Entrants is designed to serve the guidance counselor in class placement.

____ 7. Inventories cannot be used in self-rating.

____ 8. Self-appraisal is recognized to be objective in nature.

____ 9. The Ink-blot is used in the Rorschach technique.

____ 10. It is impossible, with competent raters, to have the ratings vary as widely as 70 points on a 100 point scale.

____ 11. Short-form questions should be so selected that they cover all of the subject matter to be tested.

____ 12. The essay-type test is no longer considered to be valuable.

____ 13. Standardized achievement tests can replace all other tests.

____ 14. The Thematic Apperception Test is easy to score.

CHAPTER 21

EVALUATION AND REPORTING OF PUPIL PROGRESS

To rate and report pupil progress in the mastery of information, the verbatim memorization of definite subject matter such as spelling, number combinations, formulas, or rules, and the practice of simple skills is not a difficult task. To evaluate and report to parents a pupil's growth in understanding, judgment, and problem solving, his developing attitudes and behavior patterns, or any other subtle outcomes of his learning, challenges a teacher's power of insight and his fairness of judgment.

Present-day emphasis on evaluating learner experiences and achievement according to his ability to learn increases a teacher's uncertainty concerning the accuracy of his ratings and reporting of pupil's learning progress. Assigned marks usually are not absolute measures of achievement but rather reflect the marker's philosophy concerning relative values. Hence the interpretation of test scores and other evaluating approaches is important to the teacher as well as to the learner and his parents.

Techniques for the Interpretation of Test Scores

Individual test scores have value only after they have been interpreted in terms of the entire testing situation. For example, a raw score of 75 earned by a pupil in one test may show greater relative achievement as compared to the performance of his classmates than does a score of 90 in another test.

Statistical Treatment of Data. A pupil's total numerical rating on a test, representing the number of correct responses, each having an assigned weight, is his *raw score*. In so far as the actual marking is objective and accurate, the raw score is an absolute mark that needs to be interpreted in terms of its relation to established standards. Statistical treatment of test results is a valuable technique for utilization in the interpretation of individual test scores. A teacher can discover thereby the relative success in performance of every pupil as compared with one another and with the entire group.

Many teachers are wary of applying statistical techniques; to them the term implies involved mathematical computations. The utilization of statistics in education usually is limited to the application of simple statstical approaches to the interpretation of tests and other data that have evaluative significance. The mathematical computations needed for their application to classroom situations can be mastered and applied by the teacher, with rewarding results. Some of the basic statistical concepts are presented here briefly.[1]

Basic Statistical Terms. The understanding of certain concepts as they apply to statistical treatment of data is essential. The most frequently used terms are: *range, mode, median, arithmetic mean, quartile deviation, standard deviation, normal curve,* and *correlation.*

First, the scores are ranked from highest to lowest. Starting at the top of a sheet of paper with the score of the pupil having the highest score, the other scores are arranged in descending order. For example, on a spelling test, twenty-one pupils earned the following respective scores: 70, 76, 92, 90, 88, 68, 76, 82, 94, 98, 86, 64, 66, 71, 78, 80, 84, 72, 90, 81, 76. If these scores are arranged in a descending order, starting with the highest score, the arrangement would be: 98, 94, 92, 90, 90, 88, 86, 84, 82, 81, 80, 78, 76, 76, 76, 72, 71, 70, 68, 66, 64. By referring to these data, some of the basic statistical terms will be clarified. All *numbers* included in the following brief interpretation of terms refer to the scores listed.

Range. Range refers to the spread of scores. The extent of the spread of the scores in this test is represented by the number of points on the scale that lie between 98, the highest score, and 64, the lowest score, or 34 ponits. Usually the greater the spread of scores, the *less* homogeneous are the members of the group in a measured trait or function.

Mode (M). The mode is the score made by the largest number of pupils. Three pupils have a score of 76. Hence 76 is the mode.

Median (Mdn). For the purpose of this discussion, the midscore or rough median falls at the point on the scale above which

[1] For a simple discussion of the utilization of statistics in education see L. D. Crow and A. Crow, *Educational Psychology*, new rev. ed. Van Nostrand Reinhold, 1965, Chapter 20; and also APPENDIX, pp. 329, ff. for examples that illustrate the computation of important statistical terms.

and below which an equal number of cases or scores fall. Since there are 21 cases, the score made by the *11th* pupil counting down from the highest score or up from the lowest score is 80, the mid-score or rough median. The exact median is computed by a formula. (See Appendix)

Arithmetic mean (A.M.) The arithmetic mean is the average of the scores. It is found by totaling all the scores (1692), and then dividing that sum by the number of scores (21). The A.M. is 80.57.

Quartile deviation (Q). Quartile deviation is a measure of the deviation of the scores from the median. If the number of cases were divided by 4, the number of scores falling between the lowest quartile Q_1 and the highest quartile Q_3 would equal the middle 50 per cent of the cases, ranging from about 87 to 73. One-half of this range of 14 points is 7 or Q. This means that the middle 50 per cent of the cases equal Mdn (8) $\pm$ Q (7).

Standard deviation. Standard deviation is the measure of the deviation of the scores from the mean. It represents the distance above and below the mean that includes about 68 per cent of the cases or scores. It is arrived at by subjecting the data to a formula. Standard deviation is the most commonly used measure of variability. Technically, it equals the square root of the squared deviations of the scores from the arithmetic mean. In the listed data, S.D. roughly equals 8. About 68% of the distribution equals 80. 75 (A.M.) $\pm$ 8.

Normal curve. The normal curve is the graphic representation of the distribution of phenomena in nature. Each human trait is distributed according to a bell-shaped curve, called the normal curve of distribution. The normal curve is illustrated on pages 242 and 243.

Correlation. Correlation refers to the relationship that exists between the scores of the same pupils on two different tests. For example, if one pupil ranks number one in an arithmetic test and ranks number one in a spelling test, if another pupil ranks number two in arithmetic and number two also in spelling, if another pupil ranks number three in arithmetic and number three in spelling and if the remaining ranks parallel one another, there is perfect agreement in the relative standing of each pupil in the two tests. The parallelism represents a perfect, *positive* correlation of 1.00. If each pupil performed in reverse order on the two tests, e.g., the pupil having the *highest* score in arithmetic having the *lowest* score in spelling, etc., the results show perfect *negative* correlation, or —1.00. A comparison of the results of two tests rarely, if ever, yields a perfect correlation.

Usually, however, the correlation for related learning materials is positive. For example, a correlation of .91 between the results of two tests would represent good positive agreement in the relative performance of the pupils in the tests; a correlation of .32 would indicate positive but poor agreement. A teacher may wish to know the index of correlation between two sets of scores. Formulas for computing correlation can be found in the books suggested on page 259.

Scatter diagram. The scatter diagram can be used to study two variables at one time. Various relationships between the respective data can be observed on the diagram. For example, if the scores made in an arithmetic test and the intelligence quotients of the same pupils are plotted on a diagram, the teacher can see at a glance if there is a close relationship among the data or if the scores are scattered throughout the graph. If these scores (points) are scattered throughout the graph there is little correlation or relationship among the data; if the dots tend to arrange themselves along a line that runs diagonally from the lower left-hand corner to the upper right-hand corner, the correlation is high and positive. If the data tend to fall along a line that extends from the upper left-hand corner to the lower right-hand corner, the correlation is high, but negative. The arithmetic scores and the intelligence quotients of a class of 30 pupils are illustrated graphically in Figure 10.

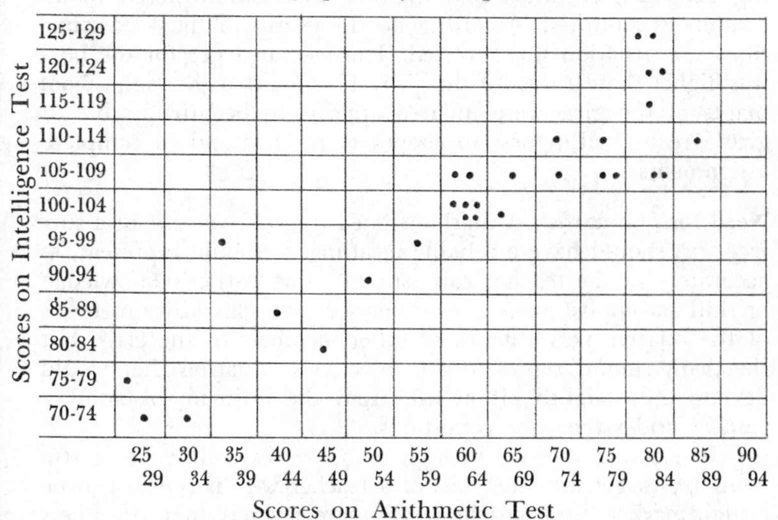

Figure 10. Scatter Diagram of 30 Paired Scores of an Intelligence Test and an Arithmetic Test.

Assignment of Marks or Grades

Important as is the proper construction or selection, and correct administration and scoring of tests, their ultimate value depends upon the interpretation and use of them. For example, during the standardization of a mathematics test for the 7th, 8th, and 9th grades, the test was administered to two members of the same family. At the time, one member, a girl, was in the 9th grade and the other, a boy, was in the 8th grade of the same school. The boy earned a better score in the standardized test than did the girl. Yet, the girl, a model school citizen, had received A's in arithmetic and in algebra, but the boy, whose behavior was less cooperative, barely achieved a B in mathematics. This disparity between the two indicates that factors other than achievement in mathematics entered into the final mark of each.

Sex Differences in Assigned Marks. On the average, the marks of girls in high school are higher than are those of boys. For many years, the entering class of ——— College consisted of 500 boys and 500 girls, each semester. In the selective process it was found that the lowest high school average of the 500 girls selected was 86; yet in order to admit 500 boys it was necessary to accept boys with a high school average as low as 78. The validity of the high school marks was checked when, for counseling purposes, entrance examinations were administered to all candidates admitted. According to the results of these examinations the situation was reversed. The median score for the boys was higher than it was for the girls. The fact that the high school marks of the girls were inflated appears to be attributable to girls' greater willingness to cooperate in class and to complete assignments.

Need for Standards. A mark assigned for achievement in a subject area should have a reliable meaning. It should represent, as accurately as the teacher can estimate, the learner's knowledge or skill accomplishment. There may be some flexibility in terms of the relative performance of other members of the class, but the mark should represent an objective evaluation that would deviate only slightly, if at all, from the estimate of another teacher under the same conditions.

In electing subjects in high school or in college, some students try to get into the class of a teacher who is reputed to be a high marker. Some teachers rate more severely than do others because of their belief that through the setting of high standards they will encourage their students to study more industriously. Equally strong is the belief of a teacher who assigns higher marks that the students thereby will be encouraged toward further application of effort. Most teachers fall somewhere between these two extremes. Students realize, however, that the teacher who "gives" many A's is not necessarily the best teacher.

There is an increasing use of distribution curves by teachers to guide then in assigning marks. As teachers come to realize that marks are not absolute but relative, they are learning how to apply the normal curve procedure in arriving at marks. If the normal curve were to be applied rigidly, however, the distribution of marks on a five-point scale would approximate the following percentage distribution of students. Too close adherence to the normal curve in the assignment of final marks might be unfair in a small class of bright, cooperative students.

A	B	C	D	F
7%	24%	38%	24%	7%

Not all grade distributions deviate from the normal curve because of the superior or inferior performance of all or most of the members of a class. Below are presented the marks in educational psychology assigned at the end of the same semester by five college instructors, respectively.

Table 4. Distribution of Letter Marks assigned by Five Instructors in Educational Psychology

Instructor	*Number of students receiving letter marks*				
	A	B	C	D	F
V (1 class)	10	15	11	0	0
W (1 class)	6	16	14	1	0
X (2 classes)	18	30	17	0	0
Y (2 classes)	4	32	27	0	0
Z (1 class)	5	7	12	4	1

Instructor Z is the most severe marker, while the easiest markers appear to be Instructors V and X. A further study of the marks assigned by these instructors over a period of years reveals that the rating tendencies of each of these instructors are consistent.

Importance of School Marks. Students want the prestige associated with receiving good marks in competition with classmates. A good scholastic record also favors the continuance of education on a higher level or the obtaining of a good job. Hence teachers' evaluations are regarded seriously by most learners. Although marks sometimes are considered to be necessary evils, they help determine promotion or failure in school. Marks earned in high school often represent the basis of college admission. In addition, the all-over grade average of a candidate for a scholarship or honor is one of the determiners of whether he is selected.

Reporting of Pupil Progress

Sooner or later, a teacher's evaluation of his pupil's achievement comes under the scrutiny of parents, other children, and supervisors. Learner progress should be reported in such way that there can be no misunderstanding of the significance of the evaluation.

Report Cards as Reports to Parents. To the recent past, a teacher's evaluation of pupil achievement was reported in the form of letter or numerical marks. Although this method still persists in most schools and colleges, attempts have been made in some schools to construct report cards that can be more functional than the customary procedure. Numerous innovations have been introduced in the form of the report so that it may be more meaningful to parents, supervisors, and the pupils themselves.

The new type report card, containing descriptive statements relative to achievement, attitudes, and specific strengths and weaknesses, has not received unqualified approval from either the teacher who prepares them or the parents who do not always understand their meaning. The items that appear on some of these report forms are similar to those listed on the report card used in Kent State University Training School, as shown here.

Report to Parents

UNIVERSITY SCHOOL

Kent State University

Kent, Ohio

__________ Grade

Report of ____

For School Year

Teacher ____

Director ____

E – Excellent

S – Satisfactory

I – Improving

N – Needs Improving

1st Quarter

Comments – Teacher:

Comments – Parent:

Parent's Signature ______________________________

2nd Quarter

Comments – Teacher:

Comments – Parent:

Parent's Signature ______________________________

ATTITUDES AND HABITS OF CITIZENSHIP

GENERAL	F	W	Sp	S
1. Takes pride in good behavior				
2. Obeys rules and regulations				
3. Expects only his share of attention				
4. Is able to manage himself				
5. Takes care of class materials				
6. Accepts suggestions well				
7. Courteous to others				
8. Gives attention				
9. Gets to right place on time				
10. Is cooperative				

PERSONAL

A. Health

1. Has clean clothes and body				
2. Uses handkerchief				
3. Has good posture				
4. Is pleasant and cheerful				

B. WORK

1. Feels pride in work				
2. Is industrious				
3. Gets needed materials				
4. Begins work promptly				
5. Finishes work promptly				
6. Assumes responsibility				
7. Follows directions				

C. Attendance

1. Days enrolled				
2. Days present				
3. Days absent				
4. Times tardy				

Fifth and Sixth Grade
SCHOLASTIC RECORD

	F	W	Sp	S
LANGUAGE ARTS				
1. Reading				
a. Comprehension				
b. Rate				
c. Fluency				
d. Word recognition				
2. English				
a. Oral expression				
b. Written expression				
c. Creative expression				
3. Writing				
a. Neatness				
b. Legibility				
4. Spelling				
a. Formal lesson				
b. Application				
SOCIAL STUDIES				
1. Knowledge				
2. Understanding				
SCIENCES				
1. General Science				
a. Observation				
b. Appreciations				
2. Health				
a. Knowledge				
b. Applications				
3. Arithmetic				
a. Skills				
b. Accuracy				
c. Reasoning				
d. Problem solving				

Parent-Teacher Conferences. The parent-teacher interview that has become a relatively common practice in early grades is finding its way into the upper grades of the elementary school. Through the interchange of ideas during these informal talks, the teacher and the parent can discover much from each other concerning the child's attitudes, abilities, accomplishments, and habitual behavior patterns. These talks usually are held at school. If the teacher can visit the home occasionally, his understanding of the child is improved through greater knowledge concerning the home background. In the home setting, the parents and pupils also become better acquainted with the teacher as a person than is possible in the school situation. In some crowded school districts, teachers' visits to the home may be neither advisable for young women teachers nor welcomed by parents.

Much good can come from school or home interviews. Parents who otherwise might be adversely critical of what the school is doing may change their opinions of the school's program. In these face-to-face conferences, either the parent or the teacher is given an opportunity to talk freely but he also can profit by listening. The interview technique has succeeded so well as applied in the lower grades that some schools have substituted it for the traditional report card in the kindergarten and through the second grade. It is the belief of the school authorities that the informal conference is all that is needed to keep the parents informed relative to the school progress of their child.

Letters as Report Cards. In some schools, when or if teachers cannot meet parents personally, they write specific progress reports in letter form to the parents of each child in the class. The letter procedure also is used in many school systems to supplement other more formal reports. Sometimes a space is provided on the report card to write what can be considered a letter-type report. Many of the letter-form reports provide a space for parents' comments concerning the teacher's report.

The teacher who habitually keeps pertinent data concerning his pupils in the form of anecdotal records is prepared to write interesting letters to parents relative to a child's behavior and school progress. The ultiziation of the letter report has several disadvantages, however. One teacher may be more skillful than another in the writing of interesting letters. Another teacher may have greater facility in the use of the personal conference. Both may be good teachers, but written letters can be compared more objectively by parents than interviews.

Visual Grading. One way to make grades more meaningful is by plotting the scores on cross-sectional paper. This enables the instructor to see at a glance how the scores arrange themselves. These scores tend to form a bell-shaped curve. In visual grading a visual rather than a statistical interpretation is used. It enables the instructor to adapt the phenomenon of normal distribution to small groups.

Some of the advantages of visual grading are given below. Visual grading:

1. Provides a uniform basis of comparison regardless of the differences in scoring procedures.

2. Helps to keep grades constant from teacher to teacher and from year to year thus making it fair to all students of all ability and grade levels.

3. Eliminates the need to be lax in evaluation procedures or to water down the content of examination.

4. Can be explained to students and parents so that the grades are easily understood.

5. Is less time consuming than many other methods since no complicated mathematical computations are involved.[1]

Value of Reports. Many aspects of reporting pupil progress must be considered. Such questions as the following enter the situation: What should be the basis of promotion—chronological age, physical and social maturity, or academic achievement? What kinds of information concerning a child should be included in the report to parents? What happens when a child takes his report card home? Should evaluating and reporting be related to degree of ability to perform. Can pupils evaluate themselves?

Some parents and teachers are working together to devise the kind of report forms that will be most serviceable to all concerned—teachers, parents, and pupils. At the same time, in some cities where the new-type reports were introduced, the parents expressed dissatisfaction because they could not interpret the report. Consequently, a few cities have dropped the modified report forms, and the parents are encouraged to help decide the type of report that should be issued.

---

[1] For examples of visual grading see L. D. Crow and A. Crow, *The Student Teacher in the Elementary School*, David McKay, 1965, pp. 366-372.

PART VI

PSYCHOLOGICAL ASPECTS OF ADJUSTMENT

CHAPTER 22

ADJUSTMENT, SELF-DISCIPLINE, AND CHARACTER

The significance of broadening educational goals lies in the fact that formal and informal agencies of education are becoming increasingly concerned with every aspect of human development and learning. School people on all educational levels realize that educational provision is needed by all children and adolescents for healthful physical, emotional, and social development as well as for subject-matter mastery.

If an adult is to be happy, economically and socially secure, and a constructively active citizen, he of course must possess a background of adequate knowledge and have needed skill competence. Perhaps more important than these are the attitudes, self-controls, and character strengths that he acquired through his pre-adult learning experiences. One of the principal responsibilities of parents and teachers, therefore, is to understand the various aspects of behavior patterning and to help young people develop self-control or self-discipline in relation to behavior expressions of their wants, urges, and interests.

Significant Aspects of Behavior Patterning

An individual's behavior may be (1) impulsive or unrestrained, or (2) controlled or inhibited. The kind of behavior displayed in a particular situation or under specific conditions may reflect a person's habitual mode of reaction, or represent a deviation from accustomed behavior, induced by unusual elments in the stimulus situation.

A person's overt behavior usually is described by those who observe it in terms of its effect upon them. Terms applied to aspects of behavior often are used loosely without regard to their psychological implications. Therefore certain conceptual relationships are explained here as background for later areas of discussion.

Adjustment and Maladjustment. According to biologists, an adjustment is an acquired characteristic, or a variation produced in an organism that is not transmittable through the genes. Psychologically, adjustment refers to an individual's characteristic or habitual understanding of, reaction to, and manner of solving problem situations which he experiences. Degree of adjustment may range from exceptionally adequate behavior to extremely inadequate behavior or maladjustment. According to popular usage, however, an "adjusted" person is one who conforms to culturally accepted mores, customs, and general ways of life; a person is considered to be maladjusted if he is unable or unwilling to adapt one or more aspects of his behavior to conform to so-called normal behavior.

Normality is a relative term. An individual may be physically or mentally able to meet his needs and to reach his goals in one environment or one societal group, but not in another. The extent to which he can or cannot reduce emotional stress in relation to his wants or ambitions is an individual experience. However, emotional stresses and conflicts or the lack of them are associated closely with the way in which the members of his group react to his behavior deviations according to their standards of conduct. Moreover, one can be well adjusted in some characteristic responses and poorly adjusted in others.

Normality can be interpreted in terms of differing criteria. Viewed according to social significance, an individual may appear to be maladjusted or abnormal because his knowledge, beliefs, or ambitions do not fit into the general thought patterns of the group. In such instances, the supposed maladjustment may be desirable in that it connotes a higher than average level of aspiration. History is replete with the achievements of noted scientists, inventors, and explorers who were judged by their contemporaries to be insane or idle dreamers. Conversely, abnormality or maladjustment can be evidenced through criminal acts that harm society as well as the abnormal or maladjusted person himself.

For the purpose of this discussion, adjustment, either relatively adequate or inadequate, represents the degree to which certain characteristics or traits are present in relationships to what might be considered a pathological norm. The personality as a whole may or may not be normal, but the extent to which a person experiences any one or more specific conditions determines his degree of adjustment. According to some psychologists, the basic determining conditions include: feelings of security, body needs and their satisfaction, self-knowledge and self-evaluation, emotional spontaneity, formulation of life goals, and emancipation from rigid cultural or group control. Accompanying positive conditions are: ability to learn from experience and to meet reasonable group requirements, a realistic approach to the meeting of problem situations, and personality consistency and integration. Malfunctioning in any of these areas may induce mild or more serious maladjustment.

Discipline and Self-Discipline. Implicit in the concept of discipline are (1) the presence of rules, regulations, standards, or other conduct determiners, and (2) the control of impulsive, overt expressions of personal desires, interests, or ambitions in accordance with appropriate and acceptable societal standards.

Discipline, as commonly regarded in connection with child rearing and school training, refers to a young person's submission to authoritative control of his behavior by parents and teachers. During early childhood, conformity to adult standards of behavior usually is achieved through utilization of extrinsic rewards for "good" conduct. The child also may refrain from engaging in "bad" or disapproved forms of behavior because of the fear of consequences (learned through past experiences), desire for approval, or the effect upon him of other externally applied behavior improvers.

Discipline or the control of behavior is needed by young and old. No one is able to exercise desirable control in all situations, especially those in which authoritarian deterrents are absent, unless he is motivated to do so by his own appreciation of what is right and good and his willingness to behave acccordingly. An individual's established habits of obeying rules and regulations formulated for the safety and welfare of all members of society, including himself, represent the achievement of self-control or self-discipline.

In its highest and most refined form, self-discipline frees one from fear of externally applied consequences of his acts as well as from the harmful effects of impulsive behavior. The self-disciplined person usually can achieve good personal and social adjustment. The development of self-discipline in all areas of behavior is difficult, however. The home's and school's responsibility in this area of learning is discussed later in the chapter.

Relation of Character and Personality. The terms *personality* and *character* sometimes are used interchangeably. Approval or disapproval of one implies a similar evaluation of the other.

Character is conceived by some to be a kind of functional aspect of personality, paralleling other personal attributes, such as physical constitution, appearance, intelligence, special aptitudes, and emotional and social reactions. According to another point of view, personality reflects the ability of an individual to "sell himself" to those with whom he comes in contact, while character is associated more nearly with his religious affiliation and his religious and moral values.

Personality and character cannot be divorced from one another. No one is born with those attributes that later are identified as constituting his personality or his character. Both are rooted in the emerging patterns of physical, mental, and emotional development, as structural growth and functional maturation are aided or hindered by environmental influences. A fundamental factor of difference in the connotation of the two terms lies in the point of reference.

Psychologically, emphasis is placed upon the developmental process. Through the utilization of research procedures, psychologists attempt to find answers to questions pertaining to the *what, why* and *how* of likenesses and differences among individuals in all phases of human growth and behavioral development. Their function is not to evaluate the rightness or wrongness of acquired conduct or attitude habits. The social stimulus value of an individual's habitual behavior has psychological implications that exclude judgments concerning the extent to which his behavior is in accord with the established behavior standards of his society.

From the viewpoint of social acceptance or rejection, an individual's consistently habitual attitudes and overt behavior as these affect the welfare of other members of his group as well as his own welfare constitute his character. Character, rooted in the total, unified integration of personality traits, functions as a complex system of inner motivators and acquired interests and beliefs, and their conduct manifestations. Character is the determiner of the choices made in relation to personal or general welfare that can be adjudged as right or wrong, according to group-accepted standards.

An individual's associates may react differently toward his personality and his character. If his overt behavior gives evidence of his strict adherence to positive principles of goodness as related to social welfare, his associates respect and admire him, but they may not like him as a person. Conversely, if his behavior sometimes is motivated by interests or attitudes that are not aimed at the common good but other aspects of his personality are attractive, his friends like him to the extent that they are willing to overlook some of his "human frailties."

Ethics and Morals. Character is closely linked with the functional aspect of ethical standards and moral values. The terms *ethical* and *moral* often are used incorrectly as synonymous. Both terms refer to behavior standards, but their implications differ. The dictionary definition of morality stresses the functional aspect of conduct as chaste, virtuous, and right, or as conforming in a greater or lesser degree with conventional rules that may or may not have religious or spiritual implications. Ethics is concerned with the philosophic aspects of conduct, including attempts to differentiate between right and wrong and to evolve basic principles of right action.

In terms of conformity to a group-formulated moral code, an individual's conduct is judged to be moral (conforming) immoral (nonconforming and detrimental to group welfare), or unmoral or amoral (detrimental to the general good, but caused by ignorance of code requirements). Whether judgment of conduct as moral or immoral is valid depends upon the narrowly specific or broadly general provisions of the moral code.

Most societal groups probably are in agreement concerning the value to individual and group welfare of adherence to certain fundamental moral standards. Character traits such as honesty, industry, loyalty, cooperation, generosity, and interest in the welfare of others as well as of oneself are generally accepted aspects of the *good life*. The kinds of behavior that are expected to be overt expressions of these concepts vary according to the traditions, mores, and customs of a cultural group, however.

If a people expect the younger generation to adhere to group-accepted standards of conduct, provision must be made for the teaching of ethical principles to children and adolescents. These principles then are to serve as ideals by which individual conduct will be governed. Most children and adolescents can master the ideas associated with rightness or wrongness of behavior. To inculcate ideals as conduct motivators is much more difficult, since all behavior is accompanied by emotional concomitants.

Life Values and Levels of Aspiration. Implicit in the meaning of life values and levels of aspiration are the concepts discussed in the foregoing pages: adjustment, discipline, personality, character, moral values, and ethical principles. The appreciation aspect of the personal and social values which motivate behavior is imbedded in experiences affecting one's attitudes toward himself and the satisfactions of his wants in relations with people, objects, situations, and conditions. His interests, ambitions, and aspirational levels or goals are influenced by the kind and extent of his physical, mental, and emotional development and by relatively favorable or unfavorable environmental circumstances. Life values and goal-pointed aspirations often are identified as (1) materialistic, (2) nonmaterialistic, and (3) self-satisfying and socially constructive balancing between concern about material achievement and nonmaterialistic interests and ideals.

A young person's value appreciations and inspirational or goal levels usually reflect adult attitudes. A competitive society which places major emphasis upon the values inherent in the possession of wordly goods, high prestige, or great power is likely to pass on, either directly or indirectly, similar value appreciations to its young people. The converse also holds. A child reared in a nonindividualistic, cooperative society tends to place group welfare above personal gain and to submit to group will or pressure.

Extremes of either type of child rearing are undesirable. The competitive, materialistic approach can induce too great individualism, undue aggressiveness, and attempted self-realization and aggrandizement at the expense of others' welfare. In a completely noncompetitive society, a child is denied the opportunity to develop special aptitudes; he remains dependent upon the group rather than learning to become self-reliant and independent. Thus he acquires an unrealistic, weakly idealistic attitude toward life.

Education toward Self-Discipline

The lay public is becoming increasingly concerned about the incidence of asocial behavior among children and adolescents. Parents and other adults tend to blame what they term "soft pedagogy" for some young people's apparent flaunting of authority, disregard for the law, acts of vandalism, and delinquent or criminal behavior.

Behavior Expression and Control. Psychological findings concerning the basic needs of children and the detrimental effects upon child development of repressions and suppressions brought about a relaxation of earlier externally applied, rigid behavior controls. Children were encouraged to give expression to their urges, wants, desires, and interests.

It was hoped that inner control of impulsive behavior would develop as a result of the suffering experienced by the child in the form of natural punitive consequences of uncontrolled conduct. Psychological objectives for granting freedom of expression to the child as a means of building inner behavior controls were misunderstood. Freedom of expression was interpreted to mean license to satisfy immediate, self-centered wants; behavior controls of any kind were believed to be undesirable.

At present, many psychologists and educators are attempting to remedy the harmful results of unduly permissive child-rearing and teaching practices. Parents and teachers are coming to recognize the value to the growing child and adolescent of a reasonable and healthful amount of physical and behavioral freedom; they also are beginning to accept responsibility for helping children develop adequate self-discipline.

Behavior Deviations among School Learners. Among the members of any class group, on any school level, behavioral patterns probably represent a wide range of differences that are overt manifestations of (1) individual developmental status—physically, mentally, emotionally, and socially, (2) home and family background, and (3) more or less serious adjustment problems, associated with psychological factors, such as threats to emotional security, and to self-esteem and the esteem of others. Many class groups include (1) active, well-adjusted, and successful learners, (2) relatively passive, well-intentioned, and hard-working pupils, (3) shy, fearful, submissive, and cooperative but unsuccessful young people, and (4) aggressive, maladjusted pupils who display little or no interest in learning and resent teacher authority.

Some forms of maladjustment among his pupils are recognized more easily by a teacher than are others. He can "spot" the troublesome pupils who interfere with the smooth running of learning activities by their inattentiveness, carelessness in lesson preparation, interruption of classroom discussion, and similar aggressive or nonconforming actions. Some of the more serious personal maladjustments among children or adolescents may not be so quickly recognized by the teacher because of the pupils' apparent conformity to class procedures. Yet these children may lie, cheat, steal, or engage in other forms of dishonest behavior.

The kind of nonconforming classroom behavior in which a pupil may engage can be motivated by more or less abnormal attitudes, such as overawareness of self, self-interest, unawareness of consequences, imitation of attention-getting devices used by other pupils, desire to be spectacular, or desire for extreme freedom of personal action or license in satisfying immediate impulses. Whatever the cause of a pupil's problem behavior may be or the form it takes, the young person must learn to control his asocial interests and their behavior manifestations. Discipline is needed, preferably developed self-discipline.

The Role of the Teacher. Probably the most effective teaching aid to help young people acquire habits of self-discipline is teacher example. The personally and socially well-adjusted teacher can exercise a tremendous influence on pupils' behavior. The significance of the teacher's adjustment status is discussed in Chapter 23. At this point, the reader's attention is directed to some of the ways in which a teacher can mold pupil attitudes apart from the example set by his own display of self-disciplined behavior.

Understanding Pupils. The teacher should know all that he can discover about each of his pupils. He can gain an understanding of a young person's needs, interests, abilities and habitual attitudes and behavior by reference to all the accumulated information concerning the pupil that is available in the principal's or dean's office, and through personal observation of the pupil's behavior in the classroom.

Suggested observational techniques that can be started on the first day of the school term or year include:

1. Identification of each pupil by name.
2. Recognition of differences among pupils in their ability and willingness to participate in class discussions.
3. Alertness to what is going on in the classroom, especially in the rear seats.
4. Awareness of differences in physical structure, posture, and health.
5. Consciousness of existing relationships among class members—the presence of closely knit cliques and of isolates (pupils not included in temporary or more permanent pupil groupings), and other evidences of pupil attitudes toward one another.

Knowing Subject Matter and How to Teach It. Many class incidents involving behavior aberrations on the part of one or more pupils can be prevented by the teacher's understanding his pupils. Another important means of helping pupils develop self-control has to do with the teacher's knowledge of the subject matter to be learned and his method of presentation. The importance of motivating learner's interest already has been discussed. Skill in fostering the aroused interest, provided the learners are mentally ready to profit from instruction in the particular area of study, prevents them from engaging in behavior not associated with learning activities. Teacher commendation for work well done and remedial help given by the teacher when it is needed are excellent inducers of continued interest in learning.

Scheduling Class Procedures. Perhaps the most potent effector of good behavior control is the pervasive influence of well-organized, democratic class management. Most young people experience emotional security in classroom situations exemplifying a well-planned schedule of activities. For the school day to proceed according to a pattern established early in the year or term frees them from possible tensions that might arise if they entered a classroom each day without knowing exactly what would happen. Usually, however, they want to have some share in the planning and control of the scheduled activities.

Many children appear willing to submit to authoritarian teacher attitudes toward regular class routines. Preadolescents and adolescents are more likely to rebel against set patterns of procedures, initiated and planned by the teacher and rigidly enforced by him. Consequently several psychological principles should function in the establishment of classroom procedures. The approach should be democratic rather than authoritarian. This does not mean that immature young people should assume complete responsibility for class management. Guidance of youthful incompetence needs to be given by a mature, experienced teacher.

For younger children, the teacher's role must be relatively positive and directive. With older children and adolescents, the teacher's approach can be more indirect. Early in the school term or year, the teacher and pupils can offer suggestions concerning the management of needed routines, schedules, recitation procedures, and related matters. The teacher's main responsibility is to discourage impractical suggestions and to encourage and expand constructive pupil plans. This technique may seem to the teacher to be time consuming and cumbersome, especially if his pupils have had no previous experience in group planning. Yet the shared project usually results in good class cooperation that stems from pride in the activities which they helped organize.

Other organizational aspects of class procedures help young

people learn to discipline themselves rather than depend upon externally administered disciplinary methods. The schedules should not be practiced so rigidly that they become boring or interfere with the achieving of habits of adaptability. Slight changes can serve as interest renewers.

In so far as possible, every member of the class should have a specific responsibility. In a large class, it may be impossible for every pupil to have a job as a permanent assignment. In fact, psychologically this would be undesirable for several reasons: (1) there would be overtraining in one type of activity and lack of experience in others, (2) job monopoly would be encouraged, and (3) decreasing interest in the job might result in careless, ineffectual performance.

To provide responsibilities for all the members of the class and to avoid psychological hazards, jobs can become committee projects, and reorganized or rotated, periodically. Moreover, whenever possible or practical, the class officers and the various job committees should be elected by the class. Certain temporary or exceptionally important assignments probably would be appropriate teacher appointments, made objectively and without personal prejudice or show of favoritism.

Treating Deviate Behavior. In spite of a teacher's utilization of psychologically sound approaches to the prevention of unacceptable behavior deviations and the encouragement of pupil self-discipline, relatively mild and more serious conduct and attitude difficulties are almost certain to arise. Even a habitually well-adjusted and scholastically successful child or adolescent occasionally may express in his classroom behavior the emotional effects of a temporary physical disorder or an annoying or disturbing experience outside the classroom.

An impulsive, still uncontrolled child may get into trouble without realizing what has happened. A boy or girl, suffering from a serious emotional disorder or possessing deep-rooted asocial, authority-resenting attitudes, cannot achieve easily and readily an adequate control of inherent impulses. Consequently, he may burst forth in uncalled-for disruptive behavior.

To prevent too great interference with regular classroom activities, the teacher may need to employ immediate disciplinary measures if or when extremely nonconforming or uncooperative attitudes are displayed by an individual pupil or a small group of pupils. The form of disciplinary procedure to be utilized should be determined according to the teacher's understanding of the offender and the seriousness of the offense. The measures used should not be completely punitive but aimed at helping the young person gain improved self-control. Sentimental appeals having personal implications must be avoided.

Tantrum behavior on the part of the teacher has little, if any, effect upon temper tantrums displayed by children, except to increase the strength of the tantrum. Threats of delayed consequences voiced by the teacher in the presence of the class are likely to incite the arousal of emotional tension and feelings of bitter resentment against the teacher, if he follows through by administering punishment after school hours. Idle threats, forgotten by the teacher after they are made, encourage attitudes of contempt for the teacher and continuance of disapproved behavior.

Disciplinary measures should be positive and constructive. Traditional forms of punishment, such as the issuance of demerits, the keeping of the offender after school to receive a lecture from the teacher concerning his offense or to sit motionless for a specified period of time soon lose their effect and have no value as motivators of self-control.

The way in which a teacher handles a disciplinary matter varies according to the offender and the offense. Whatever the treatment is, however, it should be (1) based upon an understanding of the offense, (2) directed at the offense, not the offender, (3), objective and impersonal, (4) definite, related to the offense, and understood by the offender, and (4) if possible, administered in private. There are offenders and offenses, however, that cannot be treated adequately by the teacher, without the assistance of supervisors, of school guidance counselors, and, in cases of severe emotional disturbance, of physicians, psychiatrists, or the trained personnel of child guidance clinics. A teacher should never hesitate to seek the cooperation of specialists in his attempts to help young people with their behavior problems.

Character Building

Basically, character building is concomitant to the progressive process of human development and learning. Hence most of what could be said here would duplicate the content of previous discussions. A few additional comments are needed, however, to point up some of the complex and subtle elements that effect changes in an individual's moral judgment and ethical understandings, power of self-discipline and general philosophy of life—all of which are factors inherent in the kind of character he eventually builds for himself.

Character Patterns. Character, like personality, cannot be typed. The dynamic nature of sound interrelationships constantly influences ideas, ideals, and appreciation of moral values. Long-time or intensive experience with favorable or unfavorable character molders may lead to the acquisition of particular habit patterns that become characteristic of an individual, either temporarily or permanently.

Character has unity. Specific, consistent behavior motivators that, for convenience, are identified by trait names, such as industry, sense of justice, loyalty, and honesty, interact constantly and thereby affect one another's functioning. For example, extreme loyalty to a friend may cause a man who is habitually truthful to lie or to misrepresent facts in order to help his friend get out of a difficult situation.

An individual's acquired system of values may determine the overt expression of a character trait. Most people consider it wrong to kill, yet a gentle, kind woman may kill or severly injure anyone who is about to harm her child. A sincere pacifist, on the other hand, may be extremely loyal to his country, but he is so opposed to killing other human beings that he is willing to suffer humiliation in a concentration camp rather than participate in a war.

There are certain combinations of trait trends that, in their integrated activity, constitute a person's fairly consistent character. Studies have been made of observable behavior and attitude differences between well-adjusted young people and youthful delinquents, especially in relation to authority. The findings of these studies have led to tentative conclusions concerning the character traits of socially maladjusted young people.

Delinquent boys and girls tend to resent authority of any kind. They dislike convention, have little respect for the property rights of others, are impulsive, and usually are aggressive. There appears to be little difference between the degree of dependence that distinguishes the delinquent from the well-adjusted person, however. Although social insecurity may be the cause of asocial behavior, the delinquent is unlikely to admit this fact; yet he may recognize his character defects and be dissatisfied with himself. Emotional stresses and tensions thus aroused incite him to engage in asocial acts that increase in number and seriousness until he finally suffers the consequences of his delinquencies or crimes. So strong may be his undesirable character traits that neither punitive measures nor attempts at rehabilitation and reeducation can change his attitudes or behavior patterns.

Character Education. Educational approaches to character building have been and continue to be the source of considerable controversy among educators. Some claim that "good" character, like a good attitude, is caught rather than taught. Others differ concerning the methods to be employed. Basically, all of a child's experiences in the home, the school, the neighborhood, and the larger community influence his ideals, values and appreciations, and his consequent behavior. The school program of character education represents but one area of influence. It may have relatively little effect upon a young person in comparison with other out-of-school experiences.

As is true in the development of self-discipline, example is a primary factor of influence. Consequently the consistently displayed character traits of parents, teachers, and other school personnel serve as models that consciously or unconsciously are imitated by school children. Furthermore, a young person cannot be expected to do the "right" thing unless he knows what is right, according to societal standards. Hence instruction is needed concerning moral codes, legal responsibilities, and ethical concepts. Accompanying the instruction and following it, many appropriate opportunities should be provided for repeated practice, so that adequate habits are formed. Much of what is done by the schools in character education, in addition to giving information, should be indirect and integrated into every teaching-learning situation.

In many of our colleges and universities a course in ethics is offered to students. In Japan, some educators believe that it should be offered no later than the elementary school. Consequently, after debating the pros and cons of it for a number of years, they recently decided to include a course of ethics in the curriculum. However, there are many educators who believe that ethical concepts should be acquired by learners as an inherent part of every subject taught. This seems to be a sensible point of view.

CHAPTER 23

RELATION OF MENTAL HYGIENE TO ADJUSTMENT

Since earliest times the possession of good physical health has been considered important. To pay a doctor to keep one well is an old Chinese custom. In Western cultures, however, the traditional attitude was to avoid ill health, disease, or accident in so far as it was possible, but to seek medical aid only when curative treatment was necessary. Prevention medicine and physical hygiene are identifying terms applied to relatively new concepts of health care, according to which former concern about curing physical ills has broadened to include emphasis upon the *prevention* of physical ill health and the *preservation* of good health. A similar trend is observable in present attitudes toward mental and emotional adjustment.*

Mental Health and Hygiene

Adjustment refers to an individual's mental and emotional reactions to problem situations or conditions. By substituting the term *mental* and *emotional health* for adjustment, good or adequate mental and emotional health means that the individual has achieved sufficient mental control of emotional reactions to meet a problem situation adequately. Inability to control emotional stress or strain implies that the individual is mentally weak or ill.

Concept of Mental Health. Mental health represents degree of good or normal mental functioning. A person possessing good mental health can adjust well to environmental situations and interpersonal relations. Occasionally he may deviate slightly from his accustomed mode of adjustment, but he soon returns to normality with little or no aid from others. A severe emotion-disturbing experience may so affect his normal adjustment patterns that he needs help to regain accustomed control, however.

Mental health is a matter of degree. A person who, for one

* For new insights on the behavior of the young, see Theodore Roszak, *The Making of a Counter Culture: Reflections on the Technocratic Society and Its Youthful Opposition* (New York: Doubleday, 1969).

reason or another, has become mentally ill has little or no ability to solve problems that have emotional concomitants. The resulting emotional disruption or maladjustment requires the services of a trained counselor, if curative measures are to be attempted.

Function of Mental Hygiene. Scientifically interpreted, mental hygiene is concerned with mental health and adjustment in human relationships. As in physical hygiene, the three avenues of approach are: *preventive, preservative,* and *curative.* Preventive mental hygiene is the concern of the parent and others responsible for helping a child develop adequate control of emotions. The preservative approach is utilized by those adults who, having some knowledge of the dynamics of human behavior, cooperate in promoting good adjustment. Included among adults interested in furthering child welfare are teachers, parents, ministers, psychologists, and other child and youth leaders.

The cure or treatment of serious mental illness should be left to trained specialists, such as psychiatrists, clinical psychologists, psychiatric social workers, and physical, recreational, and occupational therapists. To achieve success in any phase of its functioning, mental hygiene borrows freely from biology, psychology, sociology, medicine, religion, and psychiatry.

The Mental Hygiene Movement. The mental hygiene movement had its inception during the first decade of the twentieth century, with the publication of *A Mind That Found Itself.* Clifford Beers, the author, and Adolf Meyer, a psychiatrist who became interested in the story of Beer's experiences in a hospital for the insane, founded in Connecticut the first state Mental Hygiene Organization. The original purpose was to alert the general citizenry to the need of better treatment for patients in institutions for the insane. Shortly thereafter, a National Committee for Mental Hygiene was established. Interest in the application of mental hygiene principles spread quickly.

That the mental hygiene approach has found its way into organized education now is evidenced in curriculum construction, teaching procedures, and other aspects of schooling. The emphasis of school people is on prevention of maladjustment and mental disruption. Attempted cure of mental illness still is the responsibility of psychiatrists and the staffs of hospitals for the mentally ill.

Affectors of Mental Health. An individual's state of mental health is rooted in the interaction between his inborn characteristics and environmental forces. Much that has been said in previous chapters applies to the degree of mental health a young or older person manifests in his overt behavior. It is known that a child, an adolescent, or an adult strives to meet certain physical and social needs in ways that bring satisfaction. The relative strength of the needs and the degree to which they are fulfilled have potent effects upon physical and mental health.

Physical ill health resulting from inadequate care of tissue needs usually can be remedied through improvement in physical care or medical treatment. Emotional and social needs are conditioned by experience. The developing young person possesses strong desires for affection, good social status, and mastery of or successful achievement in learning or other tasks, with accompanying prestige. The extent to which these desires or wants are fulfilled, either through his own efforts or favorable situational conditions, or both, determines his mental health status or his degree of consistent, realistic, and positive adjustment.

Positive Mental Hygiene Approaches. The kind of attitudes and behavior displayed by parents and teachers toward the fulfillment of a child's physical, mental, emotional, or social needs is a basic factor of the young person's adjustment or state of mental health. Too much emphasis upon one area of inherent needs with disregard of others may have disruptive effects. For example, the mother of a delinquent, mentally-ill adolescent could not understand the reason for his asocial behavior. She insisted that his parents had done everything they could for him in the way of physical care, comfortable home, and fulfillment of his expressed interests. Since he was the youngest child, one want was not satisfied—the close companionship with the parents enjoyed by his brothers who were much older than himself.

The possession of good mental health is associated closely with parents' and teachers' emphasis upon a child's achieving self-discipline. Minor symptoms of poor mental health can be treated by teachers and other school guidance personnel (Chapter 24). Application of preventive and preservative principles of mental hygiene by parents and teachers, begun early in the life of a developing child, can exercise a continuing healthful influence on his personal and social adjustments. Delayed or ignored application of these principles can result in the young person's experiencing more or less serious symptoms of mental ill health or mental and emotional disorder.

Need of the Curative Function of Mental Hygiene. Although there always have been individuals giving evidence of personal or social maladjustment, present-day world unrest and disturbance appear to have intensified serious deviations from adequate adjustment. Thwartings and frustrations, leading to mental illness, are posing serious social problems. Present incidence of mental illness is great. Hospitals for the mentally ill lack sufficent beds to care for badly disordered patients. According to estimates, at least one person in every twenty is likely to need hospitalization; the number of those who may develop some form of mental or emotional disturbance during their lifetime is approximately one out of every ten.

It probably would be impossible and socially undesirable for any individual to satisfy in his own fashion every whim, fancy, or deeper urge or need that might arise during his day-by-day living. Most individuals occasionally find themselves in situations that pose problems of adjustment to conditions or relationships that seem to defy reasonable and self-satisfying solution. The influence on mental health of thwarting situations and self-attempted adjustment techniques are discussed here briefly. A more detailed treatment can be found in mental hygiene textbooks.

Influence on Mental Health of Frustrations and Conflicts

The behavior of an individual, as he attempts to adjust to conditions or people in his environment, may be detrimental to his mental health. His desires, wants, and ambitions find expression in his overt behavior and in turn are influenced by many environmental factors. Sometimes there is a conflict between the ego-satisfying and the socio-satisfying goals he has set for himself. These conflict experiences are likely to create unhappiness, discontent, resentment, or maladjustment.

Meaning of Frustration. An individual who is placed in a situation in which he is prevented from doing what he has a strong desire to do may be said to be *frustrated.* A person who has no desire to fly is not frustrated because he cannot accompany a friend on an airplane trip around the world. If the other person were planning an extended automobile trip, however, the man might strongly desire to share the trip, since he enjoys traveling by automobile. If less satisfying commitments deny him the pleasure of the trip, resulting stress conditions might produce feelings of frustration.

Frustration situations occur constantly, but mentally healthy persons are able to adjust to most of them. Every experience, such as stubbing a toe, breaking eyeglasses, misplacing a letter, being criticized, missing the bus, and similar annoying situations tend to produce temporary frustrations.

Far-reaching or deep-seated wants or desires sometimes are denied the individual by circumstances beyond his control. A severe injury, contraction of a prolonged disease, or the death of a relative may prevent or delay the fulfillment of an individual's wishes or plans. Many persons also are frustrated in their social relationships. Personality defects, lack of social experience, or excessive work may interfere with an individual's ability to establish satisfying relationships with other people.

Actual or imagined inferiority in any aspect of his personality may cause the individual to believe, rightly or wrongly, that his associates dislike him or disapprove of his behavior. An adolescent or a young adult who spent most of his leisure time during childhood in the company of adults or who as a child was restricted by his parents in play activities with other children may feel awkward and uncomfortable in peer groups.

Extreme interest in a particular form of occupational activity or excessive responsibility for the financial welfare of dependents may cause an individual to devote so much of his time and energy to his work that he fails to achieve satisfying social interrelationships. The situation is especially unhealthful if the work demands much mental concentration and is performed alone rather than shared with others, as for example, laboratory research in the pure sciences and accounting. Whatever may be the basic cause of social inadequacy, resulting thwarting of the inherent need for security in social relationships is a potent stimulator of disruptive emotional states and serious mental conflicts.

Frustration and Level of Aspiration. Many individuals are thwarted by their mediocre abilities in their attempts to attain the level of achievement toward which they aspire. Healthful progress in accomplishment depends upon an individual's setting for himself levels of aspiration beyond his immediate achievement. Yet it must be possible for him to attain intermediate aims as he struggles toward ultimate high level goals. An individual must be mentally ready, also, to change his goals if he finds that he cannot fulfill his original ambitions. If the reaching of a high level goal seems to elude him, it would be hygienically sounder for him to direct his efforts toward successful attainment of other equally worthwhile but lower goals.

The level of aspiration generally is higher for the gifted

than for the dull. Regardless of ability status, however, if an individual sets his level of goal aspiration too far beyond his ability to attain, he is likely to experience a feeling of frustration. The intellectually gifted person is responsive to more elements in his environment than are his less able peers. It is frustrating for him to evaluate situations in competition with mentally slower associates. Compared with theirs, his insights are keener, his desires and interests are more numerous, and his degree of emotional envolvement in a competitive situation may be greater.

Because of gaps between existing conditions and levels of aspiration, many frustrations of children and adolescents are associated with fear and worry. For example, adolescents report that they feel frustrated when they (1) lack sufficient money to meet their simple needs, (2) believe that they will be unsuccessful in school achievement, (3) find it difficult to form peer friendships, (4) are not invited to membership by a team, a club, or any other same-age group, or (5) are rigidly supervised by their parents or other adults.

Frustration Tolerance. There is a wide range in the degree and extent to which frustrating situations may be experienced by individuals. There also are significant differences in the behavior of individuals stimulated by the same or similar obstacles. One person may be greatly disturbed in a situation that would arouse little if any emotional disruption in another person. His degree of power to endure frustrating situations without becoming emotionally disorganized can be considered to be an individual's *frustration tolerance.*

Response to frustration depends upon motivating factors such as chronological age, health status, past experience, and the nature of the motive. The very young child may respond by physical aggression; the adolescent, exercising better physical control, reponds in more subtle ways. Ill health often makes a person irritable and may provoke temper tantrums. When a strong desire is thwarted, the individual becomes disturbed. A direct approach to a situation containing elements of thwarting usually is better than an attempt to avoid it or to delay meeting it.

If the encountering of difficulties causes an individual to stop working toward a desired goal, without applying sufficient energy for its attainment, he is said to have low frustration tolerance; conversely, if he continues to strive toward the attainment of his goal in the face of repeated failure he is displaying high frustration tolerance. For example, the behavior of a boy, having good histrionic ability, who is denied a part in a school play but who decides to prepare himself for the next tryout gives evidence of high frustration tolerance; low frustration tolerance is exemplified by the decision of another equally talented boy to withdraw from the school's dramatic club because he was not given a coveted role in the play. A more serious result of low frustration tolerance, especially among adolescents, is the committing of asocial acts because of failure to achieve desired participation in socially approved activities.

Conditions that Create Conflicts

Conflicts arise out of failure to satisfy two opposing interests or desires. Conflicting stimuli arise constantly in the daily life of an individual. When he arises in the morning, he must decide what to wear, in terms of weather conditions and his day's activities. Before he goes to bed, his next day's program influences his decision concerning the time to arise. Throughout the day he is confronted with hundreds of conflict situations which usually can be resolved easily. Some personal or social situations arise that disturb the individual mentally and emotionally and therefore cannot be resolved easily or immediately.

Bases of Conflict. The struggle for supremacy among opposing desires or drives builds up tensions that often are increased by the attempt to repress at least one of them. Many personal and social problems of adjustment are caused by the fact that repression does not lessen tensions. If the individual finds positive outlets for conflicting desires he is experiencing adequate adjustment; otherwise he may develop maladjusted behavior.

Because of a severe conflict, an individual may develop neurotic tendencies. He may attempt to adjust by retreating from the realistic situation to a world of fantasy, since thwarted desires often can be satisfied through idealistic dreams. In the case of an adolescent, fantasy or self-aggrandizing dreams are commonly used devices to escape from conflict between home or school expected submission to authority and his strong desire for independence. Emotional tensions resulting from his fundamental need for adult guidance may cause further conflict between dream satisfaction and actual dependence.

During his student teaching experiences, a person preparing

to teach is placed in numerous situations in which there is conflict. The cooperating teacher (the teacher in whose class he is student-teaching) may have definite ideas regarding teaching procedures that are diametrically opposed to those of the college supervisor who observes and evaluates the student teacher's performance. The student is in a dilemma as he is confronted with these two conflicting points of view. It usually requires a high degree of frustration tolerance to make it possible for him to live with the situation and effect a compromise between the two viewpoints that will satisfy both the cooperating teacher and the supervisor.

There is no panacea or general remedy that can be guaranteed to eliminate from the life pattern of an individual of any age the experiencing of frustration-arousing situations, or help him resolve readily and quickly whatever conflicts he may have. Most people, however, are able to rid themselves of the emotional stress and strain inherent in frustrating and conflict-inducing experiences.

An individual may engage in one of three general forms of behavior aimed at bringing about satisfying personal adjustment in a frustrating or conflict situation. He may (1) launch an attack at the believed cause of the situation, (2) attempt to effect a compromise, or (3) retreat from the situation. Whatever his approach, he is trying to do something about the situation. He may succeed in solving the problem or he may achieve temporary alleviation of emotional stress. Failing in his attempted adjustment, he becomes the victim of the situation; he is maladjusted or mentally ill.

Self-Adjustive Approaches

Attempted emotional or social adjustments or readjustments are characterized by various behavior approaches. Through their operation, some of these approaches produce a better-adjusted, stronger personality; others tend to weaken an already poorly adjusted, inadequate personality. Among significant adjustive approaches can be included the following attitudinal and behavioral patterns, each of which is explained briefly.

Compensation. The attempt of an individual to use many different forms of behaviorial adjustment to failure or inadequacy, or the adoption of a satisfactory form of behavior to reduce tensions that result from a recognized defect or lack.

Introjection. The process by which an individual unconciously acquires ideas, emotional attitudes, and ideals from those about him.

Identification. The behavior displayed by an individual when he is moved to regard himself to be another admired person. This form of imitation is a powerful force in the life of the learner.

Projection. The tendency of an individual to blame another person or object for his own shortcomings.

Rationalization. An attitude approach used to satisfy oneself that the arguments he presents, though false, effectively explain his behavior. It is a form of self-deception in which the individual finds an explanation for his behavior that he knows is not the correct one.

Sublimation. A means of guiding the individual's behavior into a different form of activity when his original desire meets with interference. For example, sublimation is used to up-step an individual's natural urges into ideals of higher thinking and social values.

Daydreaming. Attempted retreat from frustrating situations. It is harmful only if the individual habitually retreats from reality. There is a form of daydreaming which may permit the imagination so to evolve ideas that the end result may be new production in art or music, or a scientific discovery or invention.

Idealization. The tendency to place greater value on something than its real worth. Interaction between the emotions and the imagination enables the individual to believe that the object or person idealized is the most worthwhile he ever has met.

Egocentrism. The form of behavior that develops as a result of constant receiving of attention and praise, regardless of whether it is merited.

Attention-getting. An expression of thwarted egocentrism. Crying brings the baby's mother; boisterous behavior of the elementary school child commands the attention of elders who want peace and quiet; an adolescent's quiet sulking gains desired recognition.

Criticism. A false or exaggerated negative criticism of others, that is utilized because the individual does not want his own deficiency recognized by his associates.

Sympathism. A technique employed to gain the pity of others or to avoid solving a problem by convincing others that it is too difficult for him.

Conversion. The transferring of the energy needed to satisfy a socially disapproved desire into a physical symptom. The ideas and wishes in the unconscious sometimes come into conflict with those in the conscious.

Negativism. Attempted conflict resolution by deliberate refusal to recognize a real situation. Displayed behavior is characterized by rebellion against authority or suggestions offered by a superior.

Regression. An attempt of the individual to utilize behavior patterns that brought satisfaction during an earlier developmental period.

Repression. The deliberate thrusting aside, because of social inhibitions, of present drives that are striving for expression. This approach tends to limit the individual's power of adjustment to commonly experienced situations.

Neurotic behavior. Behavior displayed by an individual in an attempt to escape frustrations or conflict in real situations that is symptomatic of illness or of a physical disability. Neurotic symptoms are frequently symbolic and difficult to understand by the individual himself or by those trained persons who wish to help him.

Probably in every classroom there are a few pupils who employ one or more of the listed adjustment approaches. Such behavior often is no more than a passing phase of development, and it usually is best for the teacher to ignore its presence. If the deviate behavior persists, however, it is the teacher's responsibility to seek the help of trained guidance counselors or specialists to discover the cause and to apply remedial measures. (See Chapter 24.)

The following brief description of causes, symptoms, and forms of mental illness, including a few common therapeutic approaches, is included merely to acquaint the prospective teacher with some of the serious consequences to young people of experiencing mental health hazards, many of which could be avoided. The discussion places emphasis only on those aspects of mental illness, some acquaintance with which can help a teacher become more alert to incipient symptoms of mental ill health.

Mental and Emotional Disorders

Many frustrating experiences or conflicts cannot be resolved in a socially accepted way, with the result that the individual's attitudes and behavior become increasingly unacceptable to his associates. Failure built upon failure so reduces an individual's power to control his thinking and overt behavior that he loses contact with the world of reality. He has developed serious mental illness.

Causes of Serious Maladjusted Behavior. Some children inherit potentialities that predispose toward mental and emotional imbalance. These innate tendencies can be modified or weakened through their interaction with positive, constructive environmental influences. Unhealthy tendencies can be intensified by exposure to unfavorable environmental conditions. For example, the child of emotionally unstable parents, reared in his parents' conflict-ridden home, is the victim of poor biological inheritance and of emotion-disrupting environmental conditions.

Personal inability to achieve adequate self-control and social adjustment is a *predisposing* cause of mental and emotional disorder. Yet a relatively unstable person can achieve adequate adjustments so long as his life pattern is smooth and free from stressful stimuli. Frustrating experiences or apparently unsolvable conflicts can become *exciting* causes of mental and emotional breakdown.

Some common predisposing and exciting causes of mental illness are:

1. Fixed parental prejudices, denials, or shock experienced during childhood.
2. Inability to satisfy a fundamental want (often the sex urge) in terms of socially accepted behavior.
3. Abnormal fatigue, worry, anxiety, or boredom.
4. Physiological epochs such as puberty or the menopause.
5. Pressures arising out of disturbed economic, political, and social conditions.
6. Climatic conditions, since these indirectly produce a condition of exhaustion and toxema.
7. Diseases—especially syphilis.
8. Trauma or injuries—especially head or spine injuries.
9. Toxic infections brought about by alcohol or narcotics, or by poisons that originate in the body—especially in the gastrointestinal tract.
10. Severe emotional shock such as fright, sudden death of a beloved, or the sight of the wounded or dying (as in a severe accident or on a field of battle).[1]

[1] L. D. Crow and Alice Crow, *Eighteen to Eighty, Adjustment Problems of Adults.* The Christopher Publishing House, Boston, 1949, pp. 181-182. Copyright by Lester D. Crow and used with his permission.

Symptoms of Mental Ill Health. Significant symptoms of mental illness differ in *degree* rather than in *kind* from the behavior deviations of adequately adjusted people. Generally, however behavior abnormalities sympotomatic of serious maladjustment are fixed and persistent.

Persisting or fixed symptoms of growing mental and emotional disorders can be classified roughly as (1) physical, (2) behavior, (3) mental, (4) emotional.

1. Physical symptoms:
   a. Change in pulse, temperature, and respiration.
   b. Nausea, vomiting, headaches, and dizziness.
   c. Loss of or abnormal appetite.
   d. Extreme changes in weight.
   e. Excessive fatigue, pain (actual or imagined, coughing or pupillary activity.
   f. Motor incordination, speech disturbances, or writing peculiarities.

2. Behavior symptoms:
   a. Increased psychomotor activity, wherein the individual is impelled toward constant motion, crying, laughing, shouting, or whispering.
   b. Decreased psychomotor activity showing itself in the slowdown of motion, hesitation or indecision (abulia): rigidity, and halting speech or refusal to talk.
   c. Behavior that is impulsive or unduly responsive to external suggestion as shown by the persistent repetition of the words or movements of another, or by an attitude of refusal to respond or of doing exactly the reverse of what might be expected.
   d. Constant repetition of the same act (stereotypy).
   e. A display of unaccustomed vulgarity or profanity of language and peculiar mannerisms such as shuffling walk, queer movements of the hands or shoulders, and facial grimaces.

3. Mental symptoms:
   a. Distractibility, flight of ideas, delay or retardation of mental associations, and blocking of the thought processes.
   b. Loss of understanding or of producing language (aphasia).
   c. Loss of the power to perceive existing relationships in the world about him (agnosia).
   d. Complete loss of memory (amnesia).
   e. Phobias or strong and irrational fears that are attached to generally harmless situations such as abnormal fear of the dark, closed rooms, high places, dirt, insects, or of possible illness.
   f. Compulsions to engage in certain forms of behavior, some of which may have serious consequences such as the urge to take property

belonging to another (kleptomania); or the compelling desire to start fires (pyromania).

g. Fixed ideas or obsessions that may concern themselves with the attitude of other people toward the patient or his own attitudes toward himself or others. For example, an obsession might take the form of a fixed belief that certain foods are poisonous or that the end of the world is imminent.

h. Disturbances of perception such as *illusions* and *hallucinations.* (See Chapter 13.) Although a sane person may experience an occasional illusion, it is a common symptom of certain forms of mental illness. An abnormal mind set may lead to a distortion of what is seen, heard, or felt. A stranger may be mistaken for a close relative, a tree may become a menacing enemy brandishing a lethal weapon, the voice of an associate may be recognized as that of a deceased person who has returned to haunt him.

Hallucinations [described earlier] have no basis in immediate and actual sensory stimulation. They are imaginary perceptions and represent disorders of the imagination. The patient talks with "angels" or sees objects or persons that are nonexistent, except in his imagination. He seems to experience muscular sensations that are not present or taste sensations without food.

i. Delusions or significant disorders of judgment. There are false beliefs that cannot be corrected by an appeal to reason, that have no basis in fact and that are not justified by the individual's experience. Delusions usually are of three kinds: delusions of grandeur, delusions of persecution, and delusions of melancholia.

The patient who is suffering from *delusions of grandeur* imagines that he is a person of great power or influence. He may believe himself to be Mussolini, a noted inventor, a possessor of great wealth, a savant, or even God. His behavior reflects what he imagines to be the attitudes and actions of the one with whom he identifies himself, and he demands from others the attention that is appropriate to his exalted position.

Delusion of persecution are mental states that represent an attitude which is completely opposite from that evidenced in symptoms of delusions of grandeur. The patient who suffers from intense feeling of persecution imagines that he is the object of hatred, jealousy, and malicious influence aimed at interference with or destruction of his welfare.

A person who is suffering from an extreme case of *melancholia* tends to imagine that he has committed an unforgivable crime or that he is suffering from an incurable disease. He may spend most of his time in self-abnegating acts and in attempts to right wrongs that he never has committed. There is no joy in life or hope of salvation for the seriously afflicted sufferer from melancholia.

4. Emotional symptoms:

a. Exhibition of a state of emotional indifference or apathy accompanied by expressions of worry, sighs, crying, and an almost complete refusal to eat or to speak. The patient sits and broods, is morbid and depressed, gloomy and downhearted.

b. Display of an unnatural state of happiness that shows itself in singing, dancing, excited talking and much laughter. The patient has no cares or worries; he views the world through rose-colored glasses and seems to be unaware of anything in a situation that is not completely satisfying or is in any way undesirable.[2]

As the prospective teacher reads this list of symptoms, he must keep in mind that the temporary display of one or more of them is not necessarily an indication of serious mental disorder. At the same time, a teacher needs to realize that he should not regard as inconsequential any overt behavior aberrations among his pupils. He should not make hasty judgments, however, but be alert to its reaccurrence or increased intensity.

Psychoneuroses and Psychoses

An individual may be described by his associate as possessing a psychotic personality, implying thereby that his emotions can be aroused easily. The mildly psychotic individual usually can adjust adequately to his environmental experiences and interpersonal relationships, unless or until he experiences a severe frustration or conflict. A serious crisis can induce emotional disorder.

The Psychoneuroses. A relatively mild form of mental or emotional disorder usually is referred to as a *psychoneurosis.* It is a nervous disorder with no apparent accompanying organic difficulty. Its probable cause is the persistence of a frustrating situation or a conflict arising from societal inhibition of personal desires or ambitions. The psychoneurotic is unable to meet the ordinary demands of day-by-day living with any satisfying degree of success, but he can maintain adequate contacts with environmental conditions.

According to the similarity of their symptoms, psychoneurotic disorders can be classified as: (1) *neurasthenia* (an all-pervading and general feeling of physical and mental fatigue), (2) *psychasthenia* (obsessions, compulsions, and phobias), (3) *hysteria* (distortions of sensitivity, paralysis, tremors, etc., somnambulisms, trances, and a form of epileptic seizure), and (4) *anxiety states* (vague fears and apprehensions, especially related to death

[2] *Ibid.*, p. 182-185. Used with permission.

and insanity). Psychoneurotics rarely need hospitalization for treatment of their nervous diseases, but patients in hospitals for the physically ill may display psychoneurotic behavior.

The Psychoses. A psychosis is a serious form of mental disorder, or variety of insanity. Psychiatrists have classified the psychoses according to about 25 distinct types. Of these the most significant one from the point of view of school people is *dementia praecox* or *schizophrenia*. Its victims include children, adolescents, and young adults. Some of the early symptoms that can be identified by alert teachers are: unaccustomed idleness, excessive daydreaming, shiftlessness and lack of interest in other people (especially parents), silly behavior, hallucinations and fantasies, delusions, strongly negativistic reactions, some body rigidity, and shuffling gait. Persistent display of any of these symptoms can be significant. Parents and teachers should be aware of their presence and obtain psychiatric aid for the sufferer.

Therapeutic Treatment of Mental Disorders

Treatment of mental and emotional disorders is difficult, even for the specially trained psychiatrist. When symptoms are discovered early and treatment is started at once the chances of recovery usually are much better than if the illness has been permitted to develop gradually over a long period. Among the approved methods having mental hygiene implications are: psychosomatic medicine; psychotherapy; psychoanalysis; group therapy; and occupational, physical, and recreational therapy.

Psychosomatic Medicine. It has been discovered that almost one-half of all physical disorders are rooted in emotional disturbance. Mental and emotional symptoms cannot be separated during rehabilitation. Hence psychosomatic medicine includes physical treatment and psychiatric therapy.

Psychotherapy. Psychotherapy aims to improve the sufferer's attitudes, emotional reactions, and overt behavior through suggestion and reeducation. Physical and emotional tensions are relieved through suggestion and reassurance. Various principles and procedures of morale building are employed by the psychiatrist in his application of psychotherapy to a mentally ill patient.

Psychoanalysis. Through psychoanalysis an effort is made to elicit from a disturbed person significant information concerning his earlier mental and emotional experiences. The procedure is to attack the underlying emotional conflict by discovering those experiences which have induced the disordered state.

Group Therapy. Through dynamic group interaction the psychologist attempts to discover the emotional disturbances of individuals. Considerable preparation is needed to insure the success of this technique. All participants need to be preinterviewed, and relevant data studied. Each participant in the group situation should understand what is happening.

Occupational, Physical, and Recreational Therapy. The purpose of activity therapy is to give the patient an opportunity, under guidance, for self-expression, thus diverting attention from himself and his problem. Appropriate occupational therapy becomes a morale builder, in that the therapeutic value lies in the work activity itself rather than in the product. Physical therapy helps the patient improve his physical condition through appropriate exercise and other activities. It releases body tensions. Common forms of recreational therapy include: dancing, motion picture and television viewing, small group club projects, and other types of recreational activity.

Accepted Theories of Personality

There are certain theories of personality types that are acceptable to psychologists, psychiatrists and others who are involved with the problems of personality adjustment. They include the *four temperaments; physical types; somatotypes; sociological types; endocrine types; introvert, ambivert, extrovert types* (all of which are briefly discussed on pages 93–95); and *psychoanalytic types* that are presented here.

The *psychoanalytic types* were suggested by Freud and his followers. These types are concerned with the effect on personality of the environmentally stimulated satisfactions and frustrations as related to psychosexual development. They represent abnormal rather than normal adjustment and include the categories of *anal-erotic*—obsessions related to traits of obstinacy; *oral-erotic*—obsessions of chewing and biting as escapes from feelings of frustration including a return to infantile patterns of behavior; *genital* (with two classifications) (1) the *phallic type*—exhibitionism, boasting, self-admiration; and (2) *normal development of genital sexual maturity*—a balance between ambition and restraint, and between dependence and independence.

CHAPTER 24

TEACHER ADJUSTMENT AND LEARNER GUIDANCE

From about 800 to 1000 hours during each school year, elementary school children and high school students are under the influence of their teachers. In terms of young people's total yearly activities, the number of hours spent in school represents a relatively limited part of all their learning experiences. Yet the motivating force of teacher-pupil interaction characteristic of organized education is tremendous. By what he is, does, and says, as well as how he says it, a teacher either directly or indirectly exercises a potent influence on a learner's academic progress and his personal and social development.

A teacher who is personally and socially well adjusted can guide or help his pupils improve their own patterns of adjustment. A maladjusted teacher, on the contrary, may become an educational hazard, in so far as his behavior and attitudes interfere with the learner's school achievement, and/or arouse negative or disruptive emotional pupil reactions. Hence a teacher's personal attributes and professional relationships are fundamental factors of the kind and extent of guidance his pupils receive from him.

Basic Aspects of Teacher Adjustment

A teacher is a public figure in his school community. Some parents and other lay people seem to believe that he should be a kind of "paragon of perfection" with no frailties. He is expected to adjust adequately to community conditions and to be sensitive to and react appropriately to the differing personality characteristics displayed by those with whom he is associated in his work.

Areas of Teacher Relationships. In the fulfillment of his teaching responsibilities a teacher must adapt himself to various interrelationships.

Relation with Pupils and Their Parents. A teacher's primary and most important area of relationship is, of course, his complex interactions with his pupils. The various aspects of this relationship include his functions as an instructor of learning materials, as a guide, adviser, or director of learner activities, and as a well-adjusted person who, by earning his pupil's respect and admiration, becomes a model to be imitated. Moreover, a teacher's relationships with his pupils cannot be dissociated from accompanying relations with their parents.

The nature of a teacher's relationships with parents depends upon school and community attitudes toward one another, as well as upon the teacher's displayed interest in the welfare of his pupils. In some instances, a teacher does not meet a pupil's parents except (1) when he summons them to school because their child is failing in his work or is misbehaving, or (2) when parents bring complaints to the teacher concerning his treatment of their child, the young person's apparent failure in his school work, or other unpleasant situations or conditions.

The kind of parent-teacher relationship just described is difficult and unrewarding to both the teacher and the parents, unless the teacher is tactful and sympathetic. He then can help parents gain an understanding of their child's needs and of the teacher's desire to cooperate with them for the welfare of the child. More positive teacher-parent relationships can be achieved through the functioning in the school of a well-organized active parent-teacher organization, or of organized grade or class parents' groups. Other aspects of teachers' relations with parents are discussed in connection with teacher counseling activities.

Relationships with Other Teachers. Each member of a school faculty possesses a unique personality. Consequently, a teacher may disagree with one or more of his co-workers concerning subject-matter emphases, teaching techniques, expected learning outcomes, and disciplinary measures, in addition to the handling of the many details of school and classroom management. If the teachers involved possess a reasonable amount of self-control and are habitually cooperative, professional disagreements can be resolved amicably.

Among poorly adjusted teachers, differences of opinion may

cause conflict situations, with the arousal in some individuals of strong emotional reactions, and feelings of thwarting and frustration. Staff morale can be weakened through the display by some teachers of personality defects such as overambition; jealousy or envy caused by the apparently greater prestige of a co-worker; habits of malicious gossiping about pupils, other teachers, or administrators and supervisors; malingering on the job, and other forms of annoying or unethical behavior.

The relationships that exist between the older, more experienced members of a school faculty and new teachers, especially beginning teachers, is an important factor of teacher adjustment. Healthful, positive relationships can be established when the attitudes of the more experienced teachers reflect (1) a desire to help the new teacher become oriented in his job, and (2) a willingness to accept and perhaps adapt the neophyte's teaching approaches and techniques that are different from their own but appear to yield successful results. The neophyte can earn approval in his new school (1) by displaying an attitude of willingness to accept and profit from the help given him by the other teachers, and (2) by refraining from adverse criticism of their teaching procedures which to him may appear outmoded or inadequate.

Relationships with Administrations and Supervisors. The adequacy of teacher adjustment to administrative and supervisory control depends to a great extent upon two factors of influence: (1) the extent to which the administrative and supervisory controls are authoritarian or democratic, and (2) the degree to which the teacher's attitudes are cooperative or individualistic. The head of a school or school system is officially responsible for all aspects of the organized educational opportunities provided by it. His duties include, among others, planning for and control of: curriculum offerings, teaching procedures, programs of testing and evaluation, marking systems, class and teacher scheduling, guidance and counseling, and supervision of instructural and other activities. The teacher is responsible for carrying out the administrator's or the supervisor's policies and suggested practices. Within his limited field of activity, the teacher is expected so to perform his duties that educational outcomes will fulfill the school's educational objectives.

Adequate, congenial administrator-teacher, or supervisor-teacher relationships are difficult to achieve unless everyone concerned can approach the relationships objectively and cooperatively. Teachers resent the display of authoritarianism by the school administrators. The habitually cooperative or relatively submissive teacher attempts to meet adequately their dictatorial pronouncements and demands, even though his overtly cooperative behavior is accompanied by emotional stress. The more individualistic teacher may become openly rebellious; he may seem to cooperate but he disregards mandates and commands to as great extent as he dares, or he leaves the school.

In schools or school systems that are administered democratically, most teachers give evidence of cooperation with the administration, loyalty to the school, and enthusiastic performance of their duties. It is the policy of some school communities to have committees of teachers share in curriculum planning and construction. Policies and practices concerned with discipline, testing and evaluation, marking and pupil progress reporting, utilization of teaching aids, school guidance services, and related matters of school management are evolved as a result of faculty-shared efforts. Although teaching procedures may need to follow a relatively uniform general pattern, teachers are free to experiment with differing teaching approaches. Teachers, in common with the majority of human beings, are better able to understand and more interested in carrying out projects which they have helped develop than those jobs that are imposed on them from above.

A healthful personal relationship between a teacher and a supervisor is governed by psychological principles similar to those that condition a teacher's attitude toward school administration. Since supervision of instruction implies critical evaluation of one person's performance by another, the personality patterns of both the supervisor and the supervised are involved. Moreover, a supervised teaching situation possesses potent elements of fear arousal for the one supervised.

No matter how experienced or successful a teacher may be, the presence in the classroom of an evaluator of his teaching and his pupils' learning introduces changes in the social atmosphere of the classroom that can affect not only the attitude and behavior of a sensitive teacher but also of the pupils. An autocratic, demanding, and insensitive supervisor increases the fear-producing factors by his coldness of manner, stress on petty details, and destructively critical attitude.

Much less emotional tension is experienced by the teacher if the supervisor is sensitive to human values and has not forgotten his own past reactions to supervision. He has a friendly attitude during the period of supervision; he seeks to discover and commend the strong points of the lesson, but he does not hesitate to offer constructive suggestions for needed improvement. Even under the most favorable supervisory conditions, however, the maladjusted teacher, always believing that he is treated unfairly, is likely to become strongly emotionalized and resent any justified criticism. Moreover, he tends to accuse even an extremely reasonable critic of personal animosity toward himself.

Other Teacher Relationships. In the school itself, a teacher's activities bring him into contact with nonfaculty personnel such as librarians, clerks, and custodial staff. In general, these relationships are relatively impersonal. Yet a teacher's display of friendly and cooperative attitudes usually is returned in kind. A teacher who assumes a superior attitude toward or ignores these members of the school personnel, who demands an undue amount of their time and attention, or who criticizes them frequently and destructively receives little or no cooperation from them and is much disliked by them.

Membership in professional organizations and participation in the activities of the community in which the school is located provide the teacher with various kinds of relationships that have professional, social, and civic value. An enthusiastic teacher can become so involved in out-of-school activities, however, that their effect is physically and mentally detrimental, rather than stimulating. The more willing a teacher is to engage actively in projects and programs related to his vocational work and interests, the greater will be the demands upon him.

It is good mental hygiene for the teacher to limit himself to a healthful and interesting schedule of activities in which he can participate fully and enthusiastically. To attempt to expand one's activities too widely is as unwise as it is to avoid all professional and community participation and to devote one's entire time and energies to concern about and much extra work for one's classroom duties.

Personal Qualifications. The fact that the period of professional training has increased from no special training or a few courses in teacher education to four or five years of intensive study shows that boards of education and other community leaders recognize the importance of a teacher's being thoroughly prepared to meet his broadening responsibilities. Most teachers know the subject matter of their particular field. They are trained: (1) to become well acquainted with the principles of human growth and development, (2) to understand psychological principles of learning and their application to teaching techniques and procedures, and (3) to gain teaching skill through the study of accepted methods and by means of preteaching practice. In addition, more and more emphasis is being placed on a teacher's having a broad cultural background.

Academic and professional preparation is needed to insure good teaching. The most significant factor of teaching success, however, appears to be the teacher's personality. Institutions of teacher education are aware of the importance of a teacher's being well adjusted in his personal and social relationships. In so far as possible, they are selective in their acceptance of candidates for training, and are alert to personality improvement as a function of training. Yet, so many factors are involved in personality formation that it is difficult to: (1) determine exactly which personality qualities are favorable to teaching success, and (2) help a prospective teacher achieve a favorable personality.

Many study approaches have been and continue to be utilized to discover the personality qualities of a good or well-adjusted teacher. The evaluating techniques include: various forms of personality scales administered to teaching candidates, supervisor ratings of the teacher on the job, pupils' rating of their teachers, and teacher self-rating instruments.

As a result of these investigations it appears that the basic characteristics of a good teacher are: good health, above average intelligence (not necessarily mental superiority), emotional stability, integrity, flexibility, adequate speech and language usage, creativity, cheerfulness, sincerity, kindness, cooperativeness and social adaptability, sense of humor (laughing *with* pupils rather than *at* them), patience, and enthusiasm.

The personal qualities that predispose toward success in teaching are fundamental to the development of the kind of good teacher adjustment that functions successfully in a teacher's various professional relationships, especially in his pupil-guidance relations. Because of his own fine attitudes, he is well equipped (1) to help his pupils develop self-control, (2) to motivate and maintain pupil interest in learning, (3) to evaluate pupil potentiality and achievement objectively and intelligently, and (4) to exert a constructive influence on the school and community.

Teacher Maladjustment. All teachers experience some frustration, but most teachers are able to meet occasional thwarting situations and still maintain adequate adjustment to job requirements. It is estimated, however, that about 20 per cent of all the teachers in the United States suffer mild or more serious emotional disturbances, with a consequent display of maladjusted behavior.

Various situations and conditions are presumed to be the causes of teacher maladjustment. The primary cause probably lies within the teacher himself—his degree of frustration tolerance. Other causes are associated directly or indirectly with maladjustive teaching conditions that vary with the policies and practices of specific schools and school communities. Included among the causative factors of teacher maladjustment over which the teacher has little or no control are: (1) community restriction of teachers' activities, especially during out-of-school hours; (2) community failure to respect teachers; (3) autocratic school administrators; (4) extreme pressure of required work; (5) inadequate salary; (6) insecurity of tenure; (7) oversize of classes and too great heterogeneity of class grouping; (8) undue administrative emphasis upon petty, routine details of school and class management; (9) inadequate teaching equipment; (10) necessity to teach other subjects than those for which trained; (11) lack of sufficient recreation and rest; (12) insufficient opportunity for creative teaching; and (13) especially on the lower school level, constant interaction with immature minds.

A beginning teacher may appear to be relatively well adjusted. Gradually, however, continuing emotional strains, frustrations, or conflicts that he may experience because of the presence of one or more maladjustive factors show themselves in his behavior and attitudes. At first, he may be unduly sensitive to small thwartings, resulting in general irritability and crossness in the classroom.

The more seriously disturbed the teacher becomes, the less able he seems to be to cooperate with his co-workers or to gain satisfaction from his work. He cannot tolerate criticism from his superiors. In the classroom, either he is aggressive and faultfinding, apparently placing the blame for his own inadequacies on his pupils, or he becomes withdrawing, fearful, and overpermissive, as though the situation were too difficult for him to handle.

Mental Hygiene and Teacher Adjustment. Much is being done to prevent increase of maladjustment among teachers. In an increasing number of communities, salary schedules are being upgraded to meet living costs. Enactment of tenure and pension laws by most states is providing job and financial security. Educational policies and practices are becoming more democratic, resulting in greater freedom for teachers. The present increase in school population, however, is accompanied by an increase of unfavorable teaching conditions, such as large classes, double, triple, or more daily school sessions, insufficient teaching personnel, and other stressful conditions.

The preservation of good mental health in spite of unfavorable conditions lies in the teacher's own attitude toward his work in relation to himself, and the life values he considers worth while. To be well adjusted, the teacher needs to gain the respect and cooperation of his pupils and to experience the satisfaction of successful accomplishments. If he can regard his professional work as service to others rather than merely as a means of earning a living, and if he is self-confident rather than governed by fear, he is likely to meet frustrating situations with equanimity. Other inducers of good teacher adjustment and job satisfaction are (1) a balanced program of work and recreation, (2) healthful diet, (3) sufficient rest and sleep, (4) professional self-improvement through reading and by participation in the activities of professional organizations and small study groups, and (5) periodic self-appraisals that are followed by honest attempts at self-improvement.

The Teacher's Role in Learner Guidance

Broadly interpreted, guidance of young people includes all the activities of parents, school personnel, and other community agencies that are concerned with child and adolescent development and adjustment. Guidance is help given an individual to establish immediate and long-range goals, to plan courses of action, and to make whatever improvements in his attitudes and behavior that he recognizes to be needed.

Guidance is not direction; the counselor does not make decisions for the person being guided. Whatever goals are decided, action taken, or improvements made are the results of the individual's own self-activation.

A teacher or counselor cannot do the learning for pupils, he cannot make decisions for them concerning the ways in which their urges, desires, and interests shall be satisfied. These things must be done by the young people themselves. Intelligent parents and well-trained teachers and counselors can assist learners, individually or in group situations, by ameliorating unfavorable conditions, by exhibiting positive attitudes of understanding, and by encouraging, socially acceptable and personally satisfying learning achievement and personality formation.

Guidance Needs of Learners. Every school child or adolescent needs the help of a teacher in his learning activities. If his school experiences are to yield successful learning outcomes, the learner must know what to study and how to study it, in terms of his learning capacities and his educational goals. It is the responsibility of the teacher to guide these learning activities.

Some young people experience specific problems of adjustment that originate in situations or conditions, either directly or indirectly related to school learning. In such instances, the guidance responsibility of the teacher is to help the young person discover the cause of the problems and do whatever is possible to resolve it. The teacher's or counselor's understanding of the problem and the subject's willingness and ability to attack it positively are basic factors of guided problem solution.

The specific problems of young people vary in kind and intensity. Some are associated with personal characteristics such as physical condition or health, level of intelligence, degree of emotional control, habituated attitudes toward self and others, ambitions and interests, ethical standards and religious values, and accustomed behavior patterns. Problems growing out of attitude and behavior habits usually are products of negative adult influence and unsatisfying experiences.

Background sources of young people's special problems include unhygienic home conditions, inappropriate or unsatisfying school learning experiences, poor vocational selection and preparation, inadequate community provision for recreational facilities, and unfavorable adult example. The extent to which any of these possible areas of problem causation affect a child or adolescent is directly related to the degree of influence on him of positive, favorable elements in his environment, especially as he benefits from wisely administered guidance services in the school.

Guidance in the Classroom. Good teaching connotes good guidance of subject matter mastery. The teacher's responsibility for the guidance of individual pupils extends beyond his recognition of and provision for the learner's level of learning readiness. According to his previous experiences, each pupil is affected favorably or unfavorably by the teacher's behavior manifestations of his cultural background, his value appreciations, and his habitual attitudes toward interpersonal relations. Sometimes, without teacher awareness of consequences, the mere presence of the teacher in the room and his self-activations serve as indirect guides of pupil behavior or attitudes.

A teacher can help his pupils more directly by knowing them individually and "spotting" possible difficulties. Through utilization of sociometric techniques, he can discover the popular pupils and the isolates, and help the latter improve their social adjustments. He recognizes symptoms of poor health and physical defects, and takes measures for their improvement.

The teacher provides appropriate programs of experience for his pupils, and in many ways removes possible causes of frustration, in so far as this is possible. He encourages learners by praise and commendation when these are deserved, but consistently enforces adherence to high standards of work and behavior that are understood and accepted by the class group. Finally, he is watchful. He is alert to any incipient or actual problem of a pupil that needs special attention.

Since most young people have confidence in a well-adjusted teacher they sometimes take their problems to him, rather than to their parents. A teacher who is interested in his pupils usually finds time, in spite of his many school duties, to discuss with a pupil the latter's particular problem. In an individual counseling situation, a guidance-minded teacher is receptive and sympathetic, and a good listener, but he does not try to impose his viewpoint upon the pupil. A boy or girl who has become emotionally disturbed as the result of a thwarting or otherwise unpleasant experience often experiences emotional relaxation from talking about his problem with a friendly adult. The teacher probably can help most in such cases by listening sympathetically, occasionally interjecting a carefully phrased question that will aid the pupil in thinking through his difficulty.

Young people may experience problems that have so serious emotional concomitants that the teacher counselor is unable to give the kind of assistance needed. In such instances, help in problem solution becomes the responsibility of a specially trained counselor, a psychologist, or a psychiatrist.

Organized School Guidance Services. The provision of guidance and counseling service formerly was limited to high schools and colleges, and dealt for the most part with problems related to educational planning and vocational selection. More recently there has developed among school people an appreciation of the value to any individual of appropriate guidance services, from young childhood through adulthood. It now is believed that good personal and social adjustment can be encouraged early in the life of a child. Hence parents, and nursery school and kindergarten teachers gradually are coming to apply the mental hygiene or guidance approach in the training of young children.

On the elementary school level, guidance services are loosely organized. The classroom teacher is the most important person in the program. Provision also is made for the services of nurses, physicians, psychiatrists, and the staff of child guidance clinics, when or if their services are needed.

In some elementary schools, several teachers who are temperamentally suited and have had some guidance training are made chairmen of small committees of teachers whose function it is to work with children who appear to have learning or emotional difficulties, as well as with the latters' parents. Seriously disturbed children are referred to child-guidance clinics. In some elementary schools, special and appropriate provision for learning is made for the exceptionally bright, the mentally retarded, and the handicapped, as well as for children with reading and arithmetic disabilities.

Many junior and senior high schools have organized elaborate programs of guidance and counseling services that extend their influence into every phase of school activity. Included in the guidance staff are part-time teacher counselors and specially trained full-time educational and vocational counselors, in addition to the services of attendance officers, nurses, dentists, physicians, psychologists, and psychiatrists. The four last-named specialists serve either on a part-time or full-time basis.

In a school or school system, the guidance services offered and their organization depend upon the needs of the pupils, available financial aid, and school and community attitudes toward the value of such services. Some of the commonly used techniques are: utilization of appropriate evaluating instruments and anecdotal reports, the keeping of complete cumulative records, the application of group dynamics, individual counseling, and clinical procedures.

The goals of a well-organized, effectively functioning program of school guidance services are to help every pupil in the school achieve adequate development and adjustment in the areas of physical health, mental progress, emotional control, and interpersonal and intersocial relationships. Effective guidance should assist an individual to experience the satisfaction of performing adequately in his home and his school, and in his occupational, social, and civic activities.

The ideal concept of school guidance, of course, has not yet been realized. There are however, evidences of a growing understanding of the psychological aspect of human nature and of an increasing application of the principles of mental hygiene, both within and outside the school. Important as are the efforts and activities of school and agency specialists concerned with child and adolescent welfare, the work and influence of an enthusiastic, well-adjusted teacher are paramount effectors of good adjustment among children and adolescents. The teacher is the core of any school's program of guidance services.

The *individual inventory service* includes all of the activities necessary to obtain, record and appraise information concerning the individual. It deals with such things as identifying data, achievement, aptitudes, interests and activities, health, home background, educational and vocational goals.

The *information service* pertains to all types of information needed by the learner in determining the conditions and opportunities of his environment. It includes such things as occupational, vocational, school and college, socio-economic-cultural, and resource and referral.

The *counseling service* is the hub of the guidance program. It is a purposeful, individualized learning experience for the individual and involves a private interview between the student and the counselor on a one-to-one relationship based on mutual confidence.

The *placement service* pertains to a group of activities that provides the basic essentials to proper class placement or job placement.

The *follow-through or follow-up service* pertains to that series of systematic checks in the guidance program that help determine whether the guidance services in particular and the educational program in general are meeting the needs of the learners.

It is important that a constant *evaluation* of the school's guidance program is made. Although the other five guidance areas are concerned with direct assistance to the learner, periodic evaluation of all the services is needed.

FINAL EXAMINATION 1

(See page 357 for correct answers)

True-false Questions

Directions: Place a plus sign (+) before each statement that is true, and a zero (0) before each statement that is false.

____ 1. The amount of transfer of training that takes place does not depend upon the method of presentation, but rather on the materal presented.

____ 2. The ability to reason comes only with complete maturity.

____ 3. A plateau in a learning curve represents a period of no improvement of any kind.

____ 4. Educational research has been more successful in evaluating the quantitative aspects of capacity than the qualitative aspects.

____ 5. Horizontal growth in mental ability shows a close relationship to vertical growth.

____ 6. A correlation coefficient of —.91 ordinarily signifies a high degree of relationship.

____ 7. Good teaching and diligent study will enable any pupil to pass any course.

____ 8. The power to recall is lost less quickly than that of recognition.

____ 9. Under certain conditions, concomitant learnings may exceed the main objectives of classroom instruction.

____ 10. Negative correlations may be disregarded, since they have no practical value.

____ 11. Physical traits have a pronounced effect upon an individual's personality.

____ 12. Much of a child's learning of language usage is achieved through imitation.

____ 13. Unusually bright children tend to be physically weak.

____ 14. As a rule, level of occupational activity correlates positively with intelligence.

____ 15. Individual differences usually result from the difficulty of forming conditioned responses.

____ 16. Once a conditioned reflex has been established it is practically impossible to eliminate it.

____ 17. The individual who learns more rapidly than others usually retains longer what he has learned.

____ 18. Elementary school pupils tend to be more alike in their interests than in their learning capacities.

____ 19. A careful application of the laws of learning should make for better teaching in the next generation.

____ 20. Manual habits are generally retained longer than verbal habits.

____ 21. The intelligence quotient should be used for vertical classification of pupils.

____ 22. According to Spearman's theory of intelligence, the "g" factor is the same for all individuals.

____ 23. A skewed distribution is evidence that some kind of selection has taken place.

____ 24. The Stanford-Binet Scale is an excellent group test of intelligence.

____ 25. By reliability is meant the degree to which a test measures that which it claims to measure.

____ 26. A well-mastered skill is permanent in spite of long periods of disuse.

____ 27. After study of subject matter has ceased, forgetting sets in, at first slowly and then rapidly.

____ 28. Human beings are selective in their activity.

____ 29. Integration in learning generally takes place by mere accretion.

____ 30. Attitudes are little affected by the educative process.

____ 31. As a single criterion, the IQ is a sound basis for educational guidance and counseling.

____ 32. The curve of learning and the curve of forgetting are similar in shape.

____ 33. Correlation generally implies causes for educational phenomena.

____ 34. Learning curves are relatively similar for learners of any ability level.

____ 35. Learning frequently takes place without affecting attitudes.

____ 36. The relation between mental age and chronological age remains fairly constant throughout life.

____ 37. The differential and integrational aspects of learning are essentially independent processes.

____ 38. Although dull children develop more slowly than bright children, they continue to grow mentally for a longer period of time.

____ 39. Concentrated practice is better for retention of motor learning than is distributed practice.

____ 40. It is proper to refer to degrees of insight.

____ 41. Reflective thinking becomes effective only after a problem is clearly defined.

____ 42. In general, the limits between which an individual's IQ varies is determined by heredity.

____ 43. Superior parents tend to have offspring who are even more superior.

____ 44. Preschool children are definitely capable of simple problem-solving behavior.

____ 45. The thought process of children and of adults are very similar.

____ 46. Phonetic drills are useful for increasing the accuracy of word recognition.

____ 47. In the study of music and art, production is just as important as are the accompanying attitudes and appreciations.

____ 48. Children have a society of their own, with sanctions and taboos, and rewards and penalties.

____ 49. Psychologically, oral reading skills are the opposite of silent reading skills.

____ 50. It is possible, with skillful teaching, to help most pupils achieve some competence in drawing.

____ 51. The need of a special vocabulary in the social studies constitutes a major difficulty in that area of learning.

____ 52. Pupils either like arithmetic very much or they dislike it very much.

____ 53. Through school training desirable personalities can be developed in the majority of children regardless of their innate mental capacities.

____ 54. It is relatively easy for children to undertake mental journeys in time or space.

____ 55. Most children enjoy memorizing objective, easily-verifiable facts.

____ 56. In the teaching of spelling, words always should be presented in lists or groups, never one at a time.

____ 57. It is probable that children will improve their handwriting about as well without instruction as with it.

____ 58. Children's appreciation of beauty is no different from that of adults.

____ 59. Phrase-reading is an essential step in achieving adequate comprehension in silent reading.

____ 60. Most school work is unassociated with a child's out-of-school activities.

____ 61. When they enter elementary school, most children are not particularly interested in drawing.

____ 62. Psychologically, history probably would be easier to understand if it began with the present and worked backwards.

____ 63. In dealing with generalizations expressed in the form of words or other symbols many learners tend to accept the verbal formulation without understanding it or questioning its validity.

____ 64. Spelling games are very effective in expediting the learning of spelling.

____ 65. Less than one-half of an individual's total reading time is utilized for eye-fixations.

____ 66. To have value in the thinking process, words must carry definite attitudes with them.

____ 67. It usually is easier for pupils to understand human experiences than impersonal conditions or situations.

____ 68. Thinking in terms of space relatonships can be developed early in the child's life.

____ 69. Some high school students are able to earn passing marks in the study of geometry without understanding basic geometric concepts.

____ 70. Efforts are constantly being made to reconcile systematic bodies of accumulated cultural experiences with the needs of immature learners.

____ 71. Character and personality are synonomous concepts.

____ 72. Insight into cause-effect relationships is a mental function.

____ 73. It can be assumed that a young child who can repeat numbers in their correct sequence understands their quantitative relationships.

____ 74. Overt expression and reflective thinking must be parallel processes.

____ 75. Most adults have not developed fully whatever innate potentiality they may possess in the field of representative art.

____ 76. In most cases, the intelligence quotients of school children and adolescents give evidence of relatively slight deviations.

____ 77. There is an intrinsic unreality about the history of the early ages which may obscure the learner's concepts and distort his imagery.

____ 78. Demonstrative geometry is less abstract than either arithmetic or algebra.

____ 79. Transfer of training is greatest at the lower levels of mental development.

____ 80. In general, the concepts encountered in the study of the social studies are neither complex nor abstract.

____ 81. Associations are more closely related to the sensory processes of the nervous system than they are to the motor processes.

____ 82. Pupils manifest little difficulty in interpreting pictures and maps.

____ 83. Failure to master study materials on the high school level often is rooted in lack of appropriate skill in reading.

____ 84. The problems of socializing pupils and of acquainting them with the nature of society are essentially the same tasks.

____ 85. Cause-effect relationships are much simpler to comprehend than space relationships.

____ 86. It is correct to apply a valid statistical generalization directly to an individual case.

____ 87. Mental ability may be considered to be an independent aspect of the total personality pattern.

____ 88. Every subject studied in the school contributes to the pupil's personality.

____ 89. A child's ability to locate events in time matures earlier than his ability to locate objects in space.

____ 90. Reading a sentence problem in algebra does not require the development of a special type of reading ability.

___ 91. The validity of mathematical thinking is based on the nature of things rather than on the nature of thinking.

___ 92. Rhythmic expression is a characteristic of poetry but not of prose.

___ 93. The willingness of a pupil to work is as important in determining successful intellectual development as is mental superiority.

___ 94. There is good reason to believe that a strong social compulsion forces school children, having average ability, to achieve skill in artistic production.

___ 95. To cure fantasy, the daydreamer must be convinced that his daydreams are abnormal and harmful.

___ 96. There is little cause for alarm on the part of parents regarding petty theft on the part of their children if they meet the problem openly and frankly.

___ 97. Psychologists are opposed to all forms of identification.

___ 98. The typical stimulus for worry is a personal inadequacy.

___ 99. Teachers tend to overemphasize the significance of timid and asocial behavior.

___100. Most inferiority attitudes in adults arise from defects occurring in adult life.

Multiple-choice Questions

Directions: Select the letter of the expression which *best completes* the statement and place it before the number of the question.

___ 1. The sympathetic nervous system a) includes the autonomic system, b) is included in the autonomic system, c) is an entirely separate system, d) is a part of the central nervous system.

___ 2. Phobias a) are not transferable from an original to a derived source, b) occur soon after the causative unpleasant experience, c) must be differentiated from ordinary fears before they can be treated effectively, d) always occur in connection with a direct experience.

___ 3. An adolescent girl adopts the type of hairdress used by her favorite teacher. The term which best describes this behavior is a) compensation, b) defense reaction, c) transference, d) identification.

____ 4. The best way to deal with a temper tantrum in the classroom usually is to a) ignore it, b) isolate the child, c) discuss the situation with the child, d) punish the child.

____ 5. During an emotional turmoil the adolescent usually is a) firm and rigid in his convictions, b) not vigorously seeking the truth, c) submissive, d) passive to forceful activity.

____ 6. The most common form of delinquency among adolescent boys is a) asocial sex acts, b) truancy, c) cruelty, d) stealing.

____ 7. An individual's behavior when thwarted is determined by a) the precipitating factors, b) his personality, c) the nature of the thwarting, d) his intelligence.

____ 8. If nothing can be done about the cause of worry, it is desirable to a) put off considering it until a later time, b) refrain from thinking about it, c) develop balancing factors, d) start to worry about something else.

____ 9. Repression causes a phobia to persist chiefly because it a) prevents the extinction of the response, b) reinforces the emotional tension, c) inhibits the fear response, d) alters the individual's personality.

____ 10. The most general characteristic of stimuli eliciting emotion in infants is a) danger, b) restraint, c) intensity, d) unfamiliarity.

____ 11. The fervent activity of a reformer is most illustrative of a) regression, b) identification, c) egocentrism, d) compensation.

____ 12. A form of defense that often is encouraged rather than discouraged is a) peculiar vocalizations, b) attention-getting devices, c) fantasy, d) seclusiveness.

____ 13. The most significant basis of variation among individuals in learning ability probably is a) habit of study, b) native capacity, c) previous experience, d) effort.

____ 14. The "higher mental processes" involve a) maturity of the learner, b) perceptual learning, c) school level attained, d) individual organization of experience.

____ 15. The most extensive vocabulary of the average person is in a) writing, b) speaking, c) reading, d) spelling.

____ 16. The factor that is of greatest significance in affecting the amount of transfer that takes place in learning is a) nature of the subject, b) intelligence of the individual, c) method employed, d) presence of identical elements.

____ 17. Precocious children generally become a) normal adults, b) psychopathic individuals, c) slightly subnormal adults, d) superior adults.

____ 18. The first result obtained in scoring a paper-and-pencil group intelligence test is a) intelligence quotient, b) raw score, c) percentile, d) mental age.

____ 19. Personality probably is best measured by a) a projective technique, b) a power test, c) an inventory, d) a performance test.

____ 20. The recognition span in silent reading is a) less than, b) slightly greater than, c) much greater than, d) about the same as it is in oral reading.

____ 21. Perception is the result of a) sensory impressions, b) verbal stimuli, c) inner associations, d) passive observation.

____ 22. The net effects of school instruction depends most on a) the subject matter studied, b) the methods used by the teacher, c) the behavior of the pupils, d) the regimen of the school.

____ 23. Among techniques for motivating learning, the least desirable is a) praise, b) remedial teaching, c) ignoring, d) reproof.

____ 24. The fact that an individual tends to repeat those reactions which, on the whole, are satisfying is best explained by the law of a) effect, b) recency, c) frequency, d) readiness.

____ 25. The one of the following that is a conditioned reflex is a) sneezing, b) becoming angry at restraint, c) secreting saliva at the thought of food, d) becoming frightened at sudden loud sounds.

FINAL EXAMINATION 2

(See page 339 for correct answers)

True-false Questions

Directions: Place a plus sign (+) before each statement that is true, and a zero (0) before each statement that is false.

____ 1. Satisfaction is important in learning if it means the satisfying of a purpose not if it means being pleased through no effort or intention of one's own.

____ 2. Strong emotional states such as anger and fear have no pronounced psychological concomitants.

____ 3. Conditioned responses are stable and permanent.

____ 4. To a new type of stimulus the organism tends to respond as it does to a similar situation.

____ 5. A response to a particular stimulus often is affected by concomitant stimuli as much as if not more so than by the stimulus itself.

____ 6. Uniformity, not severity of punishment or degree of inducement, is important in the utilization of disciplinary measures.

____ 7. Insight arises from the solution of a problem.

____ 8. Insight concerns the recognition of relationships involving an agent, a goal and intervening conditions.

____ 9. The sensory-motor arc is the structural unit of the nervous system.

____ 10. In neural action, the law of least resistance refers to preferred paths.

____ 11. Emotions differ from reflexes in that emotions involve the whole body.

____ 12. The parts of a total purposive behavior pattern are never perfected until after the action as a whole has been attempted and comprehended.

____ 13. The principles of insight can be applied especially to such subjects as handwriting and spelling.

____ 14. A good social heritage can negate a poor biological inheritance.

____ 15. Every trait that an individual will exhibit as an adult is potentially present in childhood.

____ 16. Development of accuracy, precision and detailed motor skill should precede, never follow, general orientation and insight.

____ 17. Chinese speaking parents transmit to their offspring an innate capacity for learning the Chinese language.

____ 18. When there is interference with the realization of a need or a desire, an emotional state usually is aroused.

____ 19. Human beings are more alike in their physical needs and cravings than they are in ability to satisfy those needs.

____ 20. Organically, emotions are primitive emergency devices.

____ 21. Opposing emotional reactions take place simultaneously under strong pressure.

____ 22. All higher forms of behavior are independent of the simple reflex-arc.

____ 23. Motives are persistent stimuli or organic conditions which create and maintain excitement until satisfaction is achieved.

____ 24. The emotional nature of a child has an important relationship to his success or falure in mastering specific school subjects.

____ 25. Any established habit may operate to guide later learning because it acts as a drive.

____ 26. Attitudes are changed but little as a result of education.

____ 27. Praise is one of the most effective incentives to continued learning.

____ 28. Attitudes are more specific and limited in scope than habits.

____ 29. A child's mental characteristics usually are revealed in his physical make-up.

____ 30. Siblings have almost identical heredity.

____ 31. A habit, once formed, has a positive effect upon the learning of another habit.

____ 32. As twins grow older they tend to grow more alike in intelligence.

____ 33. Emotions involve the visceral and glandular systems of the body to a greater extent than do reflexes.

____ 34. Self-competition is considered to be a more desirable form of motivation than group competition.

____ 35. The best psychological practice is to permit left-handed children to remain left-handed.

____ 36. Learning through insight cannot be explained in terms of conditioning.
____ 37. Education always seeks to short-cut trial and error processes.
____ 38. In learning one always reacts to total situations rather than to common elements in total situations.
____ 39. The theory that reasoning does not appear before adolescence is now regarded as fallacious.
____ 40. Effort is justified only when its goal is attained.
____ 41. When repeated failure produces discouragement in a pupil, the teacher should substitute a related learning in which some success is attainable.
____ 42. Strong emotions influence every organ and tissue in the body.
____ 43. The intention to remember is important during the study of subject matter.
____ 44. The mental growth and development of an individual are determined mainly in terms of educational influences.
____ 45. When habit becomes fixed there is an urge to change it.
____ 46. Perceptions are first of outlines then the details are filled in.
____ 47. Each sensory neuron has its specific work to do.
____ 48. Lack of anger responses in a child indicates underdevelopment.
____ 49. Habits of attitude and emotional reaction established during childhood usually persist through later life.
____ 50. The period of adolescence becomes further prolonged as civilization increases in complexity.
____ 51. Fear is man's ally in making wholesome adjustments.
____ 52. The form of behavior displayed during anger varies with the age of the child.
____ 53. Children should be taught to develop cautious fear of certain dangerous situations.
____ 54. Some sense organs have no connection with neurons.
____ 55. Sensations could be experienced in the sense organs if the connections with the central nervous system were severed.
____ 56. A force is a stimulus even if it does not arouse a sense organ.

____ 57. The reaction of one muscle usually acts as a stimulus to other reactions.

____ 58. Some of the sense organs are contained wholly within the spinal cord.

____ 59. Brain action is a necessary correlate of consciousness.

____ 60. An idea is a conscious response to a perceived stimulus.

____ 61. Voluntary attention to one object, condition, or situation can be sustained for a long period of time.

____ 62. The teacher should never permit his pupils to "guess."

____ 63. Sense organs play a small part in learning.

____ 64. Learners demonstrate an increased power of attention with age.

____ 65. Human development usually is retarded by social contacts.

____ 66. The human cerebrum is the highest product of evolution.

____ 67. Animals tend to act on the basis of well-considered plans rather than on impulse.

____ 68. An infant, at birth, has the power of speech.

____ 69. The lower parts of the nervous system are biologically the older parts.

____ 70. Every mental state has an attitude quality as one of its essential phases.

____ 71. It is only in infancy that emotional reactions show lack of discrimination in their attachments.

____ 72. Children are more likely than mature individuals to exhibit violently emotional behavior.

____ 73. Adequate science teaching involves the presentation of problems as well as the expansion of information.

____ 74. "Whole" learning means the same thing as "unspaced" learning.

____ 75. "Battery" achievement tests test only one subject of study.

____ 76. Behavior-drives are aroused mainly by disturbances of psychological equilibrium.

____ 77. The more permanent an individual desires a product of learning to be the more he should overlearn it.

____ 78. Eye-motion while reading is continuous and uniform.

____ 79. A curve which masses its scores at the right is skewed to the left.

____ 80. Man is distinguished from animals by the complete rationality of his behavior.

____ 81. Children usually can understand the meanings of words before they can use them in speech.

____ 82. If a pupil learns to spell a sufficient number of difficult English words he will know how to spell any other word in English.

____ 83. From the standpoint of mental health, compensatory behavior is objectionable for it is a retreat from reality.

____ 84. Designating a person as an introvert tends to conceal significant facts about his personality.

____ 85. Modern psychologists tend to regard adolescence as a period in the continuity of development rather than as a definite, isolated stage.

____ 86. Usually the negativistic stage during childhood is short, after which the child resumes his former cooperative attitude toward the family.

____ 87. In evaluating classroom procedure, the psychologist asks, "Does it work?" rather than "How does it work?"

____ 88. A child's display of adult disapproved behavior should be evaluated in terms of the purpose it appears to serve the child at the moment.

____ 89. The mentally-superior child should be encouraged to select older, less able children as his playmates.

____ 90. The chief purpose of child guidance is to cure children of behavior disorders.

____ 91. It is psychologically desirable for students who fail in the academic course in high school to be transferred to the technical or commercial course.

____ 92. Lack of discipline is as harmful to integration as is excess of discipline.

____ 93. The brighter the child, the fewer his conflicts are likely to be.

____ 94. An adjustment is always a constructive solution to a behavior problem.

____ 95. The presence of a special talent does not imply the inevitability of compensatory weakness.

____ 96. The social evaluation of a defect is a more significant cause of an attitude of inferiority than is the defect itself.

____ 97. Children can be divided into types only when one is willing to ignore many significant aspects of their personality.

____ 98. Ideas of persecution are likely to arise from thwarted egocentrism.

____ 99. It is important that adults control situations to the extent that the child's initial attempts at social adjustment meet with a fair measure of success.

____100. Interests differ from attitudes in that the former cannot be measured with precision.

Multiple-choice Questions

Directions: Select the letter of the expression which *best completes* the statement and place it before the number of the question.

____ 1. When one attempts to excuse defeat by saying that others were to blame or that the teacher was not fair, he is utilizing a) projection, b) rationalization, c) exaggeration of the ego, d) introversion.

____ 2. Parents can guide their child most effectively through their a) own behavior and displayed attitudes, b) words of advice, c) ignoring of child's behavior, d) emphasis upon obedience.

____ 3. Errors of judgment are represented by a) hallucinations, b) delusions, c) daydreams, d) illusions.

____ 4. Thwarting experiences are most likely to develop a) desirable emotional controls, b) a well-balanced personality, c) a submissive attitude, d) many adjustment problems.

____ 5. Boasting or bragging is best explained as a) a result of superiority, b) an instinctive response, c) imitation, d) compensation for inadequacy.

____ 6. A ten-year-old child in your class takes the belongings of the children who sit near to him. The best way for you to handle the situation is to a) change the child's seat, b) try to convince him that he should not take things from other children, c) make a note of his stealing on his record card, d) with the help of his parents, try to discover the reasons for his behavior.

____ 7. The kind of classroom adjustment achieved by a pupil is most closely related to a) his academic success, b) his inherited personality qualities, c) the teacher's and the pupils' interrelationships, d) the teacher's giving of instruction in mental hygiene.

____ 8. Many teachers are least concerned about the a) quiet, retiring child, b) antagonistic child, c) temper-tantrum child, d) boisterous child.

____ 9. For an interview to achieve best results, the interviewee should be a) aware of the purpose of the interview, b) unaware that he is being interviewed, c) conscious of the fact that he is being judged, d) well acquainted with the interviewer.

____ 10. The making of many useless movements is typical of emotional a) diffusion, b) shock, c) transference, d) mood.

____ 11. One of the first steps in minimizing problem cases in behavior is to a) insist that pupils abide by rules, b) reduce opportunities for misbehavior, c) install a system of pupil self-government, d) avoid giving rewards and punishments.

____ 12. To emancipate an adolescent from his family means a) repudiating the family, b) outgrowing emotional dependence upon the family, c) reaching a crisis in family relationships, d) not looking to the family for advice.

____ 13. "He has been the neglected child of the school more than any other." This refers to the a) physically handicapped child, b) mentally handicapped child, c) delinquent child, d) gifted child.

____ 14. In selecting a college, an adolescent should be guided most by a) the complexity of the college environment, b) the suitability of the college to his needs and abilities, c) the vocational offerings of the college, d) the liberal and cosmopolitan offerings of the college.

____ 15. The most practical method of classifying adjustments is according to a) type of person, b) mode of response, c) cause of behavior, d) developmental sequence.

____ 16. The fact that an individual tends to repeat those reactions which, on the whole, are satisfying is best explained by the law of a) readiness, b) recency, c) frequency, d) effect.

____ 17. A general characteristic of all learning curves is a) similarity of individual curves, b) initial spurt, c) assured reduction in learning time, d) determination of physiological limit.

____ 18. At the close of what period does intellectual development, insofar as it depends on growth, commonly reach its maximum? a) senescence, b) middle adulthood, c) adolescence, d) childhood.

____ 19. The relationship between the satisfyingness of a task and the efficiency of the worker a) is not directly correlated, b) shows high positive correlation, c) shows high negative correlation, d) provides no evidence for correlation.

____ 20. The best procedure to use for controlling emotions usually is to a) let them run their course, b) talk about them, c) repress them directly, d) become active in an area that is unrelated to the cause of the emotional state.

____ 21. A child whose IQ is 89 is classified as a) a moron, b) a low normal, c) an idiot, d) an imbecile.

____ 22. The doctrine of formal discipline is based upon a) functional psychology, b) the laws of association, c) faculty psychology, d) experiments, such as that of James on memory.

____ 23. Any decrease in ability to learn from about twenty years of age until after middle age results from a) decrease in learning ability, b) forgetting specific habits of learning, c) inability to teach an old person new tricks, d) lack of initiative.

____ 24. The James-Lange theory is associated with a) instincts, b) emotions, c) laws of learning, d) habit formation.

____ 25. The genetic development of infant reactions has been experimentally traced by a) Allport, b) Hall, c) Gesell, d) Baldwin.

APPENDIX

APPENDIX

STATISTICAL TREATMENT OF DATA

In order to illustrate how educational data can be subjected to statistical treatment, examples are given for raw scores, frequency distribution, mean, median, quartile deviation, standard deviation and coefficient of correlation. The bases of these illustrations are the scores earned by 32 students on a test in educational psychology consisting of 110 short-form, objective questions and the IQs obtained by the administration of an intelligence test to those students. These are presented in Table 5.

Table 5. Scores made by 32 students in Educational Psychology and Their IQs.

Student's initials	*Scores Educational Psychology*	*IQs*	*Student's initials*	*Scores Educational Psychology*	*IQs*
C.G.	97	123	S.T.	92	131
L.D.	93	125	P.D.	88	120
R.O.	84	112	S.N.	96	135
P.T.	95	128	O.C.	91	118
A.L.	87	110	M.E.	95	130
K.F.	88	121	E.H.	99	134
H.O.	82	110	P.M.	97	128
F.R.	83	110	T.A.	90	125
L.L.	96	125	E.R.	82	112
P.J.	97	130	A.E.	84	111
O.R.	85	114	W.R.	94	122
R.T.	92	118	C.T.	100	135
C.A.	87	126	B.N.	82	110
L.C.	86	120	W.O.	84	112
M.B.	91	130	K.L.	96	127
B.C.	88	116	A.F.	92	124

Frequency Distribution. The scores given in Table 5 represent the raw scores in the educational psychology test and the IQ's of the students. Since they are not expressed in percentages they have little meaning unless and until they are subjected to statistical treatment. The first step is to arrange them in a frequency table in order to determine the frequency of their occurrence. In Table 6 are given the distribution of the data from Table 5 (ungrouped data); in Table 7 are presented the same data after the scores have been grouped in step-intervals of 3 for the educational psychology and of step-intervals of 4 for the IQs (Grouped data).

Table 6. Frequency of scores made in Educational Psychology and the IQs of the Students (Ungrouped Data)

Scores in Educational Psychology	*Talley*	*Frequency (f)*	*IQs of Students*	*Talley*	*Frequency (f)*
100	/	1	135	//	2
99	/	1	134	/	1
98		0	133		0
97	///	3	132		0
96	///	3	131	/	1
95	//	2	130	///	3
94	/	1	129		0
93	/	1	128	//	2
92	///	3	127	/	1
91	//	2	126	/	1
90	/	1	125	///	3
89		0	124	/	1
88	///	3	123	/	1
87	//	2	122	/	1
86	/	1	121	/	1
85	/	1	120	//	2
84	///	3	119		0
83	/	1	118	//	2
82	///	3	117		0
			116	/	1
			115		0
			114	/	1
			113		0
			112	///	3
			111	/	1
			110	////	4

Table 7. Frequency Distribution of Scores in Tables 5 and 6 (Grouped Data)

Educational Psychology			*IQs*		
Step-interval (3)	*Talley*	*Frequency*	*Step-interval (4)*	*Talley*	*Frequency*
100–102	/	1	134–137	///	3
97–99	////	4	130–133	////	4
94–96	//////	6	126–129	////	4
91–93	//////	6	122–125	//////	6
88–90	////	4	118–121	/////	5
85–87	////	4	114–117	//	2
82–84	///////	7	110–113	////////	8
	Total	32		Total	32

Since the scores in Table 7 represent continuous rather than discrete series, a score of 91, for example, extends from 91.0 to 91.99+. Hence the step-interval of 91.93 includes all the values from 91.0 through 93.99+ or three step-intervals, and the next interval begins with 94.0.

The Mean (*M*). The arithmetic average, called the *mean* is the ordinary average of a set of numbers and, in ungrouped data, is found by adding the scores and dividing the sum by the number of cases involved. The formula used for ungrouped data is:

$$M = \frac{\Sigma X}{N} \text{ (Ungrouped Data)}$$

In the above formula, and in those that follow, the symbol Σ represents "the sum of", *X* the individual scores and *N* the total number of scores. The mean for the ungrouped data in Table 5 can be computed by substituting in this formula.

The formula to be used when computing the mean (grouped data) is:

$$M = \frac{FX}{N} \text{ (Grouped Data)}$$

In grouped data, the mid-point of the step-interval is used as representative of all the scores of each step-interval. In the above formula *X* represents the mid-point in each step-interval and *F* the frequency. To illustrate, we are making use of the scores from the educational psychology test.

Table 8. Computation of the Mean (Grouped Data)

Step-interval (*3*)	*X*	*F*	*FX*
100–102	101	1	101
97–99	98	4	392
94–96	95	6	570
91–93	92	6	552
88–90	89	4	356
85–87	86	4	344
82–84	83	7	581

Substituting in the formula

$$M = \frac{2896}{32} = 90.5$$

(Based on grouped data)

The Median (*Mdn*). When scores are arranged in order of magnitude, the median is the point on the scale above which and below which 50 per cent of the cases fall. It is easily determined for ungrouped data by a simple count. However, when using grouped data the median is found by using the following formula:

$$Mdn = \frac{N}{2}$$

Scores in the educational psychology test are used to illustrate the method of computing the median with grouped data. See Table 9.

Table 9. Computation of the Median (Grouped Data)

Step-interval (*3*)	*F*	Substituting in the formula
100–102	1	$\frac{N}{2} = \frac{32}{2} =$ 16 cases fall above or below
97–99	4	the mid-point on the scale
94–96	6	
91–93	6	Mdn = 91 + (1/6×3) = 91.5 or
88–90	4	Mdn = 91 + .5 = 91.5
85–87	4	
82–84	7	

The number of scores divided by 2 is 16. Next we find the point on the scale above which and below which 16 cases fall. By starting at the bottom of the column marked F and counting up 16 cases we find that the median falls within the step-interval 91–93. There are 15 cases up to the 91–93 step-interval. In order to reach the 16 cases needed we must use one of the 6 cases in the 91–93 step-interval. Hence we take 1/6 of 3 (the size of the step-interval) and add the result to 91.0, the beginning of the step-interval. The median also can be found by starting at the top and counting down the 16 cases. The result will be the same.

Quartile Deviation (*Q*). Quartile deviation represents the average extent by which Q_3 third quartile (upper) and Q_1, first quartile (lower) deviate from the median. Expressed in percentiles, Q_3 is the 75th percentile, the median is the 50th percentile, and the Q_1 is the 25th percentile. The quartile deviation is computed from the median.

The formula used to compute the quartile deviation is:

$$Q = \frac{Q_3 - Q_1}{2}$$

The first step in computing the Q is to find the number of cases that are included in the lowest 25 per cent of the scores. This takes us to Q_1. By counting from the bottom it is found that the 8th case falls in the step-interval 85–87. It also is discovered that one of the 4 cases is needed to reach the 8 for Q_1. Q_1 then falls at 85 plus ¼ of 3 (step-interval) or at 85-75 as shown in Table 10. In a similar way, Q_3 is computed. We are now ready to substitute in the formula to find the Q (quartile deviation).

Table 10. Computation of the Quartile Deviation (Q) (Grouped Data)

Step-interval (3)	*F*	32 divided by 4 is 8 or the number of cases to Q_1
100–102	1	$Q_1 = 85 \quad + (1/4 \times 3) = 85.75$
97–99	4	$Q_3 = 94 \quad + (3/6 \times 3) = 95.50$
94–96	6	
91–93	6	$Q = \frac{95.50 - 85.75}{2} = \frac{9.75}{2} = 4.86$
88–90	4	
85–87	4	
82–84	7	

Standard Deviation (*S.D.*). Standard deviation is measured from the mean and is easily computed for grouped data by using an assumed mean. The formulae given here can be used to compute the standard deviation when using (1) the actual mean, and (2) an estimated mean.

$$S.D. = \sqrt{\frac{FD^2}{N}} \qquad S.D.(\sigma) = i\sqrt{\frac{\Sigma FD^2}{N} - c^2} \qquad c = \frac{\Sigma FD}{N}$$

(1) Actual Mean — (2) Assumed Mean — Correction for Assumed Mean

In these formulae, D represents the deviation from the mean (actual or assumed), i the size of the step-interval, c the correction for the mean.

Table 11. Computation of Standard Deviation (Grouped Data) (Assumed Mean is 89)

Step-interval (3)	*Mid-point*	*F*	*D*	D^2	*FD*	FD^2
100–102	101	1	4	16	4	16
97–99	98	4	3	9	12	36
94–96	95	6	2	4	12	24
91–93	92	6	1	1	6	6
88–90	89	4	0	0	0	0
85–87	86	4	–1	1	–4	4
82–84	83	7	–2	4	–14	28
	$N = 32$			Totals	16	124

Substituting in the formula for the assumed mean:

$$S.D. \text{ or } \sigma = 3\sqrt{\frac{3968}{1024} - \frac{256}{1024}} = 3\sqrt{\frac{3712}{1024}} =$$

$$3\sqrt{3.62} = 3(1.90) = 5.7$$

In this illustration, the deviation begins at the mid-point of the step-interval 88–90 or 89 and is shown in Column D. There is a deviation of *0* from the 89 in that step-interval. All step-intervals above the 88–90 deviate up (positive) by 1, 2, 3, or 4; all below deviate down (negative) by 1 and 2 step-intervals. The correction formula is used because the 89 was an assumed mean rather than the actual mean.

Computation of Correlation. The coefficient of correlation is computed by using either the *Rank-Difference* method or the *Product-Moment* method. In order to illustrate each method we shall make use of the scores of the educational psychology test and the IQ's of the students.

Rank-Difference Method. The formula used to compute the coefficient of correlation by means of the Rank-Difference method is:

$$p = 1 - \frac{6\Sigma D^2}{N(N^2 - 1)}$$

In this formula, *p* stands for coefficient of correlation, *D* represents the difference in rank between the scores of each individual on the two sets of data, and *N* represents the number of cases used.

The scores of each test need to be arranged from high to low and given a rank. By reference to Tables 5 and 6 it can be observed that in the educational psychology test the highest score is 100 and was made by one student. Hence this score is given the rank position of 1. Also since one student made the score of 99, it is given the rank of 2. However, since three students had scores of 97, each is ranked 4 in order that each student receives equal treatment in rank positions 3, 4, 5. Likewise the score of 96 was earned by three students. Hence each is given a rank of 7 to utilize the rank positions of 6, 7, 8. Continue to rank the scores of all the students. In a similar way, prepare the rank order for the IQs. See Table 12.

Table 12. Scores on the Educational Psychology Test and the IQs of the Students Arranged in Descending Order with Rank of Each.

Educational Psychology Test			*IQs of Students*		
Potential Rank	*Scores*	*Actual Rank*	*Potential Rank*	*IQs*	*Actual Rank*
1	100	1	1	135	1.5
2	99	2	2	135	1.5
3	97	4	3	134	3
4	97	4	4	131	4
5	97	4	5	130	6
6	96	7	6	130	6
7	96	7	7	130	6
8	96	7	8	128	8.5
9	95	9.5	9	128	8.5
10	95	9.5	10	127	10
11	94	11	11	126	11
12	93	12	12	125	13
13	92	14	13	125	13
14	92	14	14	125	13
15	92	14	15	124	15
16	91	16.5	16	123	16
17	91	16.5	17	122	17
18	90	18	18	121	18
19	88	20	19	120	19.5
20	88	20	20	120	19.5
21	88	20	21	118	21.5
22	87	22.5	22	118	21.5
23	87	22.5	23	116	23
24	86	24	24	114	24
25	85	25	25	112	26
26	84	27	26	112	26
27	84	27	27	112	26
28	84	27	28	111	28
29	83	29	29	110	30.5
30	82	31	30	110	30.5
31	82	31	31	110	30.5
32	82	31	32	110	30.5

Table 13. Computation of Coefficient of Correlation by Means of the Rank–Difference Method

Student's initials	*Scores Ed. Psy.*	*IQs*	*Rank Ed. Psy.*	*Rank IQ*	*Rank Difference* D	*Squares of Rank Difference* D^2
C.G.	97	123	4	16	12	144
L.D.	93	125	12	13	1	1
R.O.	84	112	27	26	1	1
P.T.	95	128	9.5	8.5	1	1
A.L.	87	110	22.5	30.5	8	64
K.F.	88	121	20	18	2	4
H.O.	82	110	31	30.5	.5	.25
F.R.	83	110	29	30.5	1.5	2.25
L.L.	96	125	7	13	6	36
P.J.	97	130	4	6	2	4
O.R.	85	114	25	24	1	1
R.T.	92	118	14	21.5	7.5	56.25
C.A.	87	126	22.5	11	11.5	132.25
L.C.	86	120	24	19.5	4.5	20.25
M.B.	91	130	16.5	6	10.5	110.25
B.C.	88	116	20	23	3	9
S.T.	92	131	14	4	10	100
P.D.	88	120	20	19.5	.5	.25
S.N.	96	135	7	1.5	5.5	30.25
O.C.	91	118	16.5	21.5	5	25
M.E.	95	130	9.5	6	3.5	12.25
E.H.	99	134	2	3	1	1
P.M.	97	128	4	8.5	4.5	20.25
T.A.	90	125	18	13	5	25
E.R.	82	112	31	26	5	25
A.E.	84	111	27	28	1	1
W.R.	94	122	11	17	6	36
C.T.	100	135	1	1.5	.5	.25
B.N.	82	110	31	30.5	.5	.25
W.O.	84	112	27	26	1	1
K.L.	96	127	7	10	3	9
A.F.	92	124	14	15	1	1
					Total	874

The initials of each student are used to identify his scores and his rank on each set of data. For example, C.G. ranks 4 on the educational psychology test and 16 among the IQs, giving a rank difference of 12 between the ranks on the two sets of data. L.D. has a rank of 12 on the educational psychology test and a rank of 13 in IQs, giving a rank difference of one. This information, together with the rank differences on each set of data and the square of the rank difference, is presented in Table 13.

By substituting in the formula for finding the coefficient of correlation by means of the Rank-Difference method, we find the coefficient of correlation to be .81.

$$p \quad 1 - \frac{6(874)}{32(1024 - 1)} \quad 1 - \frac{5244}{32736} \quad 1 - .19 \quad .81$$

Product-Moment Method. The Product-Moment method used in computing the coefficient of correlation r is sometimes called the Pearson Product-Moment method in honor of the English statistical psychologist who devised it. When the actual mean is used, the formula used to determine the coefficient of correlation is:

$$r = \frac{\dfrac{\Sigma xy}{N}}{\sqrt{\dfrac{\Sigma x^2}{N}}\sqrt{\dfrac{\Sigma y^2}{N}}} = \frac{\Sigma xy}{\sqrt{\Sigma^2 \cdot \Sigma y^2}}$$

However, when the computation is made by using an assumed mean it is necessary to use the formula which includes a correction for the mean. Hence the formula for computing the coefficient of correlation r together with the correction formula is:

$$r = \frac{\dfrac{\Sigma xy}{N} - \left(\dfrac{\Sigma x}{N}\right)\left(\dfrac{\Sigma y}{N}\right)}{\sqrt{\dfrac{\Sigma x^2}{N} - \left(\dfrac{\Sigma x}{N}\right)^2} \cdot \sqrt{\dfrac{\Sigma y^2}{N} - \left(\dfrac{\Sigma y}{N}\right)^2}}$$

The two sets of scores are set down in Table 14 for each of the students. An assumed mean of 90 was selected for the scores on the educational psychology test and of 120 for the IQs. In the x column are given the deviations from the assumed mean (90) on the first test and in the y column are presented the deviations from the assumed mean (120) of the IQs. For example, the score made by C.G. is 97 and is 7 points higher than the assumed mean of 90. This represents a positive deviation of 7 and is recorded in the x column. The score of R.O. is 84 or 6 less than the assumed mean. Hence a deviation of -6 is recorded. In the same way, the deviations of the scores from the assumed mean in educational psychology are determined and recorded in column x. Likewise, the deviations of the IQs from an assumed mean of 120 are similarly found and recorded in the y column.

The numbers in the x^2 column are found by squaring the numbers in the x column; the numbers in the y^2 column are the squares of the numbers placed in the y column. After the x, y, x^2, y^2, and xy values are found each column is added algebraically. By substituting the numbers in the correct formula, the coefficient of correlation is found to be .86.

Table 14. Computation of the Coefficient of Correlation (r) by Means of the Product–Moment Method

Student's initials	*Score Ed. Psy.*	*IQ*	*x*	*y*	x^2	y^2	*xy*
C.G.	97	123	7	3	49	9	21
L.D.	93	125	3	5	9	25	15
R.O.	84	112	−6	−8	36	64	48
P.T.	95	128	5	8	25	64	40
A.L.	87	110	−3	−10	9	100	30
K.F.	88	121	−2	1	4	1	−2
H.O.	82	110	−8	−10	64	100	80
F.R.	83	110	−7	−10	49	100	70
L.L.	96	125	6	5	36	25	30
P.J.	97	130	7	10	49	100	70
O.R.	85	114	−5	−6	25	36	30
R.T.	92	118	2	−2	4	4	−4
C.A.	87	126	−3	6	9	36	−18
L.C.	86	120	−4	0	16	0	0
M.B.	91	130	1	10	1	100	10
B.C.	88	116	−2	−4	4	16	8
S.T.	92	131	2	11	4	121	22
P.D.	88	120	−2	0	4	0	0
S.N.	96	135	6	15	36	225	90
O.C.	91	118	1	−2	1	4	−2
M.E.	95	130	5	10	25	100	50
E.H.	99	134	9	14	81	196	126
P.M.	97	128	7	8	49	64	56
T.A.	90	125	0	5	0	25	0
E.R.	82	112	−8	−8	64	64	64
A.E.	84	111	−6	−9	36	81	54
W.R.	94	122	4	2	16	4	8
C.T.	100	125	10	15	100	225	150
B.N.	82	110	−8	−10	64	100	80
W.O.	84	112	−6	−8	36	64	48
K.L.	96	127	6	7	36	49	42
A.F.	92	124	2	4	4	16	8
	Assumed Mean	Assumed Mean	83 −70	139 −87	945	2118	1250 −26
	90	120	13	52			1224

SELECTED REFERENCES IN EDUCATIONAL PSYCHOLOGY

Ausubel, D. P., *Educational Psychology: Cognitive View.* Holt, Rinehart & Winston, 1968.

Baller, W. R., and Charles, D. C., *Psychology of Human Growth and Development*, 2nd ed. Holt, Rinehart & Winston, 1968.

Bernard, H. W., *Psychology of Learning and Teaching*, 2nd ed. McGraw-Hill, 1965.

Biehler, R. F., *Psychology Applied to Teaching.* Houghton-Mifflin, 1971.

Bigge, M. and Hunt, M. P., *Psychological Foundations of Education*, 2nd ed. Harper and Row, 1968.

Blackham, G. J., *Deviant Child in the Classroom.* Wadsworth, 1967.

Blair, G. M. et al, *Educational Psychology*, 3rd ed. Macmillan, 1968.

Bower, E. M. and Hollister, W. G., *Behavioral Science Frontiers in Education*, Wiley, 1967.

Rugelski, B. R., *Psychology of Learning Applied to Teaching*, Bobbs-Merrill, 1971.

Clark, D. H. ed. *Psychology of Education.* Free Press, 1967.

Cole, L. and Bruce, W. F., *Educational Psychology*, rev. ed. Harcourt, Brace & World, 1968.

CRM Books Editorial Staff, *Readings in Educational Psychology*, CRM Books, 1970.

Cronbach, L. J., *Educational Psychology*, 2nd ed. Harcourt, Brace & World, 1969.

Crow, L. D., *Psychology of Human Adjustment*, Knopf, 1967.

Crow, L. D. and Crow, A., *Human Development and Learning*, rev. ed. Van Nostrand Reinhold, 1963.

Crow, L. D. and Crow, A., *Educational Psychology*, new rev. ed. Van Nostrand Reinhold, 1965.

Crow, L. D. and Crow, A., *Organization and Conduct of Guidance Services*, David McKay, 1965.

Cruickshank, W. M., *Psychology of Exceptional Children and Youth*, 3rd ed. Prentice-Hall, 1971.

Davitz, J. and Ball, S., *Psychology of the Educational Process*, McGraw-Hill, 1970.

De Cecco, J., *Psychology of Learning and Instruction.* Prentice-Hall, 1968.

Di Vesta, F. J. and Thompson, G. G., *Educational Psychology: Instruction and Behavioral Change*, Appleton-Century-Crofts, 1970.

Dreikurs, R., *Psychology in the Classroom*, 2nd ed. Harper and Row, 1968.

Eson, M. E., *Psychological Foundations in Education.* Holt, Rinehart and Winston, 1964.

Frandsen, A. N., *Educational Psychology*, 2nd ed. McGraw-Hill, 1967.
Gordon, E., *Psychology of Music Teaching*, Prentice-Hall, 1971.
Johnson, P. E., *Psychology of School Learning*. Wiley, 1971.
Jones, R. L., *Psychology and Education of Exceptional Children*. Houghton-Mifflin, 1971.
Kelly, W. A., *Educational Psychology*, rev. ed. Bruce Pub. Co., 1965.
Klausmeier, H. J. and Goddwin, W., *Learning and Human Abilities: Educational Psychology*, 2nd ed. Harper and Row, 1966.
Kolesnik, W. B., *Educational Psychology*, 2nd ed. McGraw-Hill, 1970.
Lembo, J., *Psychology of Effective Classroom Instruction*. Merrill, 1969.
Lindgren, H. C., *Educational Psychology in the Classroom*, 3rd ed. Wiley, 1967.
Loree, M. R., *Psychology of Education*. Ronald Press, 1970.
McDonald, F. J., *Educational Psychology*, 2nd ed. Wadsworth, 1965.
Mouly, M., *Psychology for Effective Teaching*, 2nd ed. Holt, Rinehart & Winston, 1968.
Noll, V. H. and Rachel, P., eds., *Readings in Educational Psychology*, 2nd ed. Macmillan, 1968.
Parker, R. K., *Readings in Educational Psychology*. Allyn and Bacon, 1968.
Perkins, H. V., *Human Development and Learning*. Wadsworth, 1969.
Pintner, et al, *Educational Psychology* (Outline), 6th ed. Barnes and Noble, 1970.
Powell, M. and Mangum, R. E., *Introduction to Educational Psychology*. Bobbs-Merrill, 1971.
Sawrey, J. M. and Telford, C. W., *Educational Psychology*, 3rd ed. Allyn and Bacon, 1968.
Skinner, B. F., *Technology of Teaching*. Appleton-Century-Crofts, 1968.
Starr, B., *Psychology of School Adjustment* (*Readings*). Random House, 1970.
Stones, E., *Learning and Teaching*, Wiley, 1968.
Strom, R. D., *Psychology for the Classroom*. Prentice-Hall, 1969.
White, W. F., *Psychology Principles Applied to Classroom Teaching*. McGraw-Hill, 1969.
Wilson, J. A. et al, eds., *Psychological Foundations of Learning and Teaching*. McGraw-Hill, 1969.

LEARNING AND THE SOCIAL ENVIRONMENT: SELECTED REFERENCES

Alloway, David and Cordasco, F. *Minorities and the American City: A Sociological Primer for Educators* (New York: David McKay, 1970).

Brickman, William W. and Lehrer, Stanley, Eds. *Conflict and Change on the Campus: The Response to Student Hyperactivism* (New York: School & Society Books, 1970).

Brickman, William W. and Lehrer, Stanley. *The Disadvantaged in International Perspective* (New York: John Wiley, 1972).

Burma, John H. *Mexican-Americans in the United States* (Cambridge, Massachusetts: Schenkman, 1970).

Cordasco, Francesco and Bucchioni, Eugene. *Puerto Rican Children in Mainland Schools* (New York: Grolier/Scarecrow, 1968).

Cordasco, Francesco, *et al.* *The School in the Social Order* (Scranton: Intext, 1970).

Cordasco, Francesco, Ed. *Poverty: Sources for the Study of Economic Inequality and its Social Consequences* (New York: Augustus M. Kelley, 1971). [A collection of over 100 vols.]

Crossland, Fred E. *Minority Access to College* (New York: Schocken, 1971).

[Education] *Needs of Elementary and Secondary Education for the Seventies: A Compendium of Policy Papers* (Washington: U. S. Government Printing Office, 1970).

Fantini, Mario; Gittell, M. and Magat, R. *Community Control and the Urban School* (New York: Praeger, 1970).

Fitzpatrick, Joseph P. *Puerto Rican Americans* (Englewood Cliffs, New Jersey: Prentice-Hall, 1971).

Gordon, Ira J. *Parent Involvement in Compensatory Education* (Urbana, Illinois, University of Illinois Press, 1971).

Havighurst, Robert L. and Levine, Daniel U. *Education in Metropolitan Areas*. 2nd ed. (Boston: Allyn and Bacon, 1971).

Hellmuth, Jerome, Ed. *Disadvantaged Child* (New York: Brunner/Mazel, 1969-70). 3 vols.

[Immigrant Children] *The Children of Immigrants in Schools. With An Introductory Essay* by Francesco Cordasco. (Metuchen, N. J.: Scarecrow Reprint Corp., 1970; originally, 1911). 5 vols.

Janowitz, Morris. *Institution Building in Urban Education* (New York: Russell Sage Foundation, 1969-70).

John, Vera P. and Horner, Vivian M. *Early Childhood Bilingual Education* (New York: Modern Language Association, 1971).

Jones, W. Ron. *Finding Community: A Guide to Community Research and Action* (Palo Alto, California: James E. Freel, 1971).

Levin, Henry M., Ed. *Community Control of Schools* (Washington: Brookings Institution, 1970).

Meranto, Philip. *School Politics in the Metropolis* (Columbus, Ohio: Charles E. Merrill Co., 1970).

Lupton, D. Keith. *The Student in Society* (Totowa, New Jersey: Littlefield, Adams & Co., 1969).

Miller, Harry L. and Woock, R. R. *Social Foundations of Urban Education* (Hinsdale, Illinois: Dryden Press, 1970).

Mink, Oscar G. and Kaplan, B. A. *America's Problem Youth. Education and Guidance of the Disadvantaged* (Scranton: International Textbook Co., 1970).

Passow, A. Harry, Ed. *Reaching the Disadvantaged Learner* (New York: Teachers College Press, 1970).

Passow, A. Harry, Ed. *Urban Education in the 1970s* (New York: Teachers College Press, 1971).

Piven, Frances F. and Cloward, Richard A. *Regulating the Poor: The Functions of Public Welfare* (New York: Pantheon Books, 1971).

Rever, Philip R., Ed. *Open Admissions and Equal Access* (Iowa City, Iowa: American College Testing Program, 1971).

Riles, Wilson C. [Chairman] *The Urban Education Task Force Report: Final Report of the Task Force on Urban Education to the Department of Health, Education, and Welfare* (New York: Praeger, 1970).

Rubenstein, Annette T., Ed. *Schools Against Children: The Case for Community Control* (New York: Monthly Review Press, 1970).

[Socially Disadvantaged Children] "Education for Socially Disadvantaged Children," *Review of Educational Research*, 40: 1-179, February 1970.

Stone, James C. and DeNevi, Donald P., Eds. *Teaching Multi-Cultural Populations* (New York: VanNostrand Reinhold, 1971). [Blacks; Puerto Ricans; Mexicans; Asians; and Indians].

Totten, W. Fred. *The Power of Community Education* (Midland, Michigan: Pendall, 1970).

Weinberg, Meyer, Ed. *The Education of the Minority Child* (Chicago: Integrated Education Associates, 1970). [A Bibliography of over 10,000 references].

Willingham, Warren W. *Free-Access Higher Education* (New York: College Entrance Board, 1970).

Index

Index

ANSWERS TO EXAMINATION QUESTIONS

(Pages 313-328)

Examination 1

T–F	T–F	M–C
1. 0	51. +	1. b
2. 0	52. 0	2. c
3. 0	53. +	3. d
4. +	54. 0	4. b
5. +	55. +	5. a
6. +	56. 0	6. d
7. 0	57. 0	7. c
8. 0	58. 0	8. c
9. +	59. +	9. b
10. 0	60. 0	10. c
11. +	61. 0	11. d
12. +	62. +	12. b
13. 0	63. +	13. b
14. +	64. 0	14. d
15. 0	65. 0	15. c
16. 0	66. +	16. b
17. +	67. +	17. d
18. +	68. 0	18. b
19. 0	69. +	19. a
20. +	70. +	20. b
21. 0	71. 0	21. c
22. 0	72. +	22. b
23. +	73. 0	23. c
24. 0	74. 0	24. a
25. 0	75. +	25. c
26. 0	76. +	
27. 0	77. +	
28. +	78. 0	
29. 0	79. 0	
30. 0	80. 0	
31. 0	81. 0	
32. 0	82. 0	
33. 0	83. +	
34. +	84. 0	
35. 0	85. 0	
36. 0	86. 0	
37. 0	87. 0	
38. 0	88. +	
39. 0	89. 0	
40. +	90. 0	
41. +	91. 0	
42. +	92. 0	
43. 0	93. +	
44. +	94. 0	
45. +	95. +	
46. +	96. +	
47. 0	97. 0	
48. +	98. +	
49. 0	99. 0	
50. +	100. 0	

Examination 2

T–F	T–F	M–C
1. +	51. +	1. a
2. 0	52. +	2. a
3. 0	53. +	3. b
4. +	54. 0	4. d
5. +	55. 0	5. d
6. +	56. 0	6. d
7. 0	57. +	7. c
8. +	58. 0	8. a
9. +	59. +	9. a
10. 0	60. +	10. a
11. 0	61. 0	11. b
12. +	62. 0	12. b
13. 0	63. 0	13. d
14. 0	64. +	14. b
15. +	65. 0	15. d
16. 0	66. +	16. d
17. 0	67. 0	17. b
18. +	68. 0	18. c
19. +	69. +	19. b
20. +	70. +	20. d
21. 0	71. 0	21. a
22. 0	72. +	22. c
23. +	73. +	23. d
24. +	74. 0	24. b
25. +	75. 0	25. c
26. +	76. +	
27. +	77. +	
28. 0	78. 0	
29. 0	79. +	
30. 0	80. 0	
31. 0	81. +	
32. 0	82. 0	
33. +	83. 0	
34. +	84. +	
35. +	85. +	
36. +	86. +	
37. 0	87. 0	
38. 0	88. +	
39. +	89. 0	
40. 0	90. 0	
41. +	91. 0	
42. +	92. +	
43. +	93. 0	
44. 0	94. 0	
45. 0	95. +	
46. +	96. +	
47. +	97. +	
48. 0	98. +	
49. +	99. +	
50. +	100. 0